TOMMY

First published in 2006 by

WOODFIELD PUBLISHING
Bognor Regis, West Sussex, England
www.woodfieldpublishing.com

ISBN 1-84683-026-5

Front cover illustration by
Neil Simone of Whixley, Nr York.

Tommy

*The First World War experiences of
Thomas Albert Crawford
15th Durham Light Infantry*

TOMMY CRAWFORD

Woodfield

To the memory of my boys,
who died before their time

Chief Air Technician Tommy Crawford
Southern Rhodesian Air Force

Sergeant Jack Crawford
Royal Air Force

Colin Crawford

"With the going down of the sun,
And in the morning,
We shall remember them"

Contents

Introduction .... *iii*

1. EARLY YEARS 1

2. KING AND COUNTRY 27

3. MADEMOISELLE FROM ARMENTIERS 60

4. BACK INSIDE THE ROPES 87

5. THE SOMME 118

6. BACK TO BLIGHTY 140

7. RAW RECRUITS 178

8. HONOURABLE DISCHARGE 211

9. GOING BACK 235

   From the *Harrogate Herald*: 235
   Carnage 235
   Freedom 235
   Cemeteries 236
   A letter to Brian 237

10. FINAL THOUGHTS 240

Introduction

These are the memoirs of Tomas Albert Crawford, which he wrote down whilst working on a night shift as a power station engineer in New Galloway, Scotland.

Tommy and his first wife Amy had two children: Tommy Jnr and Jack. Tragically, Tommy Senior was to lose them all: Amy died of cancer of the throat and Tommy and Jack died within five months of each other in 1957, both just thirty-seven years of age (Tommy of polio and Jack of cancer).

On the 5th September 1950, Tommy married Vera, the lady who had nursed Amy when she was in hospital. Tommy and Vera had two sons, Colin and Brian. Tragically, Colin died at twenty-eight years of age in 1980.

To lose a third son at such an early age was too much for Tommy to bear and six months later, he too passed away, at his home in Harrogate.

1. EARLY YEARS

I was born in a bleak Northern town that made its name and its wealth from its famous steel workers – most of the inhabitants being famous only for the fact that they were a hard working, hard drinking and hard fighting bunch of people – mostly Irish. I assume that I must have been an unwanted child because the only home I knew was with my grandparents and their home was my home up to the time they died. However I didn't mind that, they were good souls and they gave me the love, care and attention that should be the heritage of all children brought into this uneasy world.

I have the memory of my granddad returning home from the South African war in which he had served with a regiment of Hussars and he certainly looked quite a man to me in his khaki uniform, plume hat, and the greatest attraction his cavalry sabre by his side. I was a mighty proud kid when he put that hat on my head and let me strut around with the sabre. There were lots of people around and bands playing and everyone seemed to have a flag in one hand and a glass of something in the other. Someone lifted me into the saddle of the big black horse that my granddad had been riding and for some reason best known to itself it reared up and I came to earth with a thud. I was hurt but not injured, unfortunately the incident left an impression on my mind and from that day onwards I have given horses a wide berth.

I made a start at an ordinary elementary school at the age of five and I soon found out that the predominating feature of that school was the headmaster's inhuman ability to use a swishing cane. The classroom teachers could do their share but the headmaster was a past master at handing out punishment and he loved it! I admit that we deserved some of the hidings we received but a lot of it was cruel and unjustified and after a time I discovered a way in which I could get some satisfaction for any unjust punishment that came my way. I had put in a lot of practice with a catapult and I was a pretty good shot with it so whenever the headmaster got to work on me for something that was not just I got to work with my catapult. I found a good ambush with a sound line of retreat from which I could smash a pane of glass in the headmaster's window and by keeping it a secret no one ever knew who the guilty one was. I scored seven panes of glass while at the school and my crowning achievement just before leaving the school was to shatter the face of the school clock with a steel ball, good shooting! Teachers and their methods have changed a lot since those days. Judging by the appearance and number of callers at my home I assume that my granddad must have been a man of importance in the town, he was a bluff and hearty type and he appeared to use his money pretty freely on social events. I have vivid memories of Christmas and New Year celebrations when great long tables were built up of planks on trestles in the dining room and laden with bottles, glasses, and piles of food and fruit.

Every Christmas morning a brass band paraded on our front doorstep and played a Christmas carol, their reward being a tankard of ale for each man and a golden sovereign for the bandmaster. The first-foot at New Year got a full glass of whiskey and also a golden sovereign for wishing us 'Good Health'. All seemed to be welcome at that house and judging by the number who came they seemed to enjoy it, there was a spirit of good fellowship that it is nice to remember. When the snow lay deep enough my granddad would drive us around in a smart sleigh drawn by a high stepping pony with jingling bells on the harness and this seemed quite a ceremony. My grandmother seemed to stay in the background but I have no doubt she had a lot of work on her hands and she was always there when required. The other member of this household was their unmarried son Albert, he was my Uncle of course, but to me he was just Abby. He was, at that time a happy go lucky type, pretty fond of a good time with the boys and I'm afraid rather spoilt at home; he managed a butchering business that my granddad had bought for him. He slaughtered his own beasts for the business and I was often in the slaughter house when cattle were being killed with the swing of a spiked hammer and sheep were being held across the block to have their throats cut. It was a cruel and messy business and it made me feel a bit squeamish, but it was the only method in those days. This slaughterhouse was used as a meeting place for the local boxing fraternity at times when it was not being used for the butchering business and then I often watched another form of butchering. A few sets of boxing gloves always hung on the wall and a heavy punching bag hung from the rafters. Fighting men and their sparring partners collected here to do their training and I saw some pretty hectic milling at times. Something in this boxing attracted me, I liked to hear the thud of gloves on bare flesh, the shuffling of feet, the ducking and weaving and the smell of sweat; but I was only an interested spectator. I got to know and like a number of the professionals and I found they always had a word for me and a kindly grin on their ugly battered faces, their living was hard in those days and they fought tough battles for very little cash.

I first walked into trouble when playing football in the school playground. A boy named Connor was playing opposite me on the other team and as I trapped the ball in his rush down the field his boot took me on the shin. He was wearing heavy boots and I can still remember the shock of pain that shot up my leg. I rolled on the ground in agony and tears streamed from my eyes. To make matters worse Connor grunted, 'Come on softy get up, don't be a cry baby!' I jumped to my feet, closed my fist and lashed out at him in temper. Then there was a scramble and the next thing I knew was a hard thump on the nose and a trickle of blood. What with the pain in my leg, the tears in my eyes, and the blood from my nose I was in pretty poor shape but before any more damage could be done a teacher appeared on the scene and marched us both in to the headmaster. The headmaster added insult to injury, he gave us both the same, and that was plenty! The whole affair had been witnessed by a lot of the school and I knew that in their eyes I had put up a pretty poor show while Connor was already stepping high and sticking out his chest, he had won a fight! After tea I limped round to the slaughterhouse and found Pat Dexter leaning against the door. Pat was an ex professional who had had his day.

He grinned at me - 'Hello son, my kid Mike tells me you had some trouble at school today!'

'Yes Pat, but it wasn't my fault'.

'Never mind who's fault it was, what you going to do about it?'

I stared at him, I knew I was in trouble but I hadn't thought of doing anything.

'I don't know Pat, what can I do?'

'I'm telling you the same as I'd tell my own kid, have it out with him son an,' you'll feel the better for it after'.

'I'll think about it Pat when my legs better'.

'Never mind your leg think about it now,' grunted Pat 'here come inside and pull those gloves on, I'll show you a thing or two'.

I didn't relish it much but old Pat was a kindly soul and so for the first time in my life I pulled on a pair of boxing gloves.

They were old and battered and the stuffing had gone hard with soakings of sweat and blood, they felt like lumps of lead hanging at the end of my arms and facing me was old Pat grinning and looking like an ugly hairy ape.

'Now son do as I tell you, up on the balls of your feet, keep yourself nicely balanced, point that left toe at me, that's right, now I want you to close your fist and hit me, go on, HIT ME!'

I looked at that grinning battered face weaving about in front of me and poked out a feeble left glove.

Pat took it on the cheek and scowled 'No good, no ruddy good, I said hit me, put some beef into it, HIT ME!'

Next time I moved my left foot forward slightly as I stabbed out my left glove as I had seen the boxers doing in their training and it felt different when it landed. Pat grinned, 'That's more like it, now get moving and hit'. I stepped in and hooked my left to his chin and Pat's eyes gleamed 'There's the birth of a punch!'

Then I gave him all I had and Pat took the lot and looked happy about it as he praised me and found fault with me and corrected my mistakes.

'Right that'll do for now Tommy,' he said, pulling off the gloves 'Your right's not so hot but you've got something in that left hand of yours we'll make something of you'.

Pat was keen on making something of me and he kept me at it day after day, praising me one minute and clouting me around the next to show me where I was going wrong. He taught me how to get snap into a straight left and how to hook with the left and land my punch with the knuckle. He taught me how to block a punch and how to weave and duck and ride a punch, he taught me the vital points to land my blows and he tried to improve my right hand hitting. My right was my weakness, for some reason I often mistimed my right crosses and when I did land with it I often hurt my hand.

'Aw never mind about the right,' said Pat 'You've got a natural left and you're doing just fine'.

He made me hammer at the heavy punching bag and box fast with the punch ball and made me box with other chaps including his son Mike who was a couple of years older than me and a good boxer, keenly watching every move and every blow and criticizing all the time. I was a keen pupil and I paid more attention to Pat Dexter than I ever did to any teacher at school. I was beginning to love the glove game. At school I was having a pretty poor time of it because Connor was one of those types who kept reminding everyone how good he was and I knew my school fellows were wondering how long I was going to stand it.

At last I felt I was good enough to deal with Connor so I whispered to the boy next to me in the classroom 'Pass word along to Connor that I'll meet him after school today!' I watched the message passed from boy to boy and saw each head turn to look at me and I saw Connor start and turn towards me as if for confirmation. I nodded my head to let him know the job was on and he showed me his clenched fist from the other end of the classroom as a promise of things to come. The change in my class fellows was amazing, I felt like someone stepping out of the shadows. I wasn't worried about the outcome, I knew Connor had a bit of a reputation but I was going to lick him and that was that! When school was over I stepped into the schoolyard with Steve Robson and saw Connor at the gate with a crowd of boys around him, the word had gone round the school like wildfire, and it always did. Connor stepped out as I approached 'I'm ready when you are,' he said.

'All right Connor, but not here we'll go on the 'Rec,' I replied. The 'Rec,' was the recreation field about 300 yards from the school. The crowd of boys went dashing off to the 'Rec,' shouting and laughing and eager to see the battle and I followed with Steve. The boys had already formed a circle in the field and they made way for me to step inside and set the ball rolling. Once in there you just started fighting and you keep on fighting and mauling and tripping until one or the other cried enough. These affrays usually didn't last long but the boys of the school took them very seriously and the judgement of school depended on your performance. If you didn't put up a good fight your name was mud and it stuck! So there we were, a couple of school kids alone in a crowd, the loneliest place in the world, and may the best man win.

Connor and I faced each other and shuffled around and then crack! crack! I had snapped out a couple of straight lefts to Connor's nose. He screwed up his eyes and I saw his body tighten to jump in he was telegraphing what he intended. I met his jump with another left that started the blood trickling from his nose. Connor looked bewildered backed away and then rushed in swinging heavily. He was wide open and I swerved and crossed him with a nice right that cut his eye and as he stood dazed I belted in a couple of left hooks to his face. Connor was licked before he had started anything, and I knew it. As he went back trying to cover up I followed up tossing punches until the yelling crowd gave way and I still drove Connor back trying to force an opening to send in the winner. Suddenly there was a commotion in the crowd of boys and I found myself in the arms of a large sized policeman 'Now then me lads, what's going on here,' he shouted, and then he caught sight of Connor 'Holy Mike, is it murderin,' the boyo you're after?' The crowd scattered frantically and in a matter of seconds they had disappeared, even Connor had gone, leaving only myself, Steve, and the policeman on the field. The policeman couldn't do anything about it, had he let go of me I would have been off the mark like a shot, but he had no intention of giving me the chance and Steve stayed with me. 'Now me boyos just give me yer names and addresses, no lies mind or I'll lather yer,' hides'. I gave him mine and he stared at me, 'Oh, sur,' an,' I know yer,' now you young rascal, come on we'll see your granddad'. We trudged through the streets on the way to my home and Steve seemed to enjoy giving the policeman all the details of the fight. I didn't say anything because my mind was occupied with the kind of reception awaiting me.

'Now Malone, what's the trouble?' asked granddad as he answered the door to the policeman's knock.

'Sure an,' its this boyo of yours Sir, I found him knockin,' blazes out of another kid on the 'Rec'.

'Fighting eh, was it a fair fight?' asked granddad.

'Fair challenge fight sir,' Steve cut in - 'and Tommy won'.

Granddad's eyes ran over me 'Well, you don't seem to have taken much harm, what about it Malone?'

The policeman looked a bit uncomfortable, 'I don't want to be making trouble sir, but the other kid was a bit of a mess!'

'All right, step inside Malone I want to have a word with you, and you two clear off and get your tea'.

I didn't see the policeman again but I did see the whiskey bottle and the two glasses on my granddad's table in his room.

~ *Tommy* ~

The following morning I was at school as usual but it was a week before a subdued Connor put in an appearance and I found a considerable change in everyone's attitude towards me, it all boiled down to the fact that I had been tried and not found wanting. I kept on with my boxing lessons with the gloves and perhaps I showed a bit of cockiness after my do with Connor because one day Pat pulled on the gloves and slapped me around in good style. I tried hard but I came out of that spar with a bleeding nose and a dizzy head and I knew Pat had been laying it on.

'How'd you like that Tommy?' he asked.

'It was hard going Pat,' I gasped, 'but I'll lick you one day'.

He peered at me and laughed, 'All right kid you'll do, its a rough road an,' you've a lot to learn, but you'll do'.

At the age of ten Connor and I crossed swords once more, with the gloves this time, but I was away ahead of Connor in my knowledge of boxing by now and he called 'enough,' after two rounds. This little 'do,' took place in a barber's shop, cleared for the job after business hours, and it was properly controlled and witnessed by a number of boxing fans. My granddad was present at this event and he was all smiles when I came out on top, he came over to me and patted me on my shoulder, then his hand came out of his pocket and he gave me a golden sovereign. 'Good boy,' he said. It wasn't long after this that my granddad collapsed after running to catch a train and after a short period he died; within a matter of months my grandmother followed him and, although I didn't know it at the time, it meant a drastic change in my life. After the funeral of my grandmother a man I had rarely seen told me he was taking me home, it was my father. So far as I was concerned I was at home and I didn't relish the idea of going with him but I had no choice in the matter and off we went to the mining town about ten miles away where my parents lived with a quite prosperous business. My father was a thin wiry man, very smart in appearance and bearing, with eyes like pieces of cold blue ice; I think that cold blue ice describes the whole of the man, not only his eyes! I very soon discovered that he had affection only for himself but he was certainly a terrific showman and his front to people outside his home seemed to impress. Inside the home he was different, he ruled with an iron hand and whatever he said was law. My mother ran the business for him and she appeared to do all the work while he acted as the gentleman supervisor. I suppose it was owing to business activities that my mother didn't seem to have much time for household duties or family affairs. In my new home I found two more strangers, my younger brothers Jack and Charles, my brother Jack and I soon became pals but I didn't take to Charles and that position has lasted all through our years of life. I was a stranger in a strange land and I didn't take kindly to the change, I often longed to be back with the tough kind hearted Irish folk where I was known, and I think liked. I was one of them.

~ *Tommy* ~

I soon found that there was a chilly atmosphere in that house that nothing could break down and it seemed to have developed on a craving to make money and count every penny that had to be spent. My father was a man of unreliable temper and to speak at the table at meal times was a crime for which you left the table and said goodbye to the rest of your meal. There were no second helpings of anything, and if we made a noise during the evening we were packed off to bed. I suppose there is some truth in the saying 'there is good in the worst of us and bad in the best of us,' and its only fair to say he had some good points. He was a first class horseman, a crack rifle shot, and he rated very highly as a swordsman and lancer; he held the rank of Sergeant Major in the Hussars and every year at the military sports he came out with prizes for himself and for the regiment. He put in a lot of training at this business and he was a worthy exponent. When he was in the mood he often told me of his exploits with the gloves but I always felt a bit sceptical about this. I never saw him pull on a boxing glove and this is strange for a man who has taken an active part in the game. I've met plenty of them and no matter what their age and condition they are usually eager to pull on the mitts and demonstrate 'how they used to do it'. However on the strength of these tales I did manage to get his permission to rig up a punching bag and punchball in an old shed at the rear of the premises. Abby let me have a set of boxing gloves from the slaughterhouse so I was still able to indulge in training for the sport I had grown to love. Giving his permission was as far as he went he took no further interest in my activities. Had it not been for the keen interest within me I am inclined to think that my love for the game would have died away at this time.

We had a constant visitor to the house and I became quite friendly with him; he had been a Regimental Sergeant Major in the dragoons and had seen long and active service in northern India. He was one of those types who liked to tell the tale of his adventures and I never grew tired of sitting with him while he told me stories of his soldiering days on the sun drenched plains, charging cavalry and tight squares of British infantry fighting for the flag. Spellbound I drank it all in and I found I was stirred by the glories of battle, the horror and misery of war was hidden from me. I was sent to school now and within a month I had set an examination for a scholarship to a technical college. I failed to gain a scholarship and I don't wonder at it, I had been uprooted and tossed into a strange environment where everyone and everything was strange to me both at school and at home, I felt miserable and lonely. Even the language was strange to me, although the two localities were only ten miles apart; distance doesn't count when it comes to dialects. I was missing the soft Irish brogue I had been brought up with and trying to get use to the broad dialect of the Geordie. I settled down to the grind of preparing for the next examination due to be held six months later but in the meantime I didn't seem to be able to mix to freely with the chaps at school, the only pal I seemed to take to was a boy called Jimmy Falcus. He was the son of a professional boxer and he said he had every intention of following in his father's footsteps in the ring. He was pretty good with the gloves and we spent many hectic rounds together under the supervision of his dad and this helped me a lot in my knowledge of the noble art. I also made another friend while at that school and this was a girl called Molly; she sat at a desk in line with me across the alleyway that separated the boys section from the girls, and judging by the number of sweets Molly passed to me across that alleyway I can only assume that she had taken a liking for me. I can't remember much about her looks, I suppose it was the sweets that counted! The first time I got involved with Molly was during a playtime and I came across a couple of boys mauling a girl at the side of the school building. At first I took it for a playful romp and would have passed by but I saw the girl was on the ground and crying so I butted in with - 'Leave her alone you chaps, she's crying!'

'You go to hell out of this, mind your own business,' was the reply.

'Leave her alone or I'll report you,' I said.

That started the fun and games; they left the girl alone all right but they both jumped at me together. I squared up but I didn't stand much chance with two of them and they had a pretty tricky method of attack. One of them came in low to wrap his arms around my legs while the other chap slugged away at me with both fists. I joined in the slugging and I felt my punches landing but I couldn't move around and I couldn't get the weight into my blows with a chap hugging at my legs. This was my first experience of dirty fighting and I didn't like it, from the chap who was coming at me low down I got a hard butt with his head in the groin and that really hurt, from the chap who was slugging I got a nifty elbow jab in the eye that nearly knocked me cross-eyed. I was well and truly up against trouble so I forgot all my instructions to box clean and managed to slam down with a rabbit punch to the back of the chaps neck as he dived for my legs and thumped his face into the gravel on the ground, even then he was still groping to get a grip on my feet. A hard crack on the mouth split my lip and at that moment came blessed intervention in the form of an irate teacher. Off we trooped to the headmaster's room and I got some satisfaction from the fact that the other two got a first class thrashing while I got a severe warning about fighting at school. Apparently as soon as the brawl started Molly had run into the school and reported the affair so the headmaster knew the true details.

After this I suppose Molly was inclined to look upon me as the rescuer of maidens in distress but in actual fact it was Molly who got me out of a basinful of trouble. So I basked in the sunshine of her adoration and accepted her sweets with gusto. If you think this started a wonderful boy and girl romance you've got it all wrong, I never saw Molly after school hours and we just remained school friends until the day I left. It was a number of years later, after the war in fact, when my brother Jack informed me he had met a schoolteacher called Molly who was asking after my welfare.

I soon began to hear the threatening rumours floating around the school, those two tough boys intended taking me apart and throwing the pieces to the birds, I knew their intentions were again two to one. In order to counteract this I broadcast the fact that I would be pleased to handle them one at a time just whenever they felt like it and I'm pleased to say it came to nothing other than black looks. They gave me no further trouble and for the rest of my time at that school I was left in peace. I wasn't looking for any trouble; I liked good clean boxing but not 'rough house,' stuff. I went through with the examination when the time came and gained the scholarship for the technical college, that meant another uprooting so far as school life was concerned but I hadn't really taken root at that school so I left it without regrets. I just passed on without a 'Goodbye,' to anyone, not even to Molly!

About this time I became a member of the Church Lads Brigade, not because I had any religious inclinations but because I had seen the local company on parade with their drum and bugle band and it took my fancy. It was a happy inspiration; I made many comrades in the brigade and enjoyed many happy hours in training at the drill hall and at camp, friendships that lasted until the war saw us passing into the armed forces, and for many the beginning of the end. Parades were held every Sunday and we marched to church; during the week we paraded at the local drill hall and carried out quite a variety of training. Foot drill and arms drill as infantry, fencing with single sticks, route marches and field training and intermingled with this was a good variety of sport to indulge in such as soccer, cricket, boxing and target firing with a .22 rifle. I was pretty keen on everything we took part in and I look back with happy memories to those parades. Social evenings were also a highlight of those times and at these do's a rollicking time was had by the boys and girls of the church under the supervision of a curate, his supervision wasn't so strong that it cramped our style. The older chaps in the company were forever talking about the times they had at last years camp and I soon made up my mind this was a must. The annual brigade camp was a big affair about two thousand boys attending to live under canvas for one week of military training, and without hesitation my name went on the list for the next camp. Everything was joyful until I returned home and told my parents I was going to the camp and the cost was ten shillings, that's when my father hit the roof and told me I would have to save up the ten shillings myself. This looked like being quite a job; I wallowed in two pence a week pocket money, so I could see the camp fading away into the dim and distant future. However this snag was overcome by delivering meat for a butcher at weekends and doing odd jobs in a grocers shop after school hours. I raised the money and a bit extra for spending and paid my own way.

It was a dull and overcast morning when we marched off with our kitbags and carbines to get the train that would take us to Whitley Bay and our weeks camp by the sea, and weather conditions didn't worry us at all. This was a great day. When we arrived at the campsite it was great to see the hundreds of bell tents, row after row of them; this was our home for seven days of holiday. At the main guard entrance we were met by a Staff Sergeant who conducted us to our own company tents where we dumped our kitbags and carbines and went off to the stores for ground sheets and blankets. At the cookhouse we were supplied with tea and bully beef sandwiches and then we started getting things organized in our tents and going into details of camp life where idle hands are not welcome. We got quite a thrill watching the brigade buglers and drummers on parade that evening to sound tattoo and later as we made our beds for the night the call of the last post echoed round the camp. Looking around that tent lit by the dim glow of a candle I had a strange feeling of contentment, I was with comrades, sharing their life, away from schools and teachers and home life, things seemed to be different somehow, and I liked the change. The bugler sounded lights out and as someone pinched out the candle we huddled down with only a ground sheet and a blanket between us and mother earth to sample our first night in the rough. I dozed off into an uneasy sleep soon to be awakened by a peculiar drumming sound on the tent, it was pouring with rain, and presently there was a howl from the far side of the tent 'Hi, move around you chaps the blinking tents leaking on me!' Some unfortunate had rubbed against the canvas and now he was paying the price of carelessness. There wasn't much in the way of sleep for us that first night, we were too new to the game, the ground was too hard, and the rain drummed on and on. The stirring notes of reveille opened the flaps of the tents to a scene of watery desolation, the camp was beginning to look like a quagmire, but wrapped up in overcoats and ground sheets we sallied forth to dig trenches around the tents and carry on at soldiering. The sad story is that it rained on and off all that week and more on than off, sometimes it was a drizzle but mostly it was a good steady downpour and everything in the camp was well and truly dampened except our spirits and a week of rain couldn't lower them. We proudly brought home the silver cup we won as the smartest company in the camp for marching and arms drill, Norman Ryder of our company was winner with top score for rifle shooting, and I won the 6 stone championship of the brigade by beating a boy from York on points. The last night in camp was a boisterous affair with singsongs in the marquee's and after lights out prowlers roamed the camp loosening guy ropes and dropping the tents on the unlucky occupants. One and all had a good time despite the rain and we all swore that next year would see us all together under canvas once more. A grand spirit of comradeship existed among those boys.

Back to the old routine at home once more and the after holiday feeling wasn't so good but for weeks afterwards our talk was all of the camp. My life at the technical college was running its normal course but I was finding sitting at a desk in a classroom pretty boring. My work was about average because I soon found that the easiest way to get through schoolwork was to do it right, doing it wrong led to no end of repetition. In the school sports line I didn't cut much ice at soccer, running, or jumping but I did manage a place on the hockey team. I swam sidestroke in the swimming competitions, I was the fast bowler on the school cricket team and I was on my own at weight in boxing. Quite a number of the boys at the pits were keen on boxing and I found plenty willing to have a go for a round or two. I know I was improving fast and I was becoming pretty confident of my ability. Outside my home life I was settling down to a pretty happy time but within the family circle I struck a bad patch about this time. One holiday weekend my parents went off together and left us to take care of ourselves and seeing it was summer time I suggested we should make a camp in the yard and be real Indians. We got busy with some old wood and matting that was lying around and soon erected a wigwam, lined the floor with matting and with some bricks we built a fireplace outside the wigwam. We soon had a nice little fire going and rigged up in our war bonnets we had great fun, the fire was quite safe because the yard was concrete and we were well away from the house. Once we were on the warpath we decided to do the job properly and spent the night in the wigwam, taking turns at keeping the fire going and in the morning we cleared everything away leaving no trace of our night out. However within a short space of time after my parents return my father sprung it on me about the fire in the yard; apparently some kindly neighbour had mentioned it and he came at me in a foul temper. I told him all that had transpired but it was like talking to an iceberg, boyish games were no excuse. He ordered me into the sitting room and he followed me in with a riding crop. This thing was a thin flexible strip of steel bound with leather used by horsemen and he certainly knew how to use it. I'm not blessed with a horse's hide and I yelled blue murder. I think that is what stopped him, he was afraid someone outside might hear the racket, but I had had enough to be going on with and from that day I disliked him more than ever. I considered the punishment harsh and unjust.

The following winter I again fell from grace and again I suffered the same punishment but it caused my cup of bitterness to overflow. I was on my way home from the drill hall with some of the brigade boys when we saw a red glow away across the fields, 'That's Johnson's farm on fire!' someone said and we at once decided to make our way there to help if we could. We ploughed our way across the snow covered fields and on arrival found a rare blaze going at the farm out buildings and quite a few people milling around. A policeman was on the job and he got things organized a bit, we found ourselves forming part of a line passing buckets of water from the farm pond. It was tiring back breaking work but we kept it up until the fire brigade got on the job with pumps and the farmhouse was saved. It was about midnight when I arrived home, dirty, wet and tired, and fury met me with the riding crop. I wasn't given the chance to explain, he just laced into me and he was in a pretty vicious mood. For some reason I rather foolishly took it in silence this time, perhaps I was too tired or too disgusted to care but as I crawled painfully to my bed I knew the gap between us had widened and it would never be bridged. The following day there was an article about the fire in the local paper and farmer Johnson stated his thanks to all who had helped with mention of the school boys who had assisted by carting water to the fire. I underlined this with pencil and stuck it under my father's nose, 'That's where I was, and that's what I got punished for!' I told him. It did no good; he just stared at me and through me with those ice-cold eyes and left me feeling bitter and dejected.

The third and last time I came under the threat of the riding crop led to a show down. I broke a window at the back of the house with a cricket ball and I went indoors and confessed it was my doing but I would pay for the repairs, he said nothing, he just reached for the riding crop. I eyed him steadily as he came towards me swinging the crop against his leg, 'You see that thing you have in your hand,' I said.

He stopped and stared at me, 'Yes, what about it?'

'Someday I'll be big enough and strong enough and I'm going to use it on you,' I answered. 'I can't stop you now, but when you've finished I'm going to the police station'

He stood and stared at me for a long time and then suddenly he turned away and flung the riding crop into the corner. 'Aw, hell, what's the use,' he growled and never again did he raise a hand to me and never again did he and I have anything in common. It was soon after this that I suggested I would like to take up a career as a sea going engineer, I think this idea was based on the fact that this sort of a job would take me away from home. He promised me he would contact some shipping firm to start as an apprentice but it never came to anything and I don't think he bothered to do anything about it.

My next year's camp was held at Saltburn, the weather was good to us this time and we had a wonderful holiday. There were plenty of massed parades with drums and bugles working overtime and we were involved in night operations with the army and navy that were practicing landings along the Yorkshire coast. We had some good evenings in the town and by now we were old enough to pick up some Yorkshire lasses who were only too willing to help us spend our pocket money in the fairground. We again won the silver cup at foot and arms drill as a company, Jimmy Forrest of our company won the single sticks competition, Norman Ryder was second in the .22 rifle shooting and I was beaten on points in the final of the boxing competition. I was 7 stone 6lbs at this time but there were no entries at this weight so I was asked to box in the heavier class 8 stone 6lbs. The chap I met in the final was too good for me to give away a stone in weight, we had a good fast hard bout and he got it on points. His name was Jimmy Learoyd of Leeds and years later he held the professional lightweight championship of the North of England.

I had plenty of friends now in my life, pals at school, pals in the brigade, and pals I met in the town, but up to now, although I had heard plenty of talk about girls I hadn't bothered myself much with that side of life. I knew and liked a number of girls I had met at school and also at our social events and I was growing up so I suppose it was natural to have a certain amount of interest in them but they were something I couldn't quite understand so I was happy to stay at arms length and listen to other chaps telling their tales of conquest. Then one day something hit me with a bang and it knocked all my ideas haywire for a time. I was left groping and wondering, more puzzled than ever about the female of the species.

Olive was leaning over her garden gate as I came along the road that evening and I stopped for a chat, I knew her well enough at our school where she was a star hockey player for the girls team. She was a dark haired blue eyed wench and rather striking looking in many ways.

She greeted me with a smile, 'You're just what I'm looking for Tommy, I'm stuck with my homework, give me a hand with it will you?'

'What's the trouble Olive?' I asked.

'Math's, beastly math's!' she moaned, 'I've got my figures all tied up in knots!'

'Good job its not music,' I grinned. 'I'm no use in that line'.

'Oh come in and give me some help with these beastly figures,' she said.

I didn't feel like meeting her folk so I answered, 'No Olive we can't do math's when your people are around, nothing doing'.

'Don't be silly, anyway my folk are away, there's only granny at home and she's out at present, come in and help me'.

She grabbed me by the arm and hustled me through the doorway; I was in before I knew it and I found myself in the entrance hall of their bungalow type house.

'In here,' said Olive, opening one of the doors and I stepped forward into .... A bedroom!

'This is my room, I keep all my stuff in here,' explained Olive and I saw a single bed along one wall and beside the window a desk piled with schoolbooks. It was a nice little room but I felt a bit uneasy as I took a seat by the desk and scanned the mass of figures scrawled on sheets of paper. For about half an hour we stewed over the math's but I got the impression that Olive wasn't concentrating on the problems a bit, she kept talking about anything but math's and she didn't seem to be able to sit still, she kept wandering about the room. Suddenly she threw her pencil on the desk with a clatter and grabbed hold of me, 'Oh, blow the math's lets lie on the bed and talk!'. Before I realized what was happening I was pushed on the bed and Olive was stretched out beside me holding my hands, 'This is a lot better,' said Olive wriggling close to me and suddenly I felt my hand on warm flesh. I reared up to a sitting position and saw that her dress was disarranged and she was holding my hand on her thigh, I suppose my eyes popped because she burst our laughing. 'Not frightened are you Tommy?' Frightened, I was scared stiff! I hopped off that bed and made a beeline for the wide-open spaces. I didn't know whether I had done right or wrong, my mind was in a whirl, but I had to put distance between Olive and myself. Later when I calmed down I tried to reason it out but the answers were all wrong, male and female, who chases whom, who is the seducer?

Olive and I had been school friends for some time previous to this incident but that was one friendship that went down the drain through no fault of mine. I found that whenever we met she looked at me as though I was something the cat had dragged in so I took the line of least resistance and avoided her as much as I could. I was sorry at the way things had developed but it was something I soon put out of my mind, sex was of no importance to me at that time and I didn't intend to get mixed up with that kind of thing. However it wasn't so easy as I thought and it wasn't long before another un-looked for incident occurred in my young life. Annie was two or three years older than me and a Sunday school teacher for the youngsters at the church. She seemed to do a lot of work for the church and she was keen on the socials, we often met at these affairs and we were good friends. We were both taking part in a sketch that was included in a show being given to raise funds, and I had a pretty strenuous part to play, which included a roughhouse scene. I dashed off the stage in a bit of a sweat and sat down on a box between Annie's feet, she was sitting on a chair with her feet on the box.

'That was pretty good Tommy,' she said leaning over me and I felt her knees pressing into my sides.

'Its pretty hard work Annie,' I answered, 'Feel my back I'm soaking with sweat!'

Her hand slid under the top of my vest and rested on my back and then she suddenly jerked me close to her whispering 'Take me home tonight Tommy, across the fields!'

Before I could recover we were called for our parts in the next scene and I carried out avoiding action by going home early and lost another friend!

Roller skating had become a craze around the country and some relations of mine formed a company and built a skating rink, I found this very much to my liking and I became very fond of the sport. I also found it a means to make pocket money by assisting with the repair of roller skates that were faulty and returned to the repair shop in an endless stream. Doing this job gave me free access to the rink and I made the most of it by skating blisters on my feet until they hardened but in time became a good fancy skater, pretty fast at straight skating, and a member of the local roller skating hockey team. This was a man's team and we played against men but I held my own and I held my place in the team in spite of some pretty hard knocks at times. Occasionally boxing matches were arranged to take place in the rink and I saw a number of thrilling battles take place. When I was approached with the offer of boxing a school boys exhibition bout of three rounds I jumped at the chance and looked forward eagerly to giving an exhibition before the locals.

They lined me up with a boy from Newcastle called Griffiths and we were boxing at seven stone eight pounds, like me he was a schoolboy. As I sat in the dressing room that evening waiting my turn I was surprised and delighted to see old Pat Dexter walk in.

'Sure an,' I just had to come and see you perform Tommy,' he said, he had walked ten miles to be here.

'I want you in my corner Pat,' I told him and he beamed with pleasure.

Griffiths and I stepped into the roped square and Pat was with me with a towel around his neck and a sponge in his hand. The referee mumbled his stuff about 'no clinching nice fast boxing boys etc.,' and Griffiths and I touched gloves. 'Fight,' said Griffiths under his breath. I gave him credit for that, he warned me before we started and I nodded. Back to our corners and then the gong went and our exhibition had started. I was in full spate right from the start, I landed a couple of good lefts, ducked a return and then sent in a stream of lefts that had Griffiths going back round the ring. I was landing hard and his face showed it. I weaved to his right, blocked the right counter punch he tossed at me and got home with a smashing right to his solar plexus. He gasped and dropped his hands and I cracked home a perfect left hook to his chin that left him hanging over the middle rope. I stepped away and he pulled himself clear of the ropes but as I moved towards him he held up his hand, it was all over and it had only lasted seconds. As he moved towards his corner his knees sagged but his second was there to catch him.

Old Pat danced with glee 'Out on his feet in half a round, nice work'. Pat hadn't needed his towel and his sponge but as he removed the gloves the referee came over to my corner, 'That was supposed to be an exhibition,' he said eyeing me sadly.

Pat rounded on him, 'Exhibition!' he snorted, 'What do you want, that just was an exhibition on how it should be done!'

I got quite a thrill out of this win, it was of no importance but it created a nice little stir among the local boxing fans for a day or two and I was pleased when Mr. Tom Welsh the manager of the local collieries came into my dressing room to congratulate me.

'I see you are boxing in sand shoes boy,' he said. I nodded my head and Pat held up one of my shoes, 'Yes and look at this one, its bust!' he remarked.

It hadn't been bust when I went into the ring but it was bust now all right.

'What size shoe do you take?' asked Mr. Welsh and when I told him he wrote it down in a notebook. Four days later a parcel arrived at my home and when I opened it I was delighted to find a lovely pair of soft calf boxing boots and a bill to say account paid!

I saw Griffiths before I left the rink and one side of his face was well puffed up, he grinned crookedly at me 'You were too fast,' he remarked.

His father patted me on the shoulder, 'You're a good kid but take a word of advice from me, you'll never keep that pace up, you'll burn yourself out!'.

I boxed half a dozen times later at the rink but they never again put me in with anyone at seven stone eight pounds, the opponents were round the eight stone six pound mark in youth exhibitions, so I was giving around one stone away. I found I had to nurse myself against the heavier weight but I won four of them, boxed one draw, and was beaten on points in one match. None of these bouts created the sensation that my bout with Griffiths had done but it was all grand sport and I was learning all the way. We received no payment for these exhibitions but I got gifts which included a new punch ball, a set of boxing gloves, a pair of boxing trunks, and a pair of boxing boots so I was quite happy. I also got a wonderful black eye that lasted for a couple of weeks from the chap who beat me on points, all in the game!

I was at a church social one evening and having the usual fun and games with the rest of the gang when I noticed a stranger at the other end of the room. Something about her attracted my attention and she seemed to know it, when she looked my way our glances seemed to lock and the rest of the company just faded away.

'Who is she?' I asked Jacky, a brigade pal.

'I don't know Tommy, she came along with the Chapelhow crowd, you'd better ask Joe'

I soon contacted Joe Chapelhow and he informed me that her people had just recently come to the town and they were living a few doors from him.

'Introduce me, Joe,' I told him with my eyes still on the girl.

'After a bit Tommy, I'm busy at present,' he replied.

'Joe, introduce me to that girl now!' I retorted and I took him by the arm and steered him through the crowd.

I shook hands with Mary as Joe introduced us and he left us looking into each other's eyes tongue tied and spellbound. She was a pretty girl with thick dark brown hair and deep brown eyes that looked straight at you and had you swimming in the clouds. We talked of this and that but don't ask me what this and that amounted to because I haven't the remotest idea, all I know is that from then on there was only Mary and I in that hall so far as we were concerned. As the evening went on I became more and more convinced that Mary was the complete answer so far as I was concerned, and she certainly had something! She was good company, she had good looks, and in her walk and carriage she was a born mannequin, if such beings are born!

At last I took the bull by both horns and said 'Mary, I'm taking you home tonight if .....'

She smiled at me, 'I've been waiting for that Tommy, I'll be pleased if you will'. I felt like climbing up the wall and everything in my world looked rosy and bright. Mary and I walked and we talked and I found a great deal of happiness in her company, at her gate that night I slid an arm around her waist and kissed her goodnight, with the promise of more to come. Walking home I was treading on air, the world seemed a better brighter place to live in. Mary had brought something into my young life that had been missing for a long time; life without love can be a pretty dreary affair for both young and old. Mary and I fell into the groove of meeting twice a week come hail, rain, snow or sunshine and how I looked forward to the many happy hours we spent together! It became recognized in the locality that Mary was my girl and mighty proud I was of the fact. As I suppose happens with most couples who are sailing along on a sea of contentment the day eventually came when a ripple of trouble stirred the surface and it was no fault of ours.

One evening at the drill hall we were making arrangements about our next annual brigade camp which was to be held at Redcar, most of the company were going but a few couldn't manage it, one of the few was Jimmy Forrest.

'I'm not going this year Tommy, how about you?'

'I wouldn't miss it for the world Jimmy,' I replied, 'Too good to miss'.

'Tell you what Tommy,' he said grinning at me, 'I'll have a better time than you by staying right here'.

'How do you make that out Jimmy?'

'I'll look after Miss Regal for you while you are away'.

'Miss who?'

'You know, Mary the sweet duchess!' he laughed, 'I'm not sleeping when you're out of the way'.

There was a snigger from the group of boys who were standing around and I felt the hot blood rush to my face. Without warning I stepped in and I hit him twice, hard. I intended hurting him and I gave him all I had. He went over backwards and he didn't attempt to rise; later it was said that his nose was injured and he required medical attention. There was consternation among the boys as Sergeant Smith barged in shouting 'Hi, no fighting here,' and Jimmy was picked up and attended to. His elder brother Tommy Forrest was present and he was prompt to take up arms on behalf of his fallen brother, those two stuck together. There was a lot of slang and argument and in the end we decided on settling it with the gloves, no more bare fist brawls said Sergeant Smith. The Forrest brothers were no mugs at the boxing game and being keen on sport they were both in good condition so I wasn't taking Tommy cheaply as we laced on the gloves and started milling. Tommy was a strong tearaway type but he was lacking in science and he was in a bad temper. The opening soon came, a short right uppercut under the breastbone had him gasping for breath and the following left hook took him smack on the point of the chin. He dropped face down to the floor, a pretty sure sign that he wouldn't get up, and he didn't! Two chaps down and out was pretty good going by anyone's reckoning, but I got no joy out of it, they were both friends of mine in the brigade. My father got to know of it and kicked up a row, the vicar of the church got to know of it and he preached me a weary lecture, worst of all Mary got to know of it and expressed her disapproval. Poor old Jimmy and Tommy Forrest, perhaps I was hasty in my actions, but I was pleased it didn't break our friendship, a friendship that was cut short and final a few months later when both these boys joined the Kings Royal Rifles and gave their lives for their country fighting in France in the war that was soon to come.

I was on holiday from school and kicking my heels in idleness awaiting the time for our summer camp when I met Jimmy Falcus sporting a heavily bandaged hand, with a wry smile he pointed to it and said, 'Bust it with an axe when I was chopping wood'.

'That'll put paid to your boxing for a bit Jimmy'.

He nodded gloomily, 'It will, and just when I was due to go to Newcastle for a week on a sparring partner job, George Dando has a big fight in London and he's short of sparring partners at our weight'.

Gosh - George Dando, the great little Welsh flyweight living in Newcastle and the idol of the Tyneside. Twice he had stepped into the ring to battle with the one and only Jimmy Wilde.

'Hard luck Jimmy,' I said to Falcus 'Boy I'd like a chance like that'.

Jimmy grabbed my arm, 'If I get if for you will you take it on Tommy?'

I wavered a bit, 'I can't go to Newcastle for a week Jimmy, I haven't any money and I might not do for Dando anyway'.

'You'll do all right Tommy, I'll get dad to arrange it. You can stay with my Uncle Jim in Newcastle, you'll get your expenses paid and thirty bob for yourself, will you take my place?'

I wanted the experience and I wanted thirty shillings, 'Righto Jimmy, you fix it and I'll have a go'.

Little did I know what I was letting myself in for, but I did have the satisfaction of crossing gloves with one of this country's greats, although he was now past his best. George Dando was smaller and lighter than me but he moved like a flash, he was as elusive as a shadow and he threw punches at a bewildering speed, two rounds was as much as I could get through with him at a time and two rounds was as much as I wanted at a time! He had four sparring partners, two featherweights and one bantamweight professionals, and myself, and by taking turns of two rounds each Dando worked his way through eight rounds of boxing morning and evening. We tramped and trotted around the countryside at Jesmond Dene and outside the ropes we had a good time but once inside the ropes Dando was a holy terror. The front of my body was covered with purple bruises from those pounding gloves and by the time the week was up my lips were like sausages, my left eye was like a rainbow, I had a broken front tooth, and I felt as fit as a fiddle when I returned home with thirty shillings in my pocket. Mary took one look at my face that evening and nearly threw a fit.

'Its no use Tommy, you'll have to give it up,' Give up boxing, I stared at her, boxing was as much part of my life as she was.

I shook my head; 'I can't give up boxing Mary'.

'Have you looked in a mirror Tommy?' she asked me and I laughed.

'Don't worry about that Mary, it will be gone in a few days'.

'You're in a mess and you look a mess, you're heading to be a professional boxer Tommy, and that's no use to me'.

'I don't want to be a professional Mary, it's just the sport I like'.

'Well chuck it Tommy, before its too late,' she replied.

Shortly after this we departed for our annual camp, this year was 1914 and it was the last week in July. Once again we were greeted by the wonderful sight of hundreds of tents along the cliff tops at Redcar, and once again we were looking forward to a wonderful holiday; indifferent to the fact that in Europe the dogs of war were snapping and snarling, the tramp of jackboots was resounding on the German frontiers, and the mailed fist was poised and ready to strike. Germany where the man in the street was changing into the field grey of the imperial army! In our camp at Redcar we seemed to be isolated from international troubles and we only gave a passing thought to the rumours that were flying thick and fast, holiday, that was all that mattered. The normal routine of camp life went on, the weather was fine, the sea was blue, the beaches and the town looked good, why the hell should we bother about this emperor or that king, but behind all the fun and games we could feel a certain amount of tension among the officers and staff of the brigade, mostly army types. The guns of Austria and Serbia were already breaking the uneasy peace of the world and then on August 1st Germany declared war on Russia. Still, all this was far away from us until suddenly we heard that Germany and France were at war on Sunday August 2nd with a declaration on the same day for the mobilizing of the British fleet, things were coming nearer to us! The German armed forces were on the move and they crashed without warning into Luxembourg and Belgium at 11 o'clock at night on August 4th, word flashed around the camp that Britain was at war with Germany. There was little sleep that night, the whole camp buzzed like a hive of bees, we were in it, the British lion was awake! 'Wait till our fleet get at them!' 'The British Army and the French together - Oh boy we'd show em!' We sat in our tents by candlelight and the talk was war, war, war! Bugle calls on the battlefield, glorious charges of cavalry with lance and sword, famous British squares fighting around the colours, all the pomp and glory of battles fought through our history with our minds steeped in the bygone days of Alma and Waterloo, the knowledge of the misery and horror, the sorrowing and suffering of modern methods of slaughter was mercifully hidden from us.

'As soon as I get home I'm joining up,' someone said proudly and the echo ran through the tent 'and me!' 'and me!'

'We'll have to hurry up,' said Jacky Barrett 'It'll be all over by Christmas'.

'We don't want to miss it, we'll join right away,' said Norman Ryder.

Miss it, this was the early hours of August 5th, how could we foresee four weary years of death, pain, misery and filth. At daybreak came orders to break camp, our holiday was over and we had to return home, the camp was needed for troops. So we packed our kit and boarded the train for home, never mind, we would soon be off again in khaki. 'Look at them! There they go!' and we crowded to the windows of the train to watch and wave to a battery of horse artillery trotting down a country lane. At Newcastle as we changed trains we watched a battalion of Northumberland Fusiliers entraining, the barriers crowded with people waving and cheering and the band playing on the platform. Gosh how we envied you Tommy Atkins, a front seat in the stalls for you when there was trouble brewing. Make way for the heroes!

Upon arrival at home I found things in a state of upheaval with my mother packing up things for my father and he strutting around in his field service khaki, buttons sparkling, spurs jingling, belt and leggings glowing, he had got his papers to report. For a brief day or two he held the stage and basked in the local hero worship and then he was off, off to win the war and his last words to me were 'You stay at home and help your mother!' Like hell I would. I was just living for the day when I would be doing just as he was doing now. I couldn't bear the idea of sitting at a school desk when the country was at war so I had an interview with Mr. Welsh and he agreed to start me at the colliery power station as an apprentice trainee engineer. That was me finished with schoolwork, I thought. I soon found myself attending night classes and deeper than ever in studying while I worked eleven hours a day heaving buckets of oil for the turbine sumps, scrubbing floors, and shovelling coal with the firemen to keep the wheels turning. As a result of this I wasn't seeing much of Mary but made the best of a bad job and we still had an odd evening together. Boxing wasn't mentioned between us now, it seemed to be a banned subject, but I could sense a feeling of restraint between us that hadn't been there before our little upheaval and I think Mary was brooding a bit on her inability to turn me. The boys of the brigade were drifting away into various regiments and I was getting restless hanging around at home; eventually I said to Mary one evening as we walked through the fields:

'Mary, I'm joining up as soon as I can'.

She looked at me, 'You can't do that Tommy, you're too young!'

'I won't let that stop me, I'm going to have a crack at it, will you write to me Mary while I am away?'

We walked in silence for a bit and then Mary pointed to a seat off the path, 'Lets sit over there Tommy, I want to talk to you'.

It was a bright moonlight evening and as we sat on the bench I wondered what was coming, and hoped it was something good.

'Listen to me Tommy,' Mary said slipping her hand into mine, 'You know I think the world of you, you've become very very dear to me, but the time has come when we must come to an understanding. You seem to have a craze for fighting and I don't like it, your happiest moments seem to be when you're pulling on the gloves to fight and now you're talking of joining the army to fight, you're fighting daft!'

'Aw,' listen Mary, boxing isn't fighting, its just sport'.

'Where's it all going to end, I'll tell you, you're shaping to become a professional boxer and you'll finish up battered and broken like they all do, give it up Tommy before its too late'.

'I can't Mary, I'm boxing an exhibition for hospital funds next week'.

'Who are you boxing?'

'Kid Hunter of Gateshead, we're boxing at Birtley Miners Hall'.

'Kid Hunter's a professional isn't he?'

I nodded my head glumly.

'There you are Tommy,' explained Mary hammering home her point, 'You see the sort of company you're drifting into, George Dando and now Kid Hunter'.

'Aw', they're good chaps Mary and its just for sport,' I replied.

'And now although you're under age you want to go fighting in the war!'

'But listen Mary, the country is at war, our country needs men'.

'Men Tommy, not boys!' That shook me and I was silent.

Mary leaned back on the bench and she looked bewitching in her light summer frock in the bright moonlight, she was suddenly all woman.

'Kiss me Tommy,' she murmured, and as I leaned over her to do so I saw tears on her cheeks.

'Tommy, give up your boxing, don't go soldiering, promise me and I'm all yours!' she gasped.

Sadly I drew away from her and I knew we had reached the end of our road. Mary had willingly thrown everything on to the scales but it couldn't change my way of life. We walked home quiet and subdued and I kissed her goodnight but it wasn't the same. The following week I was rubbing my feet in the resin in the corner of the boxing ring in the miners hall at Birtley for my three round exhibition bout with Kid Hunter, and all I got out of that was a pat on the back and a split lip!

Lord Kichener's historical call for men rang throughout the country, 'Your king and country need you,' and there was nothing half hearted in the response. Lines of men formed up and outside the recruiting offices to join the army, tall and short, thin and fat, men from offices and work benches, men from shipyards and farms and pits, volunteers every one of them. But you must be over 19 years of age! I lined up with the rest at our local recruiting office and when my time came to stand before the recruiting Sergeant he just looked at me with tired eyes and said 'Come back when you're nineteen Tommy, next man'. I had forgotten I was well known locally! Everyday saw crowds of men marching off to the station to join various regents, North, East, South and West.

'Where are you going to?'

'Anywhere, we don't care, we're in the army now'.

And back I went to my work at the colliery. My father returned home in September and during this period he had crossed to France, got wounded at Ypres, been discharged from hospital and what he hadn't done to the German army during this brief period was nobody's business. He told his tale to all who would listen and he wallowed in the hero worship that came his way, he loved it! He attended church service in his flash blue and silver braid uniform, marched down the aisle with jingling spurs to a seat in the front pew where everyone would see him, and in the back seat I heard the squeaks of female admiration as he did his stuff. It's a wonder to me that they didn't offer up prayers of thanksgiving that he was back in circulation. What a showman that man was to be sure. However, he had been to the front, and me, I was still tied up at home and finding it hard to make a move. The brigade was now down to about half strength as the boys drifted away into the forces and history was being made in France with the retreat from Mons, the battle of Le Cateau, the battle of Marne, the battle of the Aisne, and the first and second battle of Ypres. The navy had battled it out with the enemy at Coronel and the Falkland Islands and at home the newspapers lists of killed, wounded and missing grew daily longer and longer. The year of 1914 was drawing to a close when the country was shocked by the news that German warships had approached our shores and bombarded Hartlepool, Scarborough and Whitby causing 671 casualties, the war was coming very near. My father went off to join a reserve unit of his regiment in Yorkshire and the New Year saw me once again in a recruiting office, this time away from home where I was not known.

The Sergeant accepted my age as nineteen and I stripped off for him to get busy with a tape measure, when he measured my chest he stepped back and grunted, 'You're in good shape son, but you're quarter of an inch short round the chest, put your cloths on'. In those days you had to be a certain size before they would accept you for the army, perhaps the idea was to give the German a better target, anyway that was me out once more and back home to the same old routine, disgusted. I got myself a pair of Indian clubs and put in an intensive course of daily club swinging; I would raise that quarter of an inch or bust in the attempt. Then I saw a poster calling for volunteers for the Royal Navy, men and boys, here we go again, dreams of bell bottomed trousers and a rolling deck, I'm having a go at this! I rode 25 miles on my bike to Newcastle where I had to report on an old training ship on the river Tyne and on arriving there I found four chaps at the gangway on the same mission as myself. We were instructed to step aboard and await instructions and it gave me quite a thrill to feel the deck of a ship under my feet. One of the chaps was having a quiet puff at a cigarette when a Chief Petty Officer appeared on the scene, and the blast of his voice nearly swept us overboard. 'Put that bloody fag out, not on the deck blast you, sling it overboard, if I see any ash about I'll rope end you!' He lined us up and glared at us, 'So you want to join the navy eh', dunno what the hell we're coming to, all right you lubbers follow me below and run, run you buggers RUN!' We doubled after him in panic and nearly tumbled head first down in iron runged ladder into the bowels of the ship, along a narrow alleyway and into a room where again he lined us up. 'Right me lads off with your clobber and make it snappy'. Within a minute or two we were standing shyly in a row, three of us in the nude and two in their underpants. The Petty Officer was writing at a table and now he looked up and approached us with a growl, 'You two birds in the pants, I said strip off and I mean strip off, do you think we got you aboard to seduce you, get those pants off!'. He eyed us balefully up and down, 'Hell, you'll look a credit to the British navy, the ladies of Naples won't rejoice much over those little titbits of yours, we'll have to make men of you, me lads, before we let you ashore anywhere, there's not enough among the five of you for one decent pair of bell bottomed trousers!' In turn we stepped on the scales and I was the lightest of the chaps. I just touched 8 stone; 'What do you feed on son, canary seed?'

I looked him in the eye, 'There's no fat on me sir,' I answered.

He ran his hand over me 'What's your line of sport son?'

'Boxing sir,' I replied, 'I'm in better trim than these chaps'.

'Good enough,' he said, 'Now I'll have your names, addresses if any, ages and all the rest of your sinful history and then we'll scare the doctor into fits by letting him have a look at you'. For the benefit of the doctor the tape measure was run over us, teeth examined, chests sounded, eye sight tested, we hopped around on one foot and then the other, more listening at the chest and then we were told to get dressed. The Petty Officer remarked, 'You look more human with your clobber on!' Maybe he was right at that! One fellow left us, his eyesight had let him down, but the rest of us were told to hang around for further instructions. After a short wait the Petty

Officer approached us with a bunch of papers in his hand giving each of us a sheet, 'You'll take that paper home with you and get it signed by your parents, you're all under nineteen so the navy won't take you for the duration of the war, you've got to take on for twelve years, but only with your parents consent'.

Then we were ushered off the ship discussing the big question, would our parents be willing to sign us away for twelve long years, personally I had my doubts and already I could see my hopes of a life on the rolling deep fading away. My mother didn't fancy the idea at all but I got her talked into sending the paper to my father who was still stationed at York, and for the next few days while awaiting his reply I spent my time living and dreaming Royal Navy. My friends Joe and Jacky had both gone into the army and our company of the brigade was sadly depleted, everyday men were marching off in every town and village throughout the land, men and more men for France was the cry. And over in France Tommy Atkins was hanging on through the battle of Neuve Chapelle, undergoing the agony of the first use of chlorine gas by the Germans in the Ypres salient, forcing a landing on the Gallipoli peninsula over the bodies of their comrades against the Turks and the Royal Navy hammering it out with the enemy in the battle of the Dogger Bank.

'Oh its 'Tommy this and Tommy that,' and 'Tommy how's your soul?'

But its 'Tommy you're a hero when the drums begin to roll'.

While awaiting my father's hoped for signature I called on Fred, an ex-brigade boy who was now training for a post as a seagoing engineer; I wanted a few tips from him on seagoing details now that I was hoping to go that way myself. I found Fred at his home all right and I also found his sister Mona, seagoing matters were at once pushed into the background and so was Fred! Mona was on holiday from college in Leeds where she was training for the teaching profession and Mona was something worth looking at. Perhaps she didn't have the same natural grace of Mary but the dark beauty of her face could have adorned any chocolate box, if Mona kept her looks she must have grown into a woman of striking beauty. I knew Fred had a sister of course but I didn't know he had kept anything like this in the background; before that evening was out I had made quite a lot of headway and found Mona was very nice to know. That night she told me she wouldn't mind having me as a boyfriend providing I went into the navy, but if I went into the army the answer was no.

'What's the idea of that Mona?' I asked her.

'Well you see Tommy, soldiers get knocked about and get some awful wounds, I wouldn't like to have a boy like that!'

Well, I ask you, I wonder what she thought happened to a sailor when his ship got a packet! Anyway it wasn't for a youngster like me to try to solve the whims and fancies of the female mind so I just accepted what was offered and I had a very happy time with Mona while it lasted. Then came my father's reply refusing his consent to my application and, although I half expected it, I took it rather badly. Mona's holiday was over all too soon and she returned to Leeds, and worst of all a rumour got around that the enlistment of men working at the collieries was soon to be stopped. It began to look to me as though I was going to miss everything. I was feeling pretty miserable about it all, the meetings of the brigade were dull with most of the old gang away in the forces, some of them were overseas, two were in hospital with wounds, and the Forrest boys, Jimmy and Tommy were dead in France. Nothing seemed to be coming my way and then to put the lid on my misfortune I got mixed up in a spot of trouble at work.

We were kicking a ball around in the colliery yard during the lunch hour one day when I kicked the ball high and it thumped against a door that was newly painted, white and wet. The ball was covered with coal dust and needless to say it made a nasty mess of the white paint. The foreman painter gaped at it for a minute and then he came over to me frothing at the mouth, 'What the hell did you do that for?' he shouted.

'Sorry,' I replied 'I couldn't help it'.

He was a tall thin chap of middle age and he was trembling with rage 'You're a bloody liar,' he cried 'You did it on purpose,' and he grabbed me by the lapels of my coat and shook me.

'Aw', chuck it, it was an accident, I'm sorry,' I said as I broke his grip on my coat, and then the unexpected happened. He swung his right arm and his open palm caught me a resounding slap on the cheek that sent me staggering back.

Temper flared up in me and I was about to rush in when my boxing experience whispered 'Steady yourself, calm down'. However I knew I couldn't leave things just like that in front of a bunch of work mates so I said 'All right if that's the way you want it I'm willing,' and rather foolishly I turned my back to him to remove my coat for the fray. With a rush he was on me before I could turn to face him and from behind his long arms were around me locking my arms to my side. For a moment I was helpless and then I realized he intended to throw me. I could feel his hot breath on the back of my head as his arms tightened their grip. I lifted my left foot and brought my heel down hard on his foot and at the same time threw myself backwards. We landed on the ground in a heap with him underneath and there was a sharp thud and a gasp from the painter. I jumped to my feet ready for the next move but there was no next move, he just lay where he had fell, his eyes closed and his mouth hanging open, he was out! The back of his head had hit the ground a terrific thump, it was cut and bleeding and it was awhile before he was brought round in the first aid room, bandaged and sent home. I was on the carpet for this affair but I got away with it, only just, owing to the fact that the foreman had struck the first blow. All the same I got a first rate dressing down from the manager.

'I hope you won't hold this against me Mr. Welsh when I come back,' I said at the end of the interview.

He looked at me 'When you come back, what do you mean?'

'I'm enlisting as soon as I can, sir'.

'You're a bit young for that Tommy, wait a bit'.

'No sir, I'm going and I'm going soon'.

'Ah,' well, maybe it will do you a bit of good, good luck anyway'.

Once more I tramped a few miles from home for a recruiting office where I wasn't known and I stood before a be-ribboned Sergeant.

'I want to join the army Sergeant'.

'How old are you son?'

'Nineteen years two months,' I lied.

'Right, strip off an,' lets have a look at you'.

Out came the tape measure once more and he went through his job without comment, I had made it! 'That's fine, now lets have your name, address, trade an,' I'll take you in for the doctor!'. In an adjoining room I faced a civilian doctor and an army officer and went through with the usual routine, eyes, teeth, ears, chest and canary hopping around the room. The Sergeant scribbled away filling in all the details and then handed the completed form to the officer, 'All complete, sir'. The officer glanced over the form and then handed me a bible, 'I'm going to swear you in now and that will complete the job'. I took the oath to serve my king and country and the Sergeant handed me the king's shilling. 'And now me lad,' he said 'Just remember this, from now on you're a soldier of the king, you can go home until we send for you, make arrangements about leaving your job and report at once when you get the word. Make no mistake, you're in the army now and from now on we can do anything with you, except put you in the family way!' They laughed at the joke and I grinned sheepishly and passed out into the sunshine, 'Glory be, I was a soldier at last!' I was walking on air, the sky was blue, the birds were singing, everything was coming up my way. I told my mother that I had enlisted in the army and she stressed the fact that I couldn't go overseas, I was under age! I reported to the colliery that I would be packing up soon as my papers came through and the only one who seemed to be excited about it was me. However I didn't worry even if they didn't run up any flags for me, for three days I met the postman at the door, and then it came, O.H.M.S. for me! 'You will report at Newcastle barracks forthwith, enclosed find railway warrant etc.!'

2.   KING AND COUNTRY

The next morning bright and early I was off, carrying all I needed in a little brown paper parcel, there was no band playing and no flags flying, boyfriends and girlfriends knew nothing of my going. I just had the feeling that I was passing from something with which I wasn't satisfied into something that was going to open out a new way of life for me. I entered the barrack gates and handed over my papers at the guardroom and a Corporal took charge of me and soon had me fixed up with a bed in a long room in the barracks. That first night in a barrack room full of soldiers was a strange one to me but I was happy and contented and I slept well. After breakfast the next morning I reported to the orderly room and after a short wait with another newly joined rookey, a Sergeant Major handed each of us an envelope and a warrant and ordered us to catch a train for Barnard Castle and report to the 15th battalion stationed there. Dick Knight had all his worldly goods stuffed in his pockets but he said the army would soon provide us with everything.

'They're letting us travel for nothing now,' he said with a grin.

'Do you think we'll get to France, Dick?' I asked him as we watched the scenery go by.

'Nothing surer,' he exclaimed, 'alf,' a mo,' Kaiser, here we come!'

'The blinkin,' war might be over before we're ready'.

'Aw,' nuts to that Tommy, this ruddy war is just starting'.

At Barnard Castle we were directed to a school occupied by the troops and in the schoolyard the cooks were busy around a fire.

'Just joined up chums?' asked an elderly soldier in overalls 'Well you don't know what you've let yourselves in for, come an,' have a drop of char, we've just brewed up'.

We sat on boxes and had a tin mug of tea each, and believe me that stuff made your hair curl; they must have measured the tea out with a shovel.

'Do we live in this school?' I asked.

'Just for tonight son, we move in the morning to Durbolt camp under canvas a couple of miles out of town, now if you've finished your tea report to the school, you'll find an N.C.O. there'.

We found a Sergeant in the school and handed over our papers to him. 'Recruits eh,' he said and then he yelled 'Corporal Jennings, where the hell are you?' A Corporal dashed in, 'Oh there you are, here's a couple of rookies for you to wet nurse, get 'em fixed up'. The Corporal got us a couple of blankets each and pointed out where we had to sleep in the school room and then we were left to our own devices, nobody was bothering much about us. At about five o'clock we heard the tramp of marching feet and we watched our company march into the schoolyard to be dismissed, there was a rush of chaps into the room to dump their equipment and soon mugs of tea and slabs of bread and bully were dished around. There was plenty to eat and drink and we sat on forms at bare scrubbed tables to enjoy it, and enjoy it we did to the rough jokes and laughter of the company. The boys in khaki looked fit and full of health and good spirits and they saw to it that the two rookies didn't go short.

'Oh, its Tommy, Tommy Atkins you're a good un,' heart an,' hand,
You're a credit to your calling and to all your native land.
May your luck be never failing, may your girl be ever true,
Oh Mister Tommy Atkins, here's your country's love to you!'

After tea someone tapped me on the shoulder and said, 'Now I wonder what the hell sent you here,' looking around I found Jacky Barrett grinning at me.

'Gosh, this is great Jacky,' I cried grabbing his hand, 'We're both in the same company'.

'Yes and Joe is here too, so is Tommy Lowery; Hi Joe,' he yelled, 'Come and see what we've got'.

We laughed and shook hands and talked of how fine it was school days together, the brigade together, and now we were in the army to soldier together. Had we been able to peer into the future we wouldn't have laughed so much, but the future was hidden from us.

The next morning we marched to Durbolt camp where rows of bell tents awaited us and after much ado we got settled down as happy as sandboys. This was no one-week camp with the brigade; this was our home for week after week of the real thing. Dick and I were detailed to fall in with the awkward squad for recruits training and we spent hours learning to march and turn, how to stand, how to form fours, how to salute etc., dead easy stuff for me owing to my brigade training but the N.C.O. in charge was spitting blood at the rest of the squad. That evening I was sitting outside my tent when Joe came along off parade and handed me his rifle 'See what you can do with that Tommy,' he said with a grin, 'You'll find it a bit heavier than our old brigade carbines'. I stood up and took his rifle, it certainly felt a bit heavier but it felt good to have a weapon in my hands once more, it was a Lee Enfield and well balanced. I had been pretty good at arms drill in the brigade and it was no trouble to go through the motions of slope order, port, present etc.

'It's the same old stuff Joe,' I said as I came back to the stand at ease position.

'Hello, what's all this?' barked a voice behind me and I turned to see the stiff figure of a Company Sergeant Major who had been watching the performance, 'Keep hold of that rifle, you, and carry out my orders, ready?'

I took the rifle to the order arms position and stood fast. Swiftly he snapped the orders at me, right through the arms drill section of infantry training, brought me to the stand easy and then stepped up to me.

'How long have you been in the army, you're still in civvies?'

'Two days sir,' I replied.

'Two days eh', an,' how the hell do you learn that lot in two ruddy days, you can tell that tale to the marines, what were you in before you came to us? Now come on lad, I want the truth an,' I'll ruddy well get it!'

An officer was approaching down the tent lines and he paused as he heard the Sergeant Majors words, 'What's the trouble?'

The C.S.M. snapped into a brisk salute as he faced the officer. 'Its this here chap in civvies sir,' he barked, 'Been with us a couple of days and he's doing arms drill like a time serving man, he's no rookey sir, he's been with some other unit'.

The officer looked me over, 'I shouldn't think so Sergeant Major, he's only a youngster, a bit too young to have served with some other crowd, you're not a deserter my lad are you?'

'No, sir'.

'Well then, just explain how you come to know arms drill'.

'Four years with the Church Lads Brigade sir'.

The officer laughed, 'That's the answer Sergeant Major, they do arms drill the same as the army, wish we had more like him'.

The officer strolled away and after a pause the C.S.M. yelled, 'Corporal Dixon!' Pass word along I want Corporal Dixon!'

The N.C.O. who handled the awkward squad arrived at the double, 'Yes, Sergeant Major?'

'Why the hell didn't you report a trained man among your recruits? This chap goes into a platoon tomorrow for regular training!'

'He's still in civvies Sergeant Major,' pointed out the Corporal.

'I don't care a damn if he's in the nude, he's wasting his time in your mob, do as I say'.

> *Linseed oil and four by two*
> *Bags of lick and spit.*
> *That's what won us Waterloo*
> *And makes our army fit.*
> *Polish brush and button stick*
> *To make our buttons shine*
> *And if our tummies are not right*
> *The cure's a number nine.*
> *Burnish up those toecaps*
> *Make that badge look bright.*
> *That's how soldier men are made*
> *To sweat, and march and fight.*
> *Blanco up that webbing*

And make those buckles glow
Oh, you've got to spit and polish
When you hear that bugle blow!

That was the beginning and the end of my recruit training. I paraded the next morning in number eleven platoon and showed I was quite capable of holding my end up on the parade ground. A hectic happy week of training went by, a week of marching and drilling and physical training, but I was still in civvies and getting a bit worried about the state of my shirt, socks and shoes. I had no change so I had reason to worry. Spud Baker was an old soldier wearing enough medal ribbons to choke a cow and sitting in the tent one night he said to me, 'You should just bugger off home Tommy, you've got a fine excuse'.

'Aw shut up Spud,' said Lance Corporal Allan 'You'll get the kid into trouble with that kind of talk'.

'Shut up yourself an,' read your kings rules and regulations,' growled Spud, 'I tell you they got no right to keep a bloke without a full kit, he's entitled to it, you can't soldier in civvies'.

'You can soldier in your bare feet if they want you to,' said Allan.

Spud glowered at him, 'What the hell do you know about soldiering, one tape up an,' you think you know all the answers. I was soldiering when your bottom was the size of a shirt button. Take the kid to the orderly room tomorrow an,' get him issued'.

After a bit of argument I asked for and got an interview with the Company Officer at the orderly room the next morning.

'Well, what's your trouble?' asked the officer when I stood before him.

'I wish to apply for leave sir,' I replied.

'How long have you been here?'

'Just over a week sir'.

'Good God man, you can't have leave just like that, five minutes in the army and you want to go home, you're a soldier now'.

'I'm a soldier sir but I object to soldiering in dirty civvies, I haven't been issued with anything and I want a change of clothing'.

He looked me over as though he saw me for the first time.

'Dear me, this is bad, very bad, Sergeant, take this man to Q.M.S. and get him kitted out at once, can't have this'.

I had paraded under that officer for a week so I can only surmise that his eyesight must have been pretty poor if he hadn't noticed that lonely civilian in a company of khaki. However within an hour I was laden with every item of kit in the book from button stick to rifle and bayonet and I lugged it back to my tent, it wasn't long before I chucked the civvies to one side and stood arrayed in khaki at last. That night the platoon Sergeant called me out and handed me a paper, 'Forty eight hours leave for you, take your civvies home with you, and get back on time, you're lucky'.

Spud Baker grunted 'Lucky hell! That's not luck Tommy, we just played the old cards right, that's all'.

The next morning I was off for home with my civvies done up in a paper parcel, my putties felt tight on my legs, my tunic collar felt rough round my neck, my cheese cutter hat felt tight on my head, but I was a happy warrior! At home I gathered together the odds and ends I now knew I would require in camp and decided I would take my boxing boots and pants back with me, I hadn't seen any boxing at the camp but according to the talk it was there at times. I soon grew restless at home, even in that short space of time, things seemed different, and after the company of my comrades in camp I was feeling lonely. I was pleased when it was time to get the train back to Barnard Castle, civilian life was a thing of the past, from now on the slap of rifles on parade and the crunch of marching feet was my life and I asked nothing more. I soon realized that the army was a strange organization. They issued you with razor and lather brush for shaving but never any soap, a button stick for cleaning buttons and buckles but never any polish, handkerchiefs and pyjamas were not on the issue list. You worked, and drilled and sweated and slept in your old grey back shirt and whatever you lost you paid for out of your one shilling a day. There was only one answer to that one, if you lost anything, from boot laces to greatcoat you just pinched someone else's before the next kit inspection and considered you had won it. After all, it was all government property and we were soldiers in the service of the government so that was made an excuse to cover a multitude of sins.

In those early days of 1915 the services were run on the lines that officers were a breed apart and this was a code that was accepted by the men in the ranks, but early in my own soldiering career I came into contact with an officer who rather changed my opinion of this class distinction. It happened on a kit inspection when everything in the tents had to be laid outside in an orderly manner and you stood by your array of worldly goods awaiting the officers,' inspection. The orderly Sergeant checked my stuff and found correct and then the officer pointed with his stick to the small canvas bag that lay alongside my kit, 'What's that for Sergeant?' he asked.

The Sergeant looked at me with raised brows 'What's in that bag?'

'Private possessions, Sergeant'.

'Turn it out, smart!' rapped the Sergeant, and as I upended the canvas bag to show my pants and boxing boots along with a couple of text books on boxing I realized that there's no such thing as private possessions in the army.

The officer turned them over with his cane and then looked me in the eye 'Professional or amateur?' he asked.

'Amateur sir,' I replied standing stiffly to attention 'I like the sport'.

'Good, Sergeant, remind me to have a word with this chap after parade, will you!'

'Very good, sir'.

Half an hour later the Sergeant came into our tent, 'Oh, you're here, get your tunic on and come with me'.

'What's brewing Sergeant?' I inquired as I stepped along with him.

'Dunno,' he grunted, 'All I know is Lieutenant Stuart Walker says I have to take you to his tent in the officers lines so I expect you're in for something'.

In the officers lines the Sergeant said 'You wait here,' and he dived into one of the tents, within a minute or two he was out again and said with a jerk of the thumb, 'Lieutenant Stuart Walker will see you in there, and don't forget to salute'.

I stepped into the tent with a snappy salute for the officer who sat on a camp bed in his shirtsleeves. He looked at me with a half smile 'All right, cut out the regimental stuff, just take a pew and we'll have a little heart to heart talk'.

I sat down and the officer lit a cigarette, 'Now tell me all about it,' he said.

'All about what sir?' I asked, not grasping his meaning.

For answer he pointed his cigarette to the tent pole and there I saw hanging from a hook a set of boxing gloves, 'They are mine and I'm proud of them, now how much of this have you done, just tell me your little story of the ring and forget the army'.

Briefly I gave him an outline of my boxing experiences and he made no comment until I mentioned the fact that I had sparred with Dando at Newcastle and then he broke in, 'George Dando eh,' - I saw him fight in London, you were crossing gloves with a good one'.

I grinned, 'A lot too good for me sir'.

'Yes, I expect so, now I wonder how you would like to have a little spar with me now and again?'

I shook my head 'Sorry sir, you're an officer'.

He stood up 'Damn it all I'm not an officer when I strip down to boxing kit. I boxed at Rugby a lot and I don't want to lose my style yet awhile, what about it?'

Again I shook my head, 'It won't do sir, someone would see us at it and word would go round the battalion, then trouble for you.

'Listen to me,' he said earnestly 'I know a farmer in Barnard Castle and he will be willing to let us use his barn, we can keep our mouths shut and no one will be any the wiser, what about it?'

For a moment I hesitated but the call of the game was too strong in me 'All right sir I'll do it, but what are you going to tell the Colonel if you turn up at the mess with a black eye?'

He laughed, 'Leave the excuses for me to find, and thanks'.

And that's how Lieutenant Stuart Walker came to cross gloves with Private Tommy Atkins to the mutual benefit of us both. He was tall and thin and didn't look like trouble but I soon found he could move around and he could box. At first I thought we would just be engaged in a round or two of fancy sparring until he changed all my ideas with a tearing uppercut that put me flat on my back. As I climbed to my feet he said 'Sorry but you left yourself wide open to that one'. I grinned ruefully and tore into him, aware now that he was good enough to give me a fight. By his arrangement we met at the old barn twice a week and we had some merry mills that did me a power of good both from a boxing point of view and also with regard to my attitude towards the men who were to lead us in battle. They might dress like tailors dummies and talk like cissies but underneath it all they could be real men. He asked me to become his batman, a cushy billet, but I turned that down flat.

'Why won't you take it?' he asked 'It will get you off these parades'.

'I don't want to get off parades,' I answered him, 'I joined the army to soldier sir, not to be someone's servant'.

He looked at me 'You're a queer chap, I believe you like soldiering'.

'Yes sir, soldiering suits me fine'.

The routine training went on from dawn to dusk and sometimes through the night and many were the miles we tramped through the country burdened with full marching order; gradually we hardened to it and felt the benefit of it. At the break of dawn the bugles sending the call of reveille echoing across the fields brought us from our tents to form up and then away at the double for our early morning run. Back to the camp and that wonderful smell of burning wood and frying bacon from the cook house and we were at that breakfast like a hungry pack of wolves. Spit and polish and out on parade once more until we were beginning to shape into something like an army should be, knitted and welded together into a fighting unit. Friday was the big day of the week, on Friday afternoon we paraded for our pay and married men stepped forward to salute for the lordly sum of three shillings and sixpence, single chaps not making an allowance draw seven shillings a week. I was one of the lucky ones and considered to be well off on seven bob a week. After pay parade the wet canteen got busy selling ale, and the fly boys got busy with the crown and anchor boards and housey, the result being that most chaps were broke before lights out. One Friday evening I returned to our tent to find Spud Baker sitting glumly on his roll of blankets sucking at his pipe.

'Hello, Spud what's wrong, canteen gone dry?' I asked.

He grunted and pulled his hand out of his pocket, 'Look at that,' he growled opening his hand and showing one shilling, 'That's what the bloody army gives me for a lousy weeks pay, that's what I had to bloody well salute for today!'

'Only a bob, how's that come about?' I asked.

'Some lousy bugger pinched me best walkin,' out tunic, an,' now I'm charged for it, worse than the 'eathens in India this bloody mob, they'd pinch yer,' false teeth if yer left 'em around'.

After a few moments sucking at his pipe he said 'Listen son, 'ave you a bob or two to spare, I promised to meet a woman tonight an,' she'll be wanting a drink?'

I shook my head 'Nothing doing Spud, you're not spending my money on a woman's drinks, its not worth it'.

He stared at me 'You're talking daft, Tommy, there's only two things that makes a soldiers life worth living, beer and women!'

'That's the reason you are always broke, Spud'.

'Do you drink Tommy?'

'No'.

'Ave,' you got a woman anywhere?'

'No'.

'Then I asks you, what the hell do you know about it?'

I grinned at him 'All right Spud, which comes first, beer or women?'

For a few seconds Spud sat chewing at the stem of his pipe gazing out of the tent, then with a shrug of his shoulders he replied, 'Aw,' hell, if you puts it that way, beer first every time'.

I pulled out a two shilling piece and spun it towards him, 'Catch Spud, go and get your lovely beer and if I hear of you spending that on a woman I'll skin you alive'.

He grinned as he climbed to his feet 'You're a good soldier Tommy, I'll look after you when we go overseas, I know the ropes'. At lights out Spud wasn't back in the tent and in the morning his bed was still rolled so I feared the worst. However I soon heard that he had spent the night in the guardhouse along with his bosom pal Nobby Clark, both put under arrest for fighting in the canteen and sentenced to 7 days C.B.

We had a pretty tough bunch of physical training N.C.O.'s who put us through our paces and, although I enjoyed this part of our training I thought their methods a bit crude, a man's age and condition did not receive any consideration from them 'You're in the army now, right, keep going!' and quite a few kept going till they dropped. Two of these instructors were quite keen on boxing, one of them stood a good six feet and weighed around thirteen stone so I just admired him from the safe side of the ropes. The other chap, Corporal Cowley, was my height with a hefty pair of shoulders. He did a lot of strutting around in his striped jersey and when he wanted the gloves on he just picked chaps out 'You, and you, and you, two rounds each with me with the gloves'. Whether they relished it or not they had to step into the ring with him, and their knowledge of boxing wasn't asked; one round with Cowley was usually enough for the novice. I kept clear of him for a time but I kept a close eye on his style, he could hit all right and if he could get a man set up to take his punch it usually finished at that, but he was slow. The day came when Jacky Barrett my old brigade pal was chosen as one of the victims, victim is the right word because I knew Jacky was hopeless with the gloves. 'What the hell am I going to do Tommy,' he groaned 'He'll murder me when he gets me in there'. There wasn't much time to advise him.

'When he lets go just duck your nut Jacky and take it on top of your head,' I replied 'Then flop down and kid you're out'.

'That's bloody fine advice from a pal,' said Jacky woefully 'There'll be no kidding about the out business!'

'Next man in, come on you look slippy!' called Cowley as they dragged his opponent out of the ring. Jacky stepped inside and the gloves were tied on, 'You know any boxing son?' Jacky shook his head and stood with arms hanging.

'Never mind, put your hands up, you'll soon learn'.

Jacky tried to duck the right when it came over but he was a week too late, it landed under his ear and slammed him into the corner of the ring, he didn't have enough sense left to fall down. Cowley moved in like an artist, a couple of lefts to the head propped Jacky up and then a snorting right landed to the body and nearly broke him in two. He went down all right this time and rolled over in agony, we dragged him out through the ropes and he was violently sick on the grass. When Cowley finished with the next man he strolled over to inquire how Jacky was feeling, poor old Jacky was still sitting on the grass as white as a sheet.

'You need a few more lessons son,' grinned Cowley.

'Listen Corporal,' I said 'Do you think this is fair, this chap can't box for nuts'.

He snapped at me 'Perhaps you can, we'll have a go tomorrow'.

'I'll have a try Corporal, will you make it three rounds?'

'Twenty three if you like,' he laughed, then he sobered up, 'Here you're not a professional are you?'

'No I'm not a professional Corporal'.

'Hell,' he laughed 'I thought you might be Billy Wells'.

This was ridicule and I retorted 'I'm no Billy Wells and neither are you, Billy Wells doesn't do this sort of thing'.

'What sort of thing?'

'Knocking mugs about the way you do'.

He glared 'All right bucko tomorrow, and that's an order'.

I was a bit worried about tackling Corporal Cowley, I was pretty sure I could handle him but he was an N.C.O. on the staff and I had been in the army long enough to know that they could make your life a hell if they had a down on a man. A hot discussion was held in our tent and the boys advised that I should mention the matter to Lieutenant Stuart Walker in order to safeguard myself against any chance of the N.C.O.'s going after my blood later on.

I felt Nobby Clark's eyes on me in speculation 'You're not very hefty Tommy, can you use 'em?'

'Enough to lick Cowley, I reckon'.

'Like to bet on it?'

I pulled out my lot, five bob, 'Cover that Nobby,' I replied.

'Aw hell, I don't mean I'm betting against you, let's rake up as much as we can an,' we'll put our money on you'.

The boys raked up their odd shillings and sixpence's and went off to lay their bets, the news had run through the camp like wildfire, I could see number eleven platoon being a sorry bunch of soldiers if things came unstuck but I was in pretty good shape and confident. I told Lieutenant Stuart Walker my story and his reaction was good, 'I can see your point all right but I don't think you need worry, tell you what I'll do, I'll get the R.S.M. to act as referee we'll make a proper show of it and we'll all be there to see it, the news is all over the camp by now'.

'Do you fancy my chance sir?'

He laughed 'Corporal Cowley is strong and he can hit, he's in good condition too don't forget that, but I fancy he's muscle bound. I know he's slow compared with you so you should box him off his feet, but don't leave any openings or he'll get you, box him all the way'.

'Thank you sir'.

'Oh and by the way, you're excused parades for today, good luck'.

I felt more satisfied now and after tea we sat in our tent and Nobby told me the bets had been laid at three to one so if I won my pals were going to be in clover. Spud grinned 'No 'ifs,' about it, I've been talkin,' to Jacky Barrett and Joe Chapelhow, this boy knows the game'.

Lance Corporal Allan came along and handed me a paper 'From Corporal Cowley,' he grinned. I unfolded it and read 'You will report for boxing instruction at 1000 hrs tomorrow'.

I handed it to Spud who read it out aloud and then he tore it across and handed it back to Allan with a glare 'You can tell him to wipe his fat arse on that,' he grated 'We don't need orders to scrap in this platoon, we're fighters see, an,' tell Cowley we're bringing a ruddy stretcher party for him tomorrow!'

They as good as tucked me into bed that night and Nobby swore he would crown anyone who made a noise with his boots 'This kid has to have a good nights sleep, see'. The next morning dawned fine, good, the grass would be dry so I could use my footwork without the danger of slipping and I knew I was going to need that footwork. As the time approached I made my way to the corner of the meadow where the boxing ring had been erected, my boxing pants were on under my trousers and Nobby Clark carried my boxing boots and a towel. My tent mates walked with me and I could see quite a crowd collected around the ropes, how it brought back memories of my first fight with Connor on the Rec', then it was school kids, now it was soldiers, but the picture was the same. I ducked under the ropes and sat on a stool in the corner to change my army boots for the boxing boots, removed my shirt and trousers and I was ready when Cowley ducked under the ropes and grinned as he shook hands with me 'You'd take a pretty photo in that rig,' he said.

'Not so pretty as that striped jersey Corporal,' I retorted. For some reason I detested those striped jersey fashions adopted by P.T. blokes, they wore them as though they were the hallmark of supermen. The M.O. stepped into the ring and came over to me 'How are you feeling?'

'I'm all right sir'.

'Put your right hand out, right out, full reach!'

I held out my right hand at arms length and noticed it shook a little.

'A bit nervous eh?'

'I don't think so sir, tense, I suppose, that's all'.

'All right, good luck,' and he stepped over to Cowley's corner.

They pulled on and laced up the gloves and the R.S.M. called us to the middle of the ring. Cowley was wearing a vest but I was bare buff to the waist.

'Where's your vest?' barked the R.S.M.

'Haven't got one sir,' I replied.

The R.S.M. turned to the group of officers at the ringside and Lieutenant Stuart Walker spoke up 'The army doesn't issue vests Sergeant Major so you'd better forego that rule'

'Very good sir,' snapped the R.S.M. again turning his attention to Cowley and myself. 'Now listen to me, I'm boss in this ring and my word is law, you're boxing three 3 minute rounds and the timekeeper is using a whistle, no holding, break clean, and no funny stuff, now shake hands and come out fighting'.

We touched gloves and retired to our corners, the whistle blew, and we stepped out into the loneliest place in the world, the place where you stand or fall entirely on your own ability, the boxing ring. I came out fast, I had to if my plan to out speed Cowley was to bear fruit, and I slipped over a good hard right that landed flush on his left eye, a sucker punch to start the ball rolling. Cowley blinked and sent over a vicious right which I blocked and again I found that eye with a right hook, then Cowley was in close and fighting with both hands to my body, he could hit all right and I was pleased to tie him up until the referee said break. As we stepped apart I saw the trickle of blood from his eyebrow, then Cowley stormed in but a couple of neat straight lefts pulled him up short. I took a heavy left to the ribs in order to get yet another right to that damaged eye and I was happy when I saw Cowley wipe the blood away with his glove, it was worrying him! Again he rushed throwing lefts and rights but I side stepped and hooked to the body as the whistle blew. End of round one! Out for the second and as we met I got home with a couple of good lefts flush on his nose but they didn't stop him, he bustled and crowded me back to the ropes and as I tried to weave away a smashing right took me under the heart and it really hurt, he could hit all right. I bobbed and weaved out of trouble and retreated fast using my left to keep him away but he wouldn't be denied and in the end we stood toe to toe slamming away at the body. He had me worked into a corner and he intended keeping me there! I was taking a lot of his blows on my arms and gloves and suddenly he must have realized my guard was low, a hard right hook came from nowhere and toppled me to the grass. Lucky for me it landed on the cheekbone and not on the chin, I was just a bit shaken and on my feet by the time the count reached six. Cowley dashed in and ran smack into a left hook that really hurt him just as the whistle went. End of round two.

In my corner as my seconds worked over me I could hear the buzz of talk around the ring and I saw Lieutenant Stuart Walker lean over the ropes beside me 'Don't try to fight him, box him, you're away ahead on points'. Was I, I didn't know. Out for the last round, Cowley missed with a right and tried a left hook that also missed. I scored four lefts on his damaged eye and slipped away to see the blood run down his cheek. He was misjudging his distance due to that eye. I gathered up a little more speed and for half the round I gave him a left hand boxing lesson, give credit where it is due Cowley kept boring in for more, and he got it! He burst my lower lip with a stinging left swing and I heard him grunt when my left buried itself in his middle. I feinted with the right and as he swung away to avoid it I put all I had into a smashing left hook to the jaw. It was a winner and I knew it, his knees sagged and I slammed in another to the point as he went down. The referee tolled the seconds and Cowley was on his knees and shaking his head at eight when the whistle blew and it was all over, would he have beaten the count? I don't think so, anyway the referee raised my arm and that's all that mattered, I had won the fight and the boys had won their bets.

Spud and Nobby climbed through the ropes and danced a wild fandango around my corner until the R.S.M. chased them out. 'Hooray,' yelled Nobby 'Beer for a ruddy week'. I wasn't interested in their prospects of beer I was feeling too sore from Cowley's body punching and as Cowley and I shook hands he peered at me with his one good eye, 'I wasn't expecting that,' he said 'I'll be ready for you next time we meet!' Lieutenant Stuart Walker directed me to the officers quarters for a shower and a rub down, during this he remarked, 'It was a grand battle, but you might have thrown it away you know, you should have boxed him!

I grinned and felt my split lip 'I thought I had his measure sir!'

'You had his measure all right but I still think you took too many chances, you needn't have done that, lets have a look at that lip'.

He examined it and smiled 'Nothing to worry about now its cleaned up, it's cut inside with your teeth, how do you feel now?'

'I feel fine sir,' I answered tenderly rubbing the angry looking patches on my body 'A bit sore, that's all'.

'Fine,' he handed me a bulky brown envelope 'That's a little present from the officers for a jolly good show'.

I opened it and saw a number of half-crowns 'I'm afraid I can't accept this sir, I'm an amateur you know'.

'Damn it, that's not payment, its just appreciation for a spot of good entertainment and Corporal Cowley gets the same'.

Back in my tent I emptied the envelope and counted out two pounds in half-crowns and Nobby Clark handed me one pound 'I got your five bob on at three to one Tommy so that's your share of the spoils, oh boy we'll paint the town a ruddy colour tonight!'

That meant that I was wealthy with three pounds in my pocket, which was money in those days to a common soldier man.

Spud Baker shook me by the hand with shining eyes 'I'd never have believed it Tommy if I hadn't seen it with my own two eyes, you don't look the type for leather slinging!'

I grinned at him 'None of you chaps seem to know the answer, can't you see it Spud?'

'You started wearing boxing gloves before you finished wearing a nappy'.

'Just about it Spud but that's not all, I've watched Cowley box a number of times and he has no variety, I knew his style so I reckon I had the job half won before we started!'

'All the same we nearly had twins when that bugger dropped you!'

'How much have you chaps picked up on the bets?' I asked turning to Nobby.

'Aw, trouble is we didn't have much cash to lay down,' answered Nobby woefully, 'I've divided it out equally and each man here gets three bob'.

'I only had a lousy tanner to bet,' moaned Spud.

'Well look here chaps,' I said pulling out a handful of half crowns, 'I've got three quid'

'You've got what? yelled Nobby.

'Three quid, the officers passed the hat amongst themselves, take thirty bob out of it Nobby and give the boys a beano tonight'.

'You mean that, boy?' cried Spud and in reply I handed over the money.

'Shoulder high round the camp!' yelled Nobby, 'Come on boys, up with him 'For he's a jolly good fellow, come on!'

They grabbed me and they meant it but just then the bugle blared.

'Fall in A, Fall in B, Fall in every company,' and we doubled for the parade ground.

The R.S.M. got his eagle eye on me and marched across the parade ground to halt in front of me, I snapped to attention.

'You will report to the battalion orderly room at 09:00 hrs tomorrow for Commanding Officer's interview, and you are excused parades for today so off you go, at the double!'.

'Yes sir!' and I doubled away under the eyes of the seven hundred men lined up on parade with mixed feelings. C.O.'s interview, what the hell had I done wrong now, it was a bit of a hair raising ordeal when one of the rank and file had to parade before this aloof being who sat on his horse and watched as from afar, the man who held the destiny of seven hundred human beings in the hollow of his hand. I got busy with spit and polish in preparation for the coming event and when the boys came off parade we discussed the matter.

'Perhaps he's going to give you a grilling over the boxing,' said Allan.

'Aw to hell with that,' said Jacky Barrett; 'I saw him and the Adjutant watching it from the verandah of the officers mess'.

Nobby grinned at me 'You haven't been getting a wench into trouble have you?'

'Nothing like that Nobby'

'Aw quit worrying Tommy, you'll be in good company when you meet Colonel Dornford Smyth M.C. tomorrow'.

Perhaps he was right, but I wasn't looking forward to it. Spud was busy with his buttons and he looked up with a smile, 'Come on Tommy boy, we're off into the town to celebrate'

'No, count me out Spud, I'm a bit too sore for that, I'm staying in camp tonight'.

'Well I go to hell! Listen to the soldier of today, we got money for beer an,' women an,' he's staying in camp. Come on boys, let her rip!'.

I saw them off and settled down thankfully in my blankets, I wasn't feeling up to their idea of a night out, enough for one day. I heard the story of their celebrations the following day and they had certainly torn the town wide open. Quite a spot of damage was done in the pub where the fun and games started and the result of their drunk and disorderly charge was fourteen days defaulters for Spud Baker, Nobby Clark, Rusty Mitchell and about quarter of number eleven platoon. Their wealth was gone and now only sackcloth and ashes for the next fourteen days in camp. I made my way to battalion orderly room the following morning and soon, with the R.S.M. stiff and erect beside me I stood before the great white chief Colonel Dornford Smyth M.C. He sat at a desk with the Adjutant beside him and I fixed my eyes on a mark on the wall behind him about a foot above his head. The C.O. fiddled with a pencil and shuffled some papers 'Ahem! So you're the chap who is pretty useful at boxing eh! You don't look much the worse for it anyway'. My eyes came down to meet his own grey eyes staring at me over his glasses and I thought I detected a twinkle in them. 'You fond of boxing, eh'?'.

'Yes sir, quite keen on it,' I replied.

'I see, I see, well now what we've got you here for is to find out if you would be willing to box in the regimental tournaments, we're looking for talent at various sports, voluntary of course'.

'I'm willing sir, under certain conditions'.

'What conditions?'

'I want to box within my own weight sir, and I want two weeks clear of parades to train before I fight!'

The C.O. and the Adjutant put their heads together and spoke in low tones, then the C.O. looked at me with a smile. 'Those conditions will be quite satisfactory, you'll see to it Sergeant Major'.

'Yes sir'.

'Good, that will be all and, er', congratulations on your recent win'.

'Thank you, sir'.

'About turn, quick march!' The R.S.M. threw in a flashing salute and we marched outside.

'Well, what do you think of the C.O.?'

'I reckon he's a toff sir,' I replied with relief that it was all over.

'Yes? Well ask your damn fool pals that one when you get back to your lines, and a word of advice my lad, don't let them lead you up the garden, and keep wearing the same size hat, away you go'.

Back in our tent I found the bunch sitting around with wry faces,

'How'd you get on, Tommy?'

'Oh, fine,' I replied airily 'The C.O. and I are just like that,' and I crossed two fingers 'He's a great chap'.

'Like hell he is,' moaned Nobby 'He's just nailed us down for fourteen ruddy days defaulters, all on account of our little spree last night'

'Aw', never mind,' said Spud 'we had a damn good night didn't we and now we pay for it, that's good old army law'.

'Balls to army law,' said Dusty Miller 'give me Civvy Street'.

'Listen Dusty,' said Spud 'If you'd been in civvy street last night I'll tell you where you would have finished up, behind the bars in a cell, we haven't come off so badly, the war won't go on for ever'.

'It'll go on two ruddy long for me, fourteen days without a break and all the ruddy dirty jobs piled on to us'.

'Aw,' shut up moaning Dusty,' growled Nobby 'We asked for it and we've got it so shove a sock in it and pipe down'.

I found the atmosphere of the battalion changed towards me, everyone seemed to know me, my platoon Sergeant Brodwick and my Company Sergeant Major Pyburn treated me in a fatherly manner and even the officers had a smile when they returned my salute. Nevertheless military training went on day and night 'on parade you're on parade my lad'; every man had to be turned into an efficient soldier. We were inoculated and vaccinated and quite a number of chaps said the M.O. would have done better if he had used a bayonet. I know my own vaccination on the wrist made me pretty groggy and after a day or two I went on parade without my rifle.

'Where's your rifle?' yelled Company Sergeant Major Pyburn and I pulled back my sleeve to show him my wrist 'Can't use a rifle with this lot Sergeant Major,' I replied.

He gazed at my swollen wrist with the two angry blemishes on it, 'Gosh! That's a mess, have you seen the M.O. about it?'

'Not yet, Sergeant Major,' I replied.

'Why the hell not? He snapped at me.

'I was hoping it would go down'.

'Go down! It looks more like busting, report to the M.O. at once!'

Off to the M.O.'s tent I went where the doctor examined it with the remark 'My word, that's a beauty!'

He bandaged it neatly and said, 'You'll be all right now, you're excused all parades and duties for seven days'.

On the way back to my tent I met Lieutenant Stuart Walker and he stopped me with 'What's the M.O. got to say about your arm?'

'Excused duties for seven days sir,' I answered.

'I was expecting something like that, you better buzz off home for a few days leave, I'll arrange it at company orderly room'.

'I'm not all that keen sir,' I replied.

He stared at me, 'Don't talk so damn silly, 'not all that keen,' everyone wants leave you ass, take the chance when you get it, anyway you're no use here with that arm!'

That was very true, I would just be in the way at the camp so I followed his instructions and collected a leave pass for five days at home, lucky for me that I did. On arriving home I found my mother had returned to her profession of teaching at the local primary school and I began to wonder how the hell I was going to spend five days in a place where I seemed to have lost touch with everyone. Then I met Amy. She was a stranger to that part of the world her home being in Norfolk, and I soon found in her company that my leave wasn't going to last nearly long enough. We spent the rest of my time together and I enjoyed every moment of her company. When my time came to depart I asked her to write to me and she agreed to do so. I wasn't writing to anyone else and I knew her letters would be welcome to me in camp. My arm was all right by the time I reported back for duty and I found they were organizing a swimming competition so I decided to have a go at that but I just wasn't good enough at that game so it didn't get me anywhere. The military training was in full swing now and it wasn't long before I was detailed to fire my course on the rifle range. The drill on the rifle range was to start your firing practice at 100 yards and work back to 600 yards range finishing up with rapid fire on moving targets back at 300 yards range! This was something I was looking forward to, I had had quite a bit of practice with the .22 rifle in the brigade and I was a pretty good shot but definitely not a marksman. However I was confident I would pass out all right with the service rifle. Imagine my dismay when at 100 yards I only scored one bull and four inners with my five rounds, a small cluster of holes just off the bull at one o'clock. 'You can do better than that me lad,' said the firing point instructor, 'You're firing high!' 'I'm not

Sergeant,' I replied 'The sights of this rifle are not right, I want it zeroed before I fire any more'. The rifle was checked by the armourer who re-adjusted the sights and my next five rounds gave me better results, three bulls and two inners. The chap lying next to me fired his five rounds and his target was unmarked, needless to say the Sergeant was on him like a cyclone, 'Wasting good ammunition, that ruddy target is four feet square, throw your bloody rifle at it, fix bayonets and charge the bloody thing!' All very funny for the rest of us, but not so funny for the poor blighter who couldn't shoot straight. My own best performance was at three hundred yards where I scored four bulls and one inner with my five rounds and I passed through my range practice as first class one grade below marksman. From the firing practice we moved on in our training to bayonet fighting and in this we doubled over rough ground, jumped trenches, and overcame obstacles like barbed wire, every so often coming across sacks stuffed with straw to represent German soldiers. Into these we had to plunge our bayonets accompanied by a howl of hate and a twist of the bayonet to make sure it killed. This was supposed to breed the right spirit in the troops but the chaps didn't take too kindly to this line of training, the usual comment being 'to hell with bayonet fighting, its too much like hard work'. We were taught the various points and parries by instructors with training sticks and I enjoyed it because there are many moves in bayonet fighting similar to the moves in boxing but I didn't approve of their methods of instruction and voiced my opinion. I told the Sergeant instructor that I couldn't see the average German soldier standing like a sack of straw awaiting the lunge of a British bayonet and I couldn't see myself rooted to the ground awaiting the lunge of an angry Jerry.

'What would you suggest?' he asked.

'I think more footwork would be a sound idea,' I replied.

However the British Army had trained on those lines since Waterloo so who was I to attempt to change it? All I got out of it was a report on keenness and orders to report to Strensall camp for a specialized course on bayonet fighting. I spent a couple of weeks at Strensall and returned to my own battalion as a qualified instructor with the information that my argument was right. The specialists at Strensall brought footwork very much into their bayonet fighting, but it still remained a specialist's job, the rank and file carried on with the same old method. Afterwards I saw that I was arguing against the spirit of the grand old British Square and the age old traditions of the British Infantry soldier and then a statement by Spud brought one to realize it was just as well to leave things alone. We sat sweating on a grass embankment one afternoon after an hours strenuous training with rifle and bayonet when Spud turned to me and said 'You know Tommy, this is just another form of physical training, when we get to the front how many of us do you think will get within sticking distance of a

Jerry, through shrapnel, machine gun fire, rifle fire and grenades?' I suppose he was right after all.

Company Sergeant Major Pyburn approached me to find out my views on promotion but I turned it down flat. My reason? I still hadn't reached the age of nineteen and I didn't feel I could accept the responsibility of taking charge of men, especially when their lives might depend on my word. Both Nobby and Spud said I had done right but they put it another way 'Once you put a tape up everyone's shouting for you and you're crawling around like a cat with kittens, don't do it!'

We knew the time was coming when we would be ready for overseas, rumour and counter rumour ran around the camp but our training went on and now I was receiving regular letters from Amy and I was contented to soldier on. The regimental sports day was fixed, company versus company, at running, jumping, swimming, soccer and boxing, my name being on the list to box for C company at 8 stone 6lbs weight. Corporal Cowley approached me with the gleam of battle in his eye, 'I see your name down for the sports,' he said. I nodded my head. 'Good, then we'll meet again'. But we didn't, he was found to scale 9 stone 4lbs and he would have had to carve off a leg to get down to my weight. In the preliminaries I met a B Company chap called Private Newburn who didn't appear to fancy his job much, he swung a wild right at me and ran slap into a left hook that spread him on the grass, and that was that!

The chap I met in the final, Lance Corporal 'Chic,' Webb of D company was a different kettle of fish; he was a southpaw and carried his chin tucked well down under his right shoulder. The result was that my favourite shot, a left hook for the chin was completely nullified and I found him a most awkward customer. Most of my attempts were landing somewhere round the back of his head and we were getting tied up in knots during the first round. In my corner after a hopeless first round Nobby Clark kept barking at me 'Use your right! Use your right!' I tore into the second round intent on using the right and found I was landing but 'Chic,' was clever at getting into a clinch whenever he was hurt and I wasn't making much headway, it isn't easy to change your style just like that. I wasn't hurt at all but I felt angry and frustrated when I returned to my corner at the end of the second and Corporal Cowley was glaring at me over the ropes 'Listen mug,' he growled, 'Step to your left and hook your right to the belly, never mind his head'. At the start of the third I did just as Cowley had advised and felt my right sink in. 'Chic,' gasped and for a split second I saw his chin, my left landed true enough on the point and as he went down I slammed in another right to the stomach. He rolled over and over claiming a low punch but no one took any notice of that, it wasn't low and I knew it, so did everyone else. Corporal Cowley won his 9 stone 6lbs regimental title and I felt bound to thank him for his spot of advice, 'A southpaw isn't easy kid,' he replied, 'And when you're outside the ropes you can see things better than when you're inside. Anyway you won, good luck to you'.

The day came when the whole battalion turned out on parade in full marching order for an inspection by a Major General and the amount of polish used for that parade must have been fantastic. We were lined up on the parade ground at 10:00 hrs under a scorching sun and at 11:00 hrs the brass-hat made his appearance, what was said on that parade ground by the rank and file about brass-hats was nobodies business. Slowly he passed down the ranks and he had a word or two with the old soldiers like Spud and Nobby who flashed a good display of service ribbons. Then he mounted a horse and sat at the saluting base while the battalion marched past with band playing and arms swimming, and sweat running out of us by the pint. Again we were lined up, company by company, and again he passed down the ranks to moans of 'This old bugger is having a field day!' 'Perhaps it's his ruddy birthday!' But this time it was different, here and there a soldier was tapped on the back, and that man stepped forward two paces and stood fast. I felt the tap on my back and stepped forward, 'what the hell was wrong?' button undone, hair-cut, I just didn't know'. About two dozen of us were picked out and grouped together while the rest of the battalion moved off and we were left wondering. For half an hour we hung around awaiting the axe to fall.

'It wouldn't be so bad if we knew what the hell it's in aid of!' grumbled Ginger Thomson.

'Perhaps the brass-hat wants a special body-guard,' someone suggested.

Just then a Sergeant doubled across the parade ground with a paper in his hand and halted in front of us.

'Orders for you chaps from battalion H.Q.,' he barked.

'The General isn't satisfied that you fellows are old enough to go on active service, your posted to staff jobs'.

'That old geezers wrong Sarge, I'm nineteen turned,' said Ginger.

'And me', 'And me,' went up the chorus; I ran my eye over the group and I thought the old geezer hadn't guessed far wrong.

'Aw', shut up,' growled the Sergeant 'You! Report to the cookhouse, You! Report to the Sergeants mess, You! Report to the officer's mess', that was me. Sadly I moved away towards the officers mess and there I reported to Sergeant Watkins. 'Hello what do you want?'

'I was ordered to report to you Sergeant, I don't want anything'.

'I see,' said Sergeant Watkins, 'Time I had some extra hands'.

'What's the idea, Sergeant?' I asked.

He grinned, 'The idea is, my lad, you now work here, you wash a thousand dishes a day, you clean cutlery, you sweep and polish the floor in the dining room, and when the officers are feeding you wear a mess jacket and wait on them and your hours are from seven o'clock in the morning until midnight, that's the ruddy idea'.

I stood and gaped at him 'Listen Sergeant, I don't know anything about this racket'.

'You'll learn me lad, you'll learn, and consider yourself lucky, no more square bashing for you, away you go and bring all your kit here, you sleep here now'.

I was shocked into replying hotly, 'Aw,' to hell with your officers mess, I joined up to soldier not to be anyone's flunky'.

'You'll do as you're told me lad,' roared the Sergeant, 'Get that kit here and start work in half an hour or I'll put you on a charge. Now don't waste my time, get moving!'

Back in my tent I sadly broke the news to the boys, finishing up with 'To hell with it, I'm not going to do it!'

Spud removed his pipe and tapped me on the chest with it, 'Listen to me son, you're talking daft, you're a soldier and a soldier obeys orders whether he likes 'em or not, see? You've only got one comeback, you're pally with Lieutenant Walker so you might lodge an objection through him, it's worth trying anyway. Meanwhile its not a bad billet, you'll get the same grub as the officers an,' you might manage to snuffle a spot of whiskey out for us now an,' again. Come on boys help Tommy to move his kit'.

Dusty Miller grinned at me as he carried my blankets along, 'Going to live on the fat of the land Tommy, some blokes have all the luck!'

'I'll swap you right now Dusty, how about it?' I answered.

'No thanks Tommy, when we're drinking our wine with the sweeties in France we'll think of you washing dishes in Barnard Castle'

'Like hell you will, this mob isn't leaving me behind'.

And that's how I got landed into a job I despised and detested, the food was good, drinks and cigarettes were left lying around in the mess, the officers were a decent bunch, but every time I saw the troops march past on parade my heart went with them. For two long weary weeks I gritted my teeth and stuck it and then I buttonholed Lieutenant Walker and poured my tale of woe into his willing ear.

'If I don't get out of this sir I'll either bash Sergeant Watkins and do time or I'll pour the soup down the C.O.'s neck and get a firing party'.

Lieutenant Walker grinned 'I'll try to get you an interview with the C.O. but you won't find it easy to change his mind'.

He got me the interview after a few more days of waiting and once more I stood before the Commanding Officer in battalion orderly room. The great white chief sat behind his desk and looked at me with a worried frown on his face 'What's this man here for, Sergeant Major?'

The R.S.M. rapped out 'Lodges an objection to being employed in the officers mess sir'.

'What! This won't do. What have you to say for yourself?'

'I volunteered for the army sir, to soldier, not to be a waiter'.

'But damn it, you're under age for active service'.

'I'm over nineteen sir and I'm a trained soldier, you're putting a square peg in a round hole'.

He leaned back in his chair 'Now listen to me, this battalion will soon be going overseas and there's going to be hardships for every man and death for some of us. The youngsters were picked out on the parade to remain in this country until they reach the age. How old are you?'

'Nineteen years three months sir'.

'Can you get a birth certificate to prove it?'

'Yes sir, I came from a soldiering family and I want to soldier'.

The C.O. sighed and handed a paper to the R.S.M.

'Well, you are returned to duty and I hope you won't regret it, good luck to you, carry on, Sergeant Major!'

'About turn, quick march!'

I didn't send home for a birth certificate, I couldn't because it would have given away my true age but shortly afterwards our C.O. was replaced by a younger man, Lt. Col. Edward Townshend Logan (3rd Cheshire)[1], to take the battalion overseas and in the changeover I suppose the matter was forgotten for more important things. I was back in the tent with the boys, back on parade with the battalion, slogging it out on route marches with an ache in my back and tired feet, firing on the range and throwing grenades, dashing over rough country and crawling along ditches, and in my heart I was content, happy to be just one of the poor bloody infantry! We were issued with gas respirators which were simply impregnated bags that totally enclosed your head having a pair of goggles to see your way around and we were also issued with identification discs to be slung around your neck, these stated briefly your name, number and religion.

'That's very nice,' remarked Dusty Miller, 'but what happens if you get your ruddy head blown off, away goes your disc, what then?'

'Then, Dusty, you're dead,' answered Spud with a grin.

'Don't suppose it will matter much to you Dusty once your nuts off,' said Nobby.

'Cheerful lot of blighters you are,' grunted Dusty; 'I was just raising a point'.

'Well don't raise points like that Dusty,' I said, 'It sounds a bit too messy to me'.

Later that evening Dusty and I went for a stroll together and we sat on the riverbank enjoying a smoke as the sun was setting. From where we sat we could overlook the lines of white tents and the parade ground of our camp and all looked peaceful and quiet. Then we saw figures move to the

---

[1] Lieutenant Edward Townshend Logan, Commanding Officer 15th Battalion died 26th September 1915. Son of Edward and Emily Logan; husband of Hilda Logall (21 King Street, Chester) Served in South African War, twice mentioned in Despatches. Loos Memorial Panel 49 and 50.

flagpole in the centre of the parade ground, a roll of drums reached our ears and the Union Jack was slowly lowered to the ground.

'They're beating the retreat,' said Dusty and Spud came along the path to squat down beside us.

'I've watched that ceremony in a few different countries in my time,' remarked Spud as he sat scraping out the bowl of his pipe.

I glanced at his ribbons 'What countries Spud?' I asked.

'Oh, South Africa, Egypt, the Sudan, Burma, India and China,' he replied, 'I've been around a bit'

'Hell,' said Dusty, 'Have you been soldiering all your life Spud'.

'Most of it,' answered Spud blowing out a cloud of vile tobacco smoke, 'I joined up as a drummer boy and I've done twenty five years up to now'.

'In the army all the time?'

'No, I came out after I done twelve, but I couldn't stick civvy street an,' I don't think civvies had much use for me, anyway I was soon back into uniform again'.

He gazed at the parade ground and the lowered flag and said softly -

> *'There's many of your kinsmen son*
> *Have looked up at that flag:*
> *They fought for it and died for it*
> *They suffered, cheered, and cried for it*
> *They saw it torn and tattered*
> *Just a coloured bloodstained rag.*
> *But somehow it keeps flying*
> *The Red and White and Blue,*
> *And what is it that keeps it there*
> *The likes of me and you'.*

For a while we just sat and gazed at the camp now disappearing into the shadows as night fell, and a feeling of pride came to me that I was in khaki and along with men like these. Men were going off every day now on their embarkation leave, the last leave we would have for a long, long time; and on their embarkation leave both Spud and Nobby fell foul of the law and came back under escort. They were hard case soldiers but good soldiers all the same when they had no money for drink and women. Amy was at the station to meet me when I arrived home for my last four days and we had an enjoyable time in each other's company. Everyone else was forgotten, even the war was pushed into the background and my hometown seemed a brighter more cheerful place. The time went by on wings and soon came our last evening together and as we stood in the moonlight to say goodbye I had a feeling that there was a bond between us that would endure the worst the future could do.

'Do you think its France, Tommy,' she asked quietly.

'I don't know Amy, but wherever it is, its coming soon'.

'I suppose you are keen to go?'

'Well, I'm a soldier and I'm trained so it's really duty now,' I replied, 'Will you keep on writing to me Amy?'

'Of course I will if you want me to, I'm going back to Norfolk soon but I won't forget you', she slipped her hand into mine.

'Goodnight Tommy, and good luck, I won't forget you, and I'll see you when you come back again!'

And that is how we parted, it was twelve long months before we met again, twelve months of blood and sweat, of hope and despair, and through it all her promise held good, her letters and parcels arrived to cheer me up and through it all the echo of her words came back to me, 'I'll see you when you come back again'. Did she know that I would live to come back?

Back in the camp I was swept into a bustle of activity, we were on the move, and it wasn't long before we were marched to the station and crammed on the train. After a long journey we stepped off the train at Rugby formed up and marched to our camp at Cannock Chase. Cannock Chase was voted by one and all, without fear of contradiction, to be a first rate dump and the general hope was to get away from it as soon as possible. It was a mass of army huts away in the hills and moors of Staffordshire, very different to our clean white tents at Barnard Castle. Military training and field operations were now carried out as brigades, and we slogged many a weary mile over the moors, and then like a bolt from the blue came the information that brigade sports were to be held that week and my name was up to meet a Sergeant Ryland of the West Yorkshire Regiment. I set up a howl about this, 'Colonel Smyth promised me time off parades and facilities for training and now they're slinging me in without any preparation at all!' Spud grunted, 'Once they get you in these rackets son they've got you just where they want you'. Corporal Cowley laughed it off, 'We're in the same boat Tommy they're in a hurry before we go overseas'.

I wasn't feeling very happy about it and when I stepped into the ring with Sergeant Rylands I sailed in to get the job over. I found him wide open to left hooks and I had him dizzy and on his knees at the end of the first round. The second round was short lived; the gallant Sergeant threw in his hand pleading a damaged nose. The doctor later verified this was true and I wasn't surprised my left landed on it often enough goodness knows. Cowley made a quicker job of his, he slammed over a vicious right under the heart that dropped his opponent like a log and it was all over for him in a matter of seconds. Cannock Chase knew we had arrived! The next bouts were to be held the following week, but I told Lieutenant Stuart Walker that I had no intention of carrying on in this haphazard manner; he agreed with me and promised he would see to it, but there was no need, by the time the next bouts were due the following week we were all heading for a more serious bout, in France. That weekend we were issued with first aid field dressings, 150 rounds of rifle ammunition, and orders to stand by ready to move at one hours notice. Spud and Nobby strolled into the hut as I sat on my bed carefully packing 150 rounds of nice bright cartridges into my ammunition pouches, and I looked at them with a grin, 'It won't be long now boys!'

'Hell Spud,' said Nobby 'look at the glint in his eye, you'd think he was off to meet a dame!'

Spud looked at me 'You're looking forward to this ain't you Tommy?'

'We all are Spud'.

'Yes, I suppose we are, but don't kid yourself it's a picnic that's all'.

'Aw,' hell, Spud, you've been under fire before,' I answered.

'Yes I have, I've been under fire from native bows and arrows, single round rifles, maxims that kept jamming and throwing spears, but I ain't been under the kind of stuff that's being chucked around in France, I'm telling you, it ain't no picnic!'

A bugle rang out close at hand sounding the fall in. 'That's us,' grunted Nobby swinging on his equipment 'Those buglers are working overtime in this ruddy camp'. Our parade kit was inspected, ammunition checked, rifles examined and then we were issued with 'emergency rations,' and informed that we would parade in full marching order at twelve o'clock in the afternoon, the excitement was growing. With the band at the head of the parade we marched to Rugby station and boarded the train, not sorry that we had seen the last of Cannock Chase and we settled down for what we were told was going to be a long journey.

'Have you made your will, Spud?' shouted Dusty Miller.

'I've got no next of kin,' grunted Spud 'Anyway I've got damn all to leave so it doesn't matter'.

'What about your pipe Spud?' asked Dusty, 'won't you leave that to me?'

Spud fondled his pipe lovingly.

'You smoke fags Dusty, what would you want the old pipe for?'

'Well I might get sent to the Middle East and I'm damn sure the fly hasn't been born that could live through that stench!'

'You go to hell Dusty, this is my only comfort'.

'Use that comfort in the trenches Spud,' I said 'And Jerry will be sounding his gas alarm'.

The train jogged on and on, sometimes it stopped but never at a station.

'Not a cat in hells chance of getting a bottle of beer,' groaned Nobby, 'I reckon the officers have told that lousy driver just to stop where there's only green fields'.

Once towards evening the train stopped where we could see a little village in the distance and the boys joined chorus in yelling to try to attract someone's attention, someone that would get a bottle for them, but only the birds replied.

'There's bound to be a pub in a place that size,' said Nobby gazing wistfully at the distant scattering of cottages.

'Listen Nobby,' said Spud 'I reckon one of these youngsters could run that distance in ten minutes'.

'Good idea!' exclaimed Nobby, 'Come on Tommy, what about it?'

'You can do your own running Nobby,' I replied, 'I'm not doing any running into trouble'.

'Dicky Knight's the fastest runner in this compartment,' said Dusty Miller, 'Come on Dicky, four bottles of the best'.

Dicky looked up startled 'Aw, the hell, you don't expect me to do that, what about if the train starts again?'

'Oh just shout out,' said Spud 'the driver or the guard will see you and then they'll have to stop the damn thing to pick you up'.

'No, damn it all I can't do that,' exclaimed Dicky in alarm.

Nobby already had the window down leaning out to open the carriage door, 'Bugger me, they've locked us in, we're ruddy prisoners that's what we are!'

'Let's have him out of the window,' cried Spud grabbing at Dicky, 'Come on son, the quicker the better'.

'Here pack it up you damned fools,' protested Lance Corporal Allan, 'If he gets left behind he'll be booked for a court martial!'

'He won't be left behind,' snorted Nobby 'You know what that little cord up there is for, that's to stop ruddy trains an,' we can always use that can't we?'

'Then we'll all face a court martial, pack it up!'

Despite all the protests poor old Dicky was heaved to the window, lucky for him the train started up again before they could carry out their drastic intentions.

'We missed a golden opportunity Spud,' moaned Nobby; 'these kids are too damned slow that's what's the matter with 'em!'

'I know what's the matter with you, you're a pair of ruddy maniac's,' growled Dicky from the other end of the compartment. Night fell and still the train rattled along while we tried to snatch a bit of sleep in our cramped positions and at long last the train rattled to a halt and the carriage doors were unlocked.

'Come on me lucky lads out you get'.

We staggered out with our equipment on the cold dimly lit platform; there was a chilly breeze blowing and that unmistakable tang of sea air. As our eyes grew accustomed to the dark we saw the towering bulk of ships close by; we were on the quayside of Folkestone harbour. As we sat on our kit on the quayside we were issued with mugs of hot tea and bully beef sandwiches and shortly afterwards we tramped up the gangway of the troopship that was to take us overseas. Once on board a roll call was taken company by company and to our dismay Spud and Nobby were missing.

'Where the hells Baker and Clark?' yelled Sergeant Broadrick, 'Anyone seen those two half baked swaddies?'

'Fallen overboard I expect,' someone answered.

'Bloody good riddance if they have,' growled the Company Sergeant. Just then two figures doubled across the quay and scrambled up the gangway, Spud and Nobby.

'Where the hell you two been?' roared Sergeant Brodwick, 'I'll put you on a charge!'

'Aw,' have a heart, Sergeant,' said Spud grinning 'We just went after a drop of mule's milk, salt water don't agree with us'. How they managed it I don't know but Spud proudly displayed a bottle of whiskey and Nobby two bottles of beer. The gangway was raised and we were issued with life belts and told to make ourselves comfortable down below decks. It wasn't long before we heard above us the shouting of orders, the clanging of the engine room bell, and then the steady throb of the engines told us we were on our way. A number of the troops, including myself, made our way back to the deck in time to see the dark outline of England disappear, and along the rails from where I stood someone was singing softly -

'Homeland! Homeland! When shall I see you again?
Land of my birth, the dearest place on earth.
I'm leaving you, to recall your songs with a sigh -
It maybe for years, and it maybe for ever -
Dear homeland, goodbye'

As our ship throbbed on over a choppy sea I caught a brief glimpse of a low shadow ploughing along some distance from us, coming and going, our destroyer escort and suddenly a searchlight flashed out from the warship and settled on a ship that was approaching, lighting up the huge red cross on the side of the vessel. A ship full of broken men coming home, a ship full of fit men going out to take their place; the searchlight went out and the ships passed like shadows in the night. I stood by the rails for a while staring into the darkness, dreaming of the past and wondering about the future 'I'll see you when you come back again!' Ah, well, this was it! I found the wind across the sea a bit too chilly for comfort and I made my way below decks once more. My company was in what had been the dining saloon on that ship and I found them, some sitting smoking on their packs, others stretched out on the floor with their great coats around them, a ghostly band of khaki clad figures seen in the dim light of a solitary lantern. These men were no plaster saints, and no crusaders either, just ordinary people from the pits and work benches; miners, labourers, teachers, clerks, engineers, farmers, men from every walk of life thrown together and trained to fight a common enemy, and every single one of them was a volunteer offering his all for his country. I was in worthy company.

As I sat down on my pack and lit a cigarette Nobby turned to me and said 'Can you swim mate?'

'A little bit Nobby,' I answered 'What's biting you?'

'Nothing at present,' he said moodily 'but if this damned ship goes down its fish that will be biting me, I can't swim a ruddy stroke'.

'Now's your chance to learn Nobby,' grinned Dusty 'You've got a blinkin,' life jacket on so you can't sink'.

'Gor,' - the shock of that water would kill me'.

'Aw shut up Nobby, the navy's got its watchdogs out,' said Spud. 'Cheer yourself up with one of those bottles of beer'.

I stretched out on the floor with my greatcoat around me, my pack serving as a pillow and to the steady pulsing of the ships engines and the sway of the vessel I soon fell into an uneasy sleep, and as I slept the troopship carried me away from my own country, away into the unknown. A rough hand shook me awake and through the porthole I saw the grey light of dawn 'Come on son show a leg,' said Spud, 'We're within sight of land'. I stretched the stiffness out of my bones and made my way up on the deck where a lot of the boys were already at the rails, 'There she is Tommy,' laughed Jacky Barratt as I joined him at the rails 'good old France waiting to welcome us'.

'As long as they have breakfast ready that's all the welcome I want,' said Joe gazing at the land we were approaching. Soon the troopship was tied up alongside and we were mustered on deck, down went the gangway and we moved slowly along to set foot on another land. Here and there French poilus (French Infantry) in blue overcoats stood guard with rifles and fixed bayonets on the quayside.

'French soldiers,' someone cried 'Gosh! Look at the length of their bayonets, long as ruddy swords!'

Spud looked the guards over and sniffed 'Not much of the Buckingham palace stuff about them anyway'.

'Aw hell, Spud, there's a war on in this country'.

We formed up along the quayside for another roll call and then we were told to take things easy, off came the equipment again and we sat on our packs and smoked while officers and N.C.O.'s had fun and games dashing all over the place looking important.

'You see what I mean when I run down promotion, Tommy,' said Spud.

'Those buggers with their stars and tapes dashin,' around like blue arsed flies while we sits and takes it nice an,' cushy'.

'I wonder what this place is,' I remarked.

'I heard an officer say its 'Boulogne,' said Nobby 'and if that's a fact then I hopes we stay here'.

'What for?'

'Haven't you heard about Boulogne?' cried Nobby, 'its the best place in France for pubs an,' wild women'.

'I don't know about pubs Nobby,' I remarked 'but here's one of your other weaknesses coming along the quay now'.

Along the quay she strode, tall, dark, well built, and bold looking with a smile for everyone and a basket on her arm 'orange, choc-o-let, you buy Tomee?'

She was selling oranges and chocolate at about double their worth and she was soon surrounded by a crowd of laughing soldiers buying for the novelty of it and addressing her with rude remarks to which she answered with a laugh 'no compree, Tommee'. All the same I have a sneaking fancy that she understood every word but she wasn't giving anything away, she soon sold out and then she strolled away with the money, she had no further interest in Tommy Atkins. Mugs of tea and army biscuits were issued and we sat and enjoyed our first meal in France while officers and N.C.O.'s still flapped around. Spud leaned back on his pack, puffing contentedly at his pipe and watching with interest the bustle of our superiors.

'If we just sit here nice and quiet,' he mused 'those silly buggers will make themselves so dizzy they'll go off an,' forget all about us'.

I laughed 'I don't want to stay here for the duration Spud!'

'You might do worse son, you might do worse!'

However it was not to be and soon we were on the march through the cobbled streets of the town with a few grimy kids trotting alongside the column begging for coppers, chocolate, biscuits, souvenirs, anything you like to give them. We put on a good show marching through Boulogne but it didn't create much interest among the inhabitants, just a flutter of a handkerchief here and there. Boulogne was well used by this time to the coming and going of British troops. Once we were out of the town and in open country we marched at ease and soon the old marching songs like John Brown's body, whiter than the whitewash on the wall, take me back to dear old Blighty, here we go again, etc. were echoing down the column to the tramp of marching feet. Two hours of steady marching brought us to a huge army camp on sand dunes and about three miles away we could see the glint of the sea. Soon we got settled down in tents and after tea Nobby Clark suggested a trip out of camp to see a bit of French life. We cleaned ourselves up, Spud, Bobby, Dusty and myself and marched off down the main road through the camp until we came to the place where the guard was mounted, and here we were brought to a halt by a red capped military policeman.

'Where are you chaps going?'

'Just down the road for a stroll,' answered Nobby.

'Like hell you are, where's your passes?'

'We've got no blinkin,' passes,' snorted Nobby; 'we just come into camp today'.

'Right,' said the M.P. 'well, just be good little boys and get back into camp'.

'You mean we're not allowed out?' cried Dusty .

'That's just what I do mean'.

'Can't we just go into town for a quick couple of pints?' asked Spud.

'You can't go into town for anything without a pass!'

'Well what about that place?' said Nobby pointing hopefully to a cluster of red tiled houses over the dunes towards the sea 'There'll be a pub there I expect'.

'That village is out of bounds to troops,' answered the M.P.

'You'd be court martialled if you were caught there'.

'Well this is a damn fine set up,' grunted Spud 'Where the hell can we go in this dump?'

'You can't go anywhere, you just stay in the dump, soldier,' said the M.P. with a grin 'if its beer you want try the canteen'.

'Strikes me this is going to be a bloody fine war we've landed in,' growled Nobby as we tramped back to our lines, 'here we are in France, a country famous for its wine and its women and we can't even have a night out'.

'I bet it's not out of bounds to the ruddy brass hats,' snorted Dusty.

'Well we're not brass hats we're just common soldier men,' sighed Spud, 'I suppose we don't need women and wine'.

'Aw to hell with it, we haven't much money anyway,' I said, there'll be plenty more towns later on'.

'That's what you think, but I wouldn't be too sure'.

The following day we marched to a railway siding and boarded a train made up of cattle trucks, no cover to the troops and only the floor to sit on, and as we waited for our train to start a red cross train pulled up alongside us full of wounded.

'What's it like at the front mate?' we questioned eagerly.

The walking wounded grinned and made a thumbs up motion, 'Not too bad chum, if you keep away from Ypres and Hooge'.

The stretcher cases took no notice of us, they just lay grim and grey and silent staring at nothing or with their eyes closed and I wondered what their thoughts were on, past pleasures, present suffering, future hardships, only they knew. Then our train pulled slowly away and we raised a cheer for the broken men we were leaving behind. The novelty of travelling in France soon wore off, it was slow and monotonous and most uncomfortable, we were well fed up by the time the train pulled into some godforsaken siding in the St. Omer area where we left the train and marched to some billets for our first taste of sleeping in cow sheds and feeding in a stinking farmyard.

The next day was spent cleaning, oiling and inspecting rifles and grenades. After tea came the order fall in, full kit and once more we were marching along the straight, dreary, cobbled roads of France, and on and on, mile after weary mile, night after weary night until at last on the night of September 25th in pouring rain we tramped through the town of Vermelles with the glare of star shells in the sky and the thunder of guns ahead. The rain continued to pour down on us and we were hungry, tired and footsore.

~ *Tommy* ~

Wet to the skin we came to a halt outside Vermelles and sank to the sodden ground too weary to care. There we lay for the night without shelter of any kind and without food or drink, just waiting for the dawn and all night the boom of guns and the crash of shells. Some near, some far, intermingled with the crack of rifle fire and the stutter of machine guns.

At break of day we saw the road was crowded with troops, transports, guns, and ambulances. Officers, N.C.O.'s and military police seemed to be working themselves into a frenzy; in fact it was a complete state of chaos behind the front. 'If they don't kill us one way they'll kill us another,' growled Nobby. 'Hi, Sergeant, when the hell do we eat? My stomach says my throat was cut three days ago,' The Sergeant shrugged his sodden weary shoulders 'I hear the bloody transport has gone and got lost, God knows where the grub is!'. Eventually we got some tea and one biscuit for each man and we lay in that sodden field in wet clothing while the rain pelted down and we were too exhausted to care. At dusk the rain ceased and each man got a little soup and a piece of bread, and then once more we were on the move, forward and halt, forward and halt, nearer and nearer to the hell of noise that was going on ahead of us. Now and then there was the howl of shells passing over our heads and occasionally the crash and flash of one exploding near by. At long last I found myself in a trench and breathed a sigh of relief at the bit of cover it gave against the flying shrapnel.

'Where the hell are we?' I asked Spud who crouched beside me.

'Dunno son, but there's merry hell to pop,' he replied 'Just listen to those ruddy guns, Gawd! I'm dyin,' of hunger!'

We lay in the water logged trenches while officers and N.C.O.'s tried to get things straightened out, I saw Lieutenant Walker pass and I called out to him 'Any idea where we are sir?' He gave me a weary eyed, harassed look 'So far as I can gather we're on the Loos front, right in the middle of a battle but nobody knows anything, left flank not known, right flank not known, German positions not known, contact with artillery, nil. It's just a hideous balls up from start to finish!'

'What about grub sir?' asked Spud.

'God only knows, our transports missing, and Jerry is shelling blazes out of everything on the roads'.

'In other words we're in one hell of a mess,' grunted Spud.

'That's just about correct Baker, but now we're in it we'll see the job through all right eh!'

'Its carry on and carry on and carry on all day,
And when you cannot carry on they carry you away
To slumber sound beneath the ground
Poor soldiers dead and gone,
Till Gabriel sounds on Judgement Day'
Get out and carry on!'

~ Tommy ~

The shells howled and shrieked overhead every so often crashing in and around the trenches where we crouched with the vicious whip and phut of bullets striking the sandbags and every so often the cry from right or left of us for stretcher-bearers! Men pushed past us with muttered growls and curses in the darkness and as day was breaking I peered over the sandbags to see men in khaki lying everywhere on the sodden ground. Away to our right was a rise in the ground and as I watched I saw men in kilts rise from our trenches and move forward with fixed bayonets over the bullet swept slope of Hill 70. The men of the highland regiment were cut down left, right, and centre but the rest went on and I saw the gleam of their bayonets in the morning light as the remnants reached the German trenches. N.C.O.'s dashed down our trench with white strained faces, 'Prepare to advance, fix bayonets, prepare to advance!' All hell was breaking loose and the noise was nerve racking as I fumbled to get my bayonet clamped on my rifle, Spud looked at me with a wry grin as he tucked his pipe away in his pocket.

'For what we are about to receive this day, Oh Lord make us truly thankful!' he murmured. Old soldiers, old rascals, but in the face of death they took their place as men worthy of their motherland. A little to our right a solitary figure climbed over the sandbags and stood upright, it was our own Commanding Officer, Lt. Colonel Logan. He waved his cane and shouted 'forward the 15th!' And forward he went with never a glance behind, forward into a storm of machine gun and rifle fire and we scrambled over the sandbags to follow into an inferno. I was weary and soaked, hungry and feeling sick at the horror of it all, men were on the ground and now more were falling as we moved forward. I could see nothing but piles of khaki, hear nothing but the crash of shells and the hiss of bullets, where the hell were we going, where the hell were the Germans? Blindly we struggled on with Lt. Colonel Logan still in the lead, and then he went down. As we passed him I saw him feebly raise his arm to wave us forward, and then Major Babbage our second in command was out in front urging us on, so died our Commanding Officer. Suddenly we were up against a coiled mass of barbed wire, unbroken and intact, our advance was halted.

'Wire cutters, cut the bloody stuff, cut a way through,' went up the shout as we sank to the ground hunting for cover against the storm of bullets. I lay behind a dead soldier and as I raised my head I saw some figures in grey running about seventy yards beyond the wire, my first Germans!

'There they are,' I shouted, 'Rapid fire!'

I fired and reloaded as fast as I could and some men beside me did the same, some of the grey figures staggered and fell and I hoped some of my bullets had found their mark. 'Retire! retire! the right flank is broken!' came the order and back we went in the direction of the old British trenches, back over the ground we had just covered at such a terrible price, raked all the way with rifle and machine gunfire and shrapnel tearing gaps in the ranks, staggering over the broken bodies of men in khaki and kilt, shaken, dazed, bewildered and filled with despair at the utter futility of our sacrifice. I toppled over into a trench and lay in the mud like someone dead. I felt I had gone past the limit and then I felt someone raise my head 'Try a wee drop o,' this laddie,' a gruff voice said and I opened my eyes to see a kilted Sergeant beside me holding his water bottle to my lips. I took a gulp and gasped for breath, 'What's that?'

'That's rum laddie, the real MacKoy, feel better noo?'

'Not so bad Sergeant,' I gasped as I felt the rum burn its way through me, 'where's the rest of our chaps?'

'Maist o,' them ower yonder,' he replied jerking his thumb over the sandbags 'Ye'll find the rest some place, ye dinna ken where a body is these days, well guid luck, I'm awa,' and he calmly mounted that bullet swept parapet and strolled away across no mans land. I stood up and shook my head; the calmness of that Sergeant brought sanity back to me and steadied my tottering nerves. I moved along the trench and soon contacted some of my own battalion, officers and N.C.O.'s were collecting the remnants and organizing the stragglers into some kind of a unit and once more we stood on duty at the parapet on the alert for any move of the enemy, and still the shells rained down on our positions and the call for stretcher-bearers went on and one.

'Stretcher-bearers,' growled Spud 'If they turned the whole bloody army into stretcher-bearers we couldn't clean up this mess'.

During the afternoon we were banded with the remnants of a battalion of the Kings Own Yorkshire Light Infantry and once again came the order for the line to advance. Hungry, weary, thirsty and dazed we pushed forward once more, forward over that body strewn hell that was no mans land and once more we were raked and beaten and hammered to the ground by a storm of bullets with never a chance of success. Someone's hair brained idea was hopeless from the start, and back we went to the cover of the trenches leaving more dead and dying to pile up on that ghastly battlefield. Soon afterwards the Germans launched a counter attack and as we lay behind the sandbags working the bolts of our rifles and watching the grey ranks stagger and fall we felt we were doing some good at last. All that day and all that weary night we hung on to our position suffering tortures from hunger and thirst and then at long last we were relieved by the Brigade of Guards and we staggered back and out of the trenches, dirty, bloody, grey faced and weary-eyed, the remnants of a battalion that had gone far past the limit of human endurance and still lived.

When the roll call was made it was found that we had left behind on the blood soaked fields of Loos 12 officers and 450 men, more than half the battalion.

By slow stages we moved clear of the chaos of the battle dragging our weary way back along the battered road which was lined with wrecked transports, blasted guns and limbers, and men dead and shattered lying thick at the side of the highway. At last we were collected in a field and issued with hot soup and bread with mugs of strong tea to follow and still our eyes and ears were turned back towards the thunder of the guns over the battlefield of Loos.

> 'When you move in to attack you know you're for it
> The hungry guns are waiting to be fed.
> Your legs shake like a jelly,
> You're squeamish round the belly,
> But you stick it, son, you're game until you're dead.
>
> When there's miles and miles of misery behind you
> And miles and miles of misery ahead.
> Let your pals see you can make it,
> Just shown them you can take it,
> And stick it, son, you're game until you're dead.

3. MADEMOISELLE FROM ARMENTIERS

We shuffled along in short stages until we came to the outskirts of Vermelles and stopped by the roadside; we sat and watched the stream of fresh British youth marching past on their way to the slaughter we had just left behind. On every side I heard the muttered words 'Have you seen ....?' and in my turn I said to Spud as he sprawled beside me sucking at an empty pipe 'Seen anything of Nobby, Spud?'

Spud looked at me with weary bloodshot eyes and jerked his thumb in the direction of Loos 'He's back there on that bloody muck-heap along with the rest, poor old Nobby won't march no more'.

'Was he killed?'

'Was he killed!' Spud's voice was hoarse and gruff 'I saw Nobby in a shell hole, he wasn't only killed, he was shattered, a horrible mess, and at home they'll say he died a hero's death, my Gawd!'

For awhile we sat staring at nothing, wrapped in our thoughts. War in all its dirty, horrible misery had come home to us. The pomp and glory that is written was dead, I had seen them, husbands, fathers, brothers, sweethearts torn and battered and huddled into the filthy mud in death a soldiers death!

'Well Tommy,' said Spud 'What do you think of it now?'

'It is ghastly Spud,' I replied 'I was scared stiff, that was just a bloody slaughter house for us!'

Spud nodded 'Yes, just a bloody slaughterhouse and there's thousands more marching into it. The blasted brass-hats make their plans and it doesn't matter a damn after that, the show must go on. That job up there is just hopeless, but do they stop it, like hell they do! No, they'll just go on pouring men into the furnace until half the ruddy army is wiped out and not a cat in hells chance of showing anything for it'.

Later I heard that the battle of Loos gave us a casualty list of 2,000 officers and 48,000 men, all for a few hundred yards of dirty, stinking, shell battered ground soaked with the life blood of the youth of Britain, and that was its only value!

Spud pointed to his cap badge, 'you see that!' he growled, 'if I lose that there's hell to play, its important equipment, but lose a man, lose a company of men, lose a bloody battalion of men and does the army worry, not so bloody likely, there's plenty more men in England. To hell with the army!'

Lieutenant Stuart Walker had been picked up on the field with a bullet through the arm and shrapnel wound in the face, Company Commanders Moir, Green, and Atkins were dead. Lieutenant Elford, Devenish, Westerman, Humble and Mullens would march no more.

~ *Tommy* ~

Company Sergeant Major Pyburn came along, usually so spruce and smart now as dirty and scruffy as the rest of us, handing out a packet of cigarettes to each man, and turning to me he said 'You can get a tape on your sleeve son, you're promoted to lance jack'.

I stared at him 'I don't want it Sergeant Major'.

Spud grunted 'Tell him to stuff it, Tommy'.

The C.S.M. squatted down beside us with a sigh 'Shut up Spud. Now listen to me. This company has only three N.C.O.'s left and I've got to have N.C.O.'s to get things moving again. I'm not ordering you, I'm asking you to help me!'

'Where's Lance Corporal Allen?'

'He's back there dead, he was last seen hanging on the German wire, its his place I want you to take'.

'Aw hell, give it to Dusty Miller'.

'Dusty Miller was picked up with a hole through his chest, he's in hospital and doubtful!'

I stood up 'Oh, all right Sergeant Major, I'll have a go at it but I don't ruddy well want it don't forget that!'

'Good boy, I knew you wouldn't let the team down,' said the C.S.M. and he walked on, handing out the cigarettes.

Jacky Barratt came along with a bandage on his head, 'Nothing much, tore it on some wire,' he said 'I've just been to the dressing station to have it done up, gosh! You should see the wounded down there, thousands of them! By the way Tommy you won't be crossing gloves with Cowley anymore'.

'How's that Jacky?'

'I saw him down there on a stretcher, he's lost an arm'.

On our feet once more we dragged ourselves wearily along the cobbled road at last with much cursing and grumbling we reached the outskirts of Noeux-les-Mines where again we fell out at the roadside. The men were in an ugly mood and hard to handle. It was deep in their minds that so many of their comrades had been killed on a useless, hopeless task and they were bitter in their resentment. As we lay at the roadside with drooping heads a strange noise came down the road 'What the hell's that?' Major Babbage stepped out on the road and roared 'fall in!' We stood up and lined the roadside 'battalion 'shun!'

And we sprang to attention as they marched past us. Two pipers at the head of about one hundred dirty battle scarred Seaforth Highlanders, the remnants of a battalion playing their way out of the jaws of death. What men! What soldiers! A thrill of pride ran through me, pride at belonging to the same army as these men who could still play their pipes and march despite the mauling they had received, this was no beaten army! This episode did something to us, we were soldiers once more and no longer a bitter resentful mob as we stepped out behind the Seaforth's and entered Noeux-le-Mines where billets and rest awaited us.

> *The dead men lay on the shell torn plain*
> *Where death and autumn held their reign,*
> *Like banded ghosts in the heavens grey*
> *The smoke of the conflict died away.*
> *The boys whom I knew and loved were dead*
> *Where wars grim annals were writ in red*
> *On the field of Loos in the morning.*
>
> *The dead men lay on the cellar stair*
> *Toll of the bomb that found them there.*
> *In the street men fell to the snipers aim*
> *A field of death on the field of fame.*
>
> *'Stiff in khaki the boys were laid*
> *Food of the bullet and hand grenade,*
> *This we saw when the charge was done*
> *And the East grew pale to the rising sun*
> *On the field of Loos in the morning'*

Our billet was at the usual French farm and we settled down in the usual French cowshed beside the usual stinking cesspool that seems to be the outstanding feature of French farm life. We slept and ate and lounged around talking and smoking and making very little effort at doing anything other than getting our rifles cleaned and oiled and in good working order. After nearly a day of idleness we were called out on a battalion parade and Major Babbage didn't mince his words when he told us what we looked like, 'A mob of dirty ruddy scarecrows, get some of that muck off your boots, equipment and uniforms and the next time I call a parade I want to see soldiers not tramps, get moving!'

We sat around and scraped and scrubbed and did the best we could but even our best didn't have much affect on the gluey muck that plastered us, and as daylight faded we said 'To hell with it,' and retired to our cow shed, all we wanted was sleep. After breakfast the next morning we paraded in full kit and marched to a railway siding where we climbed on board the cattle trucks of the waiting train. 'Wonder where we're off to this time,' I remarked to Spud as we settled down in a corner of the truck.

'Hope for the best Tommy,' replied Spud 'and expect the worst'.

However things turned out all right this time, we disembarked at a place called Caustre, were directed to our billets and then paraded by platoons for hot baths. This was luxury indeed, the huge tanks of hot water were in a factory, and we just stripped off everything and climbed into the hot steaming tanks. While we soaked, our filthy clothing was taken away for fumigation and after the bath there was a pile of clothing to pick from, if you were lucky you got your size, and if you didn't you swapped around until you got something near enough to satisfy.

'How do you feel after that lot Tommy?' asked Spud as we lounged outside the factory.

'Its great to feel clean again Spud,' I answered 'the last wash down I had was at Cannock Chase'

'So you think you're clean an,' wearing a nice clean shirt and uniform once more eh?', grinned Spud ' 'Well boy I know something about fumigation, it doesn't kill lice it just puts 'em to sleep, you wait until they wake up hungry an,' they'll give you merry hell!' I didn't believe him at the time but alas his words were very true, the lighted candle flame was the only answer to that nightmare.

Letters from home and parcels started to arrive for us, we drew two weeks pay, our food rations became regular, once more our badges and buttons took on a shine and day after day fresh faces joined us to bring us back to battalion strength. The newcomers looked upon us with a kind of respect, in their eyes I suppose we were veterans, we had fought through a major battle. A new man arrived to take charge of the battalion, Lieutenant Colonel Fitzgerald, and fresh platoon and company officers appeared to take over the reins of those who had fallen. There are higher ranks than those in a battalion of infantry, but to us there are no higher people, whenever things became grim and deadly, in cold wet misery and danger your battalion officers are in it with you and the average time an infantry officer lasted at the front was about four weeks. With a stroke of luck he may go back with wounds but all too often he went for keeps. Spud gave me his explanation and I think he was right.

'Look at them, they just ask for it, they wear different tunics and trousers to us, Sam Browne belts and revolvers and they lead the way once we go over the top. German snipers are looking for them and by hell they advertise their rank all right'.

Our new platoon officer Lieutenant Ramsey looked a young and lanky schoolboy and Spud's opinion was moodily expressed 'Bet the only woman he ever slept with was his mother!' So the young officer was crudely and harshly judged by the men in the ranks but usually it wasn't long before he had the chance of justifying the rank he held, providing he lived that long.

Once again we took the road as a battalion and on October 10th we marched into Armentieres in Flanders where billets awaited us in school rooms and empty buildings, and for these billets we felt very thankful, they were a vast improvement on the broken down leaking cow sheds and October nights were cold. We soon settled down to town life in Armentieres although shells crashed into the town and the rattle of machine gunfire wasn't far away. We just had time to find our way around while kit was inspected and replaced and then on October 19th we were struggling through the rain and mud to take over the trenches in Plugstreet (Ploegsteert) Woods during the hours of darkness. Plug Street was a weird spot on the left flank of Armentieres a mass of shell shattered trees where bullets slammed into the tree trunks, but those trees gave us a certain amount of cover and the wood was handy for shoring up trenches, dugouts, and also for making fires in the reserve trenches. And in Plug Street we spent a couple of weeks, one week in the reserve trench and one week in the front line getting used to the wet, filthy, stinking animal existence that was to be our lot for months to come. We slept in holes in the ground often in slimy mud with rats scampering in the darkness, our food came to us like swill and we ate it like pigs standing in mud and water. At night on duty we huddled up to the sandbags shivering in the cold and always the whine of the bullet and the crash of the shell to tell us death was very near. A couple of weeks of physical misery and then we were relieved and we marched away from Plug Street leaving behind us one officer and four men buried among those shattered trees.

We were pleased enough to find the end of our march was our billets in Armentieres and we were happy as we got fires going to dry our clothing and we could get busy getting rid of the muck of a fortnight in the trenches. Armentieres was a dull drab Flemish town but the troops who got billeted there considered themselves lucky, at least there were a few shops, some beer houses and eggs and chips could be bought anywhere. A lot of the houses were closed and shuttered but quite a number of the people had hung on, despite the nearness of the fighting line, and they were making a good living out of the troops selling anything they could get hold of.

We paraded for our pay and Spud said 'Come on lets see what this ruddy towns like, we've seen enough of the other stuff'.

We smartened up, Spud, a new chap who had joined our section called Ron Delany and myself and as we strolled down the street we saw approaching us a girl all curves and colours.

'Ah this is it,' grinned Ron 'Just the sort of French bit I've been dreaming about'.

As she drew level with us Ron stopped and saluted with a flourish, but her head went up and she looked down her nose at him as she passed under full sail.

'And that is that,' grinned Spud, 'come on Ron lets see the bottom of a tankard of French beer!'

'Well I go to hell!' said Ron scratching his ear.

I had moved on and I stopped at a small cafe, through the window of which I saw a young girl serving chips and eggs.

'I'm going in here for a feed,' I said, 'What about you two?'

'Aw I dunno, I feel more like a pint,' said Spud.

'No good on an empty belly, come on get some grub inside you'.

Into the cafe we went and seated ourselves on forms at a table beside the window where we could watch people go by, and believe me, after our experiences it was a pleasure just to sit and watch people walking upright instead of crouching in trenches. The smiling pleasant looking young girl came over to us wiping her hands on a cloth and cocking an inquiring eye.

'Go on Ron give her the order,' said Spud, 'you reckon you know the Flemish lingo, I want chips, eggs, bread and a pint of beer'.

Ron blew out his cheeks, grinned at the girl and muttered something that sounded like 'Pomme de terre, caufs, panne de buerre, and, 'er, a bucket of ale, sil vous plais!'

The girl laughed merrily and replied in clear distinct English, 'You Tommy's can have chips and eggs, yes, bread and butter, yes, but ale, no compree, only coffee, that do? Yes - No!'

We laughed with her at Ron's discomfort and I said 'Yes that will do us fine little lady, wheel it out!'

She looked at me a bit puzzled and then nodded and tripped away to prepare our meal while Spud remarked 'This is a hell of a country Ron. They don't understand you if they don't want to, but when it suits them they know English as good as we do'.

Looking out of the window I said 'Look out Ron, here comes your fancy piece with an officer'.

It was her all right hanging on to the arm of a Major of the artillery and when I took in his smart cut uniform, brightly polished belt and leggings and compared it with Ron's rigout as an infantry private I knew why she looked down her nose. Ron disappeared under the table as they passed by the window and when he came up he grunted 'Hell of a chance a private has against that kind of thing'.

The girl of the cafe brought our grub and as we ate I told her of Ron's experience, she laughed and pulled a face, 'Ah that one no bon-compree, she only want money, no good!'. That is how I came to meet 16 years old Victoria the Flemish girl who served chips and eggs to the troops in Armentieres, all that winter we moved in and out of the trenches in Flanders and always we came back to Armentieres for a few days rest and that little cafe became my regular port of call. Victoria told me her father was fighting at Verdun in the French Army and her mother looked at me for a time with a question in her eyes but she soon got used to me and made me welcome at the cafe. There I would sit for hours just talking to Victoria when she wasn't busy, telling her of England and she would tell me of France and Belgium. We never went anywhere away from the cafe and we were always under her mothers watchful eye, but I found a lot of peace and happiness in that second rate cafe away from the cold and misery of the trenches.

Early in November we marched away from Armentieres to a village called Houplines and there we took over the trenches between the main road to Lille and the Lys River. Conditions in the trenches were terrible. The winter was really with us now and the nights were bitterly cold, it was impossible to find a dry place anywhere and most of our time was spent knee deep in frozen water, some of the trenches were waist deep and others had to be abandoned. During our week in the front line Captain Campbell and four men were killed and seven men were wounded but on the whole things were pretty quiet, the Germans must have been just as wet and miserable as we were. It rained heavily and in many places if a man got stuck in the mud in a trench he was stuck until help arrived to pull him out. Getting a wounded man back under these conditions was an ordeal; it could take you hours to get a stretcher along a length of trench and God help the man on the stretcher. No wonder I looked forward to the day when we would be back in Armentieres for a rest spell and I could push all this misery into the background with the help of a young girl of Flanders, after all I think the cafe was better than some establishments, swilling beer, or some hole and corner brothel of cheap, scented women. Out of the trenches we trudged laden with our kit like a column of grim grey ghosts, after our two weeks duty in the water logged line, back to Armentieres and our billets. After a week and general clean up I made my way to the little cafe and pushed open the door. I hadn't told Victoria we were going into the line, I had just faded away two weeks previously, but she knew well enough where I had been, and for a moment she stared at me as though she couldn't believe here eyes.

'Hello Mademoiselle Viccy, how's things?!' I greeted her with a grin; her hand fluttered to her mouth as her eyes roamed over me 'Ah m'seiur Tommee, you come back, Yes! Mamma, Tommee, he return from the trenches'.

And as her mother came from the rear premises Victoria came up to me and kissed me lightly on the cheek and to my astonishment her mother smiled and kissed me on both cheeks. I was pleased Spud and Ron were not there to witness that! Soon a plate of chips and eggs with bread and hot coffee was laid out for me. Her mother was looking at me and speaking rapidly to Victoria, who turned to me and said, 'It was not nice up there Tommee, Mamma say you fatigue, how you say it, weary! Yes!'

I nodded my head, 'It was pretty bad Viccy,' I replied.

'Les Allemands!' Viccy spat out, 'The dirty bloody Boche!'

I grinned at her troopers English 'Not much the dirty bloody Boche Viccy, more your dirty bloody weather!'

> It isn't the foe that we fear
> It isn't the bullets that whine,
> It isn't the business career
> Of a shell or the burst of a mine.
> It isn't the snipers who seek
> To nip our young hopes in the bud,

No, it isn't the guns, and it isn't the Huns,
It's the rain, and the cold, and the mud!

Oh the rain, the mud and the cold,
The cold, the mud and the rain,
With weather at zero it's hard for a hero
From language that's rude to refrain.
With porridgy muck to the knees
With sky that's a,' pouring a flood,
Sure the worst of our foes are the pains and the woes
Of the rain, the cold, and the mud!

I was finding that carrying a tape on my sleeve curtailed my time off duty quite a bit, often when the boys were free on an evening I would find myself tied up with guard duty, fire picket, orderly room duty etc. when back from the line.

'And it serves you bloody well right, I warned yer,' said Spud, as he and Ron went off into the town, 'I'll give your love to the wench in the cafe'.

'You can go to hell,' I replied despondently 'but the first chance I get I'll peg you two for guard duty'.

Six days of relaxation and back we went to Houplines and squelched our weary way through the mud into the reserve trenches and for six days we toiled along the communication trenches carrying food, ammunition, rolls of barbed wire, loads of sandbags etc. up to the front line and re-building the sodden parapets that were forever collapsing through shellfire or water rotting the sandbags. Then into the front line to man the parapet day and night and most of us were pleased enough to be finished with the donkey work of the reserve trenches. We lived in mud, fed in mud, slept in mud and at night we shivered up beside the frosted sandbags and gazed at the cold twinkling stars overhead our thoughts far away in some corner of England wondering 'How long oh Lord, how long?' It was on this turn of duty that I did my first patrol of No Man's Land with Lieutenant Nicholson and although things were pretty quiet owing to the weather conditions it was a bit of a hair raising experience crawling around between the two lines of fire, and whenever a star shell burst overhead you felt horribly exposed. In the darkness you had to keep a tight check on your imagination and when at last we lay beside the German wire Lieutenant Nicholson gripped my shoulder and whispered in my ear 'Listen, you can hear them!'.

I could hear them all right beyond the coils of wire, the occasional stamp of boots on duckboards and the grunt of lowered voices, then someone started to laugh. I wondered what the hell anyone had to laugh about on a night like this! Then I felt the tap on my back, the signal to withdraw, and I was quite pleased when we got started on our crawl back towards our own trench. Half way back and Lieutenant Nicholson suddenly stopped and murmured, 'Keep still and listen!'

I heard the thud of heavy gun fire away on our flank, the crisp crack of rifle fire nearer at hand, and then I caught what he meant when I heard the sound of movement and low voices. Lying flat on the ground we could see the faint outline of figures moving at the German wire and Lieutenant Nicholson whispered to me, 'Working party on the wire, come on'.

We crawled back to our own trench and Lieutenant Nicholson checked his position at the parapet 'Right, company H.Q. and we'll get that little bunch of square-heads'. Into the company dugout we dived and he made his report, swiftly messages were passed and as I made my way along the trench to contact my own section I saw a number of bright star shells sour up from our own trench accompanied by a sudden savage burst of machine gun and rifle fire. At dawn Lieutenant Nicholson came into the bay where I stood on the fire step, 'We got that working party Corporal, nice clean job'.

'How do you know sir, you been out again?'

He laughed 'Here, have a look with my glasses, a bit to your left, about ten o'clock, you'll see some of them hanging on their own wire,' I turned the field glasses in the direction indicated and saw them all right, and a bullet slapped viciously into the sandbag at the side of my head, I wasn't the only one looking!

I ducked hastily and handed him his glasses, I had been in the line long enough to take a hint!

Lieutenant Nicholson was a chap who seemed to spend most of the hours of darkness crawling around in No Mans Land and he must have been a pretty useful officer but the battalion lost him on his next patrol when he was brought in with a severe wound in the chest. He wasn't dead, but his chances were pretty slim. We did six days and nights in the front line and nobody was sorry when the time came to pack up as the relief battalion of the South Staffords stumbled past us to take over the good work.

'What's it like mate?' someone growled in the darkness.

'Pretty cushy chum, Jerry won't bother you but the trenches are bloody awful!' It had been a pretty cushy trip; we had only lost one officer killed and one wounded, three men killed and five wounded during our couple of weeks in. Relief was a grim slow business either coming in or going out and it was just breaking daylight when we reached the last length of trench that would see us clear of the lines when suddenly there came the horrible shriek of shell which we knew by instinct would burst very, very close. It did, right in the trench where we were crowded together. I saw the terrific flash of the explosion and felt something hit me a severe blow on the chest as I was hurled to one side. 'God, this is it,' I thought as I lay in the mud 'I'm hit in the chest'. In the confusion I managed to pull my head clear of the mud and water and I heard someone shout 'Get these wounded men out of this, blast you!' And then I must have passed out because the next thing I knew I was lying on cobbles at the side of a roadway and Spud was kneeling beside me unbuckling my equipment 'Take it easy boy,' he grunted as he saw me move 'Where are you hit?'

'I think it's the chest Spud,' I gasped struggling for the breath that seemed to have left me.

'All right, be still and we'll soon have you fixed up Tommy', his fingers unbuttoning my tunic. As he uncovered my chest I was sick over him but he took no notice and I felt better when the sickness passed. I felt his hands roam over my flesh under my shirt back and front and as he stood up I said 'Is it a bad one Spud?'

He eyed me severely, 'Tommy, you're a bloody false alarm, that's what you are, there's not a drop of blood or a hole anywhere, just a bloody big bruise on your tits, sit up and have a look yourself'.

Spud was right, there was a huge purple bruise forming on my chest where something had hit me, perhaps a stone or piece of wood, perhaps a sandbag, perhaps a piece of someone else, I would never know. The shell killed two officers and eight men and four men were wounded in the shambles.

I saw our platoon officer Lieutenant Ramsey sitting at the side of the road awaiting a stretcher, a cigarette in his ashen lips and a bloody stump where his right arm had been. It wasn't so cushy after all! Back to Armentieres once more where the M.O. gave me a brief inspection and suggested that seven days light duty would see me all right so I made the most of it and besides visiting my cafe I also spent a bit of time with Spud and Ron. Their idea of hitting the high spots seemed to be visiting as many establishments as they could in the dingy side streets and drinking a good load of beer while they had the money to, but I'm afraid I didn't get much joy out of this. One evening after a spell of drinking Spud suggested going to a house he knew where we could get a good supper pretty cheap and we followed him like good little boys.

Down a lane we staggered until Spud pulled up at a house and bashed on the door with the beer bottle he carried, 'This is my little home from home boys,' he cried as the door opened and a hard faced female looked us over, 'open up Lola I've brought some of the troops tonight'. We grinned sheepishly as we stepped inside and a crackle of female voices greeted us in French. I blinked around the dimly lit room and saw about half a dozen girls sitting around the place. 'What the hell's this joint?' I asked Ron.

'I dunno Tommy, but I can make a damn good guess,' replied Ron, 'The old bugger hasn't brought me here before!'

'Come on boys,' cried Spud waving a hand towards the bunch of females, 'pick which you like, but leave me that ginger one'.

A dark haired wench with cold eyes and a fixed smile sidled up to me 'Anglais soldat nice, you like me, yes!'

I looked at her and felt a trifle sick 'Look Mademoiselle,' I said desperately pulling out a couple of francs 'I want coffee, compree, coffee, sil vous plais!'

She grabbed the money and looked at me with wonder, 'Ah, oui,' she said and as she moved away I said to Ron 'You can do what the hell you like Ron but I'm getting out of this'.

Ron looked unhappy 'I don't want to stay either Tommy but I don't like leaving Spud, the silly old mucker will finish up with his bleeding throat cut or something'.

'Let him,' I grunted 'serve the old bugger right, anyway you can have my coffee when that tart brings it, I'm off!'.

As I opened the door I heard the chatter of shrill cries behind me but I was out in God's clean air and legging it for the part of Armentieres I knew best, where a plate of chips and eggs awaited me and the face I looked at was not painted and powdered to cover up the markings of vice. That was my only experience of a peep behind the scenes at the nightlife of France, it was a sorry affair.

Christmas 1915 saw us back in the front line once more on the Houplines front, and we made the best of a bad job helped along by a good flow of parcels from home and extra rum rations to keep us from brooding too much over the festive season. Our sector remained fairly quiet until December 30th and then suddenly there was a drastic change. The German artillery fire increased and shells of all sizes poured into and around our trenches, parapets were blown down, dugouts collapsed, water from the flooded River Lys poured into the trenches, men were wounded and drowned and blown to pieces. We were cut off and isolated by gunfire and all we could do was crouch and curse and wait, without sleep and almost without food. By the time Jerry was satisfied that he had brought in the New Year to his liking we had four officers and 29 men killed, two officers and 43 men wounded. It was a weary eyed grey faced column of men who were relieved on January 3rd to trudge along that cobbled road from Houplines to Armentieres.

'Dunno what the hell Jerry wanted to mess things up like that for,' grumbled Spud 'There we were nice and quiet, as happy as pigs in shit and he has to come along and knock hell out of us'.

'Perhaps it was some of the German brass hats who suggested it,' I replied as we tramped along.

'Yes, just the sort of bloody silly thing the brass hats in any army would think up,' said Spud, 'they sit miles back drinking their tots and then one of them points to a sector of the line and says 'I think we'll give that sector a pasting'. That sets the ruddy ball rollin,' and the pearly gates open for a few more poor bloody infantry'.

I received a warm welcome from Victoria and her mother when we arrived at the cafe for a meal, they could hear the thud of guns and the crash of shells in the Houplines sector and they knew there had been merry hell to play while we were up there. 'No good up there Tommee,' said Victoria 'the dirty Boche!' and she hovered around us as we sat and ate and talked and smoked just thankful to be out of it once more.

Spud sat and sucked at his pipe blowing out clouds of smoke and then he turned to me saying 'She's a nice kid this Victoria you've got hold of Tommy'.

I laughed 'She's nice as you say Spud, but I haven't got hold of her'.

'Aw to hell, Tommy, she's fallen for you, can't you see it?'

'Don't talk like a bloody fool Spud, she's only a kid'.

He waved his pipe 'Oh, and of course you're not, you're a full grown man I suppose, well let me tell you boy, if you can't see what's in her eyes you've a hell of a lot to learn'.

Ron grinned at us, 'Its right what Spud says Tommy, she's scared stiff every time we're in the trenches and she's all over you every time you come back alive'.

'That's because we're good friends,' I replied.

'Friends hell,' grunted Spud, 'there's no such thing with the male and the female, I know what I'd do if I was you, I'd ruddy well sleep with that wench and bring her joy'.

'You would, you old bugger, I reckon you'd also sleep with her mother in your spare time,' I grunted.

Spud's eyes roved over Viccy's mother, taking in her buxom curves, 'I might do a hell of a lot worse than that with my spare time, do you think there's a chance?'

'Oh come on, you old reprobate,' I replied, 'Lets see the shops'.

> *Standing up to the sandbags*
> *Its funny the thoughts that come,*
> *Staring into the darkness*
> *Hearing the bullets hum.*
> *Leaning against the sandbags*
> *With a rifle under my ear,*
> *Oh I've had more thoughts on sentry go*
> *Than I use to have in a year.*
>
> *Shivering up to the sandbags*
> *With an icicle there for a spine,*
> *Don't it seem funny the things you think*
> *Here in the firing line.*
> *Hunkering down when a star shell*
> *Bursts in a splutter of light,*
> *You can jaw to your soul by the sandbags*
> *Most any old time in the night.*

~ Tommy ~

I was pleased to get them away from the cafe because I could see Spud was just in the mood to start anything, the joy of still being alive I suppose and the urge to grab any pleasure that was available, there might be no next time. When the angel of death is fluttering his wings over you every minute of every hour, every day you are in the trenches you have a frantic desire to squeeze every last drop of pleasure out of the few days you have, knowing full well as each day passes that it is one day nearer to the time when you'll buckle on your equipment and march once more into a dirty stinking world of death and destruction. We wandered into Chapelle Armentieres buying silk post cards to send home and I stopped at a shop window with a display of leather gloves, belts, slippers etc. and pointed to a set of boxing gloves hanging in the corner. 'Its a long time since I pulled a pair of those on, Spud,' I said.

Spud sighed 'Yes Tommy, remember those days at Barnard Castle!'

I saw some photo postcards of Georges Carpentier, Eugene Crique, and Charles Ledoux, famous French Boxers and we went into the shop to price them. The old man behind the counter could speak good English and as I selected my post cards we talked of boxing. 'Ah m'sieur, that one he fly for France,' pointing to Carpentier, 'and that one,' pointing to Crique, 'he, how you say, wounded bad at Verdun - les sales Boche!'

I paid for the cards and the old man came around the counter, 'I show you m'sieur, I show you,' and he opened a door exposing steps leading down to a cellar, 'you follow me, oui'.

We followed him down the steps and found ourselves in a large cellar in the centre of which was rigged up a boxing ring and around the walls various gear used by boxers in training. Memories came flooding back to me, the slaughter house boxing of my childhood days, the gym at school, the boxing rings at the brigade camps, the exhibition bouts at the rink, the open air boxing in the army training camps.

'Gosh, how I'd like to get the feel of it again,' I cried as I felt the sagging ropes of the ring.

'I'll have a go with you Tommy if you like,' said Ron quietly.

'I stared at him 'Do you box Ron, why the hell haven't you told us about it?'

He looked uncomfortable 'Aw, I'm not much good now, I used to do a lot in the Boy Scouts but I've gone to seed, still I'll have a go just to please you'.

We pulled off our tunics and shirts and kicked off our heavy army boots and as Spud and the old Frenchman laced on the gloves I eyed Ron in speculation. He would be about a stone heavier than me and he looked pretty good around the shoulders. As we shook hands and sparred he shuffled round in a useful manner. I stabbed in a light left to the chin tried a left to the body that he blocked and took a crisp right in return that made me blink. We swapped lefts and I heard him grunt as I hooked my next left to the body and then we were together belting away merrily with body punching. As we came apart I hooked left and right to the chin and took an overarm right on the forehead that sent me back on the ropes. Lucky for me that one landed high. Ron rushed in but I stabbed him off with straight lefts to the face and slid off the ropes. 'Round one,' yelled Spud and as I stepped to the corner I saw the old Frenchman's face beaming with excitement.

After a brief rest, 'Round two,' and as we met in the centre Ron made the mistake of slinging a round arm right. I ducked it changed feet and hooked a hard left that landed hard under the breastbone, he gasped and I saw his mouth open as I followed in with a solid right under the heart.

Ron held up his hand and grasped the rope with his other hand; 'Enough old boy,' he gasped panting for breath.

I dropped my hands, 'Are you all right Ron?' I asked.

He grinned 'I'm all right from the neck up but my guts have caved in, no more for today Tommy'.

As we unlaced the gloves I said 'Thanks for the spar Ron I enjoyed it'.

He was still gulping air 'So did I Tommy, but a little bit goes a hell of a long way with me these days'.

We dressed, thanked the Frenchman, and made our way back to our billet Spud remarking on the way 'You haven't lost much, Tommy'.

I looked at him and shook my head 'I've lost a hell of a lot Spud, I'm rusty and my timing has gone, I was in there and I know, its a good job Ron wasn't in good fighting condition'.

January went by in wet and cold and misery and throughout the month the trench routine went on until on January 22nd orders came to us to arrange a raid on the German trenches. Fourteen men and myself under Lieutenant Smith and Sergeant Brodwick were going to cross No Mans Land, enter German lines through a gap that was to be blasted through the barbed wire by gunfire, and if possible bring back a German prisoner. At midnight the raiding party collected in the company H.Q. dugout and Lieutenant Smith briefly informed us that we would cross No Mans Land when our gunfire lifted from the German front line.

'There's about one hundred and fifty yards to cross to their wire and we'll go fast, our shells should be dropping on their reserves and keeping them pinned down. When we get into his trench my party will turn left and Sergeant Brodwick's party will turn right. Don't do any more than one hundred yards and use grenades on their dugouts, get a prisoner alive if you can and we'll meet at the starting point in Jerry's trench and come back together. Now empty your pockets and remove your badges, all you need is your identification discs. Get your faces and hands blackened, each man will carry a couple of grenades, rifle and bayonet and twenty-five rounds, all clear? Good luck to you!'

Soon we were ready for the show and we moved along the trench to our starting point where a section of barbed wire had been removed in the darkness to let us pass through. As we crouched against the sandbags a thin drizzle of cold rain started and our artillery was slinging over an occasional shell, but nothing to make Jerry alarmed. Lieutenant Smith stood beside me checking the time on his wristwatch 'Keep your heads down, it will start any minute now'. Suddenly there was a series of heavy thuds behind our trenches and the howl and shriek of our own shells passing close overhead made us crouch deeper in the trench. 'Right on target sir,' cried Sergeant Brodwick as the shells exploded in a fiendish tattoo on the German wire and front line trench ahead of us. 'Good shooting gunners,' said Lieutenant Smith and for ten minutes the infernal row went on intermingled with bursts of machine gun fire. Suddenly it ceased and for a minute there seemed to be complete silence and then it started again but the range had been elevated to the enemy rear trenches.

'Come on boys, here we go!' cried Lieutenant Smith as he scrambled over the parapet and we were on our way, keeping close so as not to go astray in the darkness and our hearts thumping in our chests. In a short space of time we were through the shattered remnants of the German barbed wire and tumbling breathless over the broken down parapet of the German front line, we were in!

Someone laughed and said in a high pitched voice 'Never a bloody shot fired, they've buggered off!'

'Shut up and get a move on,' ordered Lieutenant Smith and we trailed after him to the left along the trench while Sergeant Brodwick took his party to the right. There seemed to be no Germans in that bit of trench to meet us as we pushed along, and then Lieutenant Smith stopped at the dark entrance of a dug out. 'Come out,' shouted the officer but there was no response and we were about to pass it by when we heard a cough from below. I pulled a pin out of a grenade and threw it in the dark entrance and the man following me did the same. There was a satisfying muffled thump as the grenades exploded and we carried on around traverse after traverse but still making no contact with the enemy. Suddenly there was the sharp crash of exploding grenades along the parapet, fortunately for us they didn't fall in the trench, and Lieutenant Smith pulled up.

'Sling a few grenades,' he ordered 'and then back we go!'

Grenades were thrown left, right and forward in the darkness and then we scrambled back the way we had come until we met Sergeant Brodwick's party.

'We've got one of the bastards sir,' gasped the Sergeant.

'Good, get him over the top and rush him back to our own trench, we'll follow behind you, steady now, keep moving!'

Just before we reached our own trench, fire from a German machine gun swept through us and Lieutenant Smith and two men went down, they were carried in but Lieutenant Smith died as he lay in the mud at the bottom of the trench. I saw the German prisoner at dawn as he was being escorted back to H.Q. and I saw the blanket covered form of Lieutenant

Smith on the stretcher as he was being carried away for burial, in my opinion a very poor exchange. I could visualize the report in the newspapers at home 'A successful raid was carried out by our troops in the Armentieres sector and a prisoner was captured'. It makes nice reading when you're sitting at home at breakfast, but you see things different when you are actually in it.

As I sat on the fire step of the trench munching a slab of bread and a piece of greasy bacon Spud and Ron came along and squatted down beside me.

'How did things go Tommy?' asked Ron.

I shrugged 'How the hell do I know Ron, you go over in pitch blackness, barge around in the dark, sling a few grenades, and then leg it like hell for home sweet home'.

He nodded 'I know, I heard them asking for volunteers, and that's just where you go wrong in this mans army, see?'

'Aw hell Spud, someone's got to do these jobs or we're going to be stuck in this damned country for ever and ever'.

'Listen boy,' said Spud 'the last time I fell for that volunteering racket was in 1914 and I swore I'd never volunteer for anything else while I was in the army, I haven't!'

'What happened Spud?' I asked lighting a cigarette and leaning back on the sandbags.

'We were on parade, square bashing, when the Sergeant Major comes along and asks for some musical volunteers,' answered Spud 'I thinks this is a cushy do so I steps forward, I used to be a drummer boy when I was a kid; four of us steps out of the ranks and the Sergeant Major looks us over and he says, 'You're all musicians eh?' 'Yes sir,' we chorus in a happy little bunch. 'Right, you four are detailed to go to the station, you'll find a piano there, carry it into the officers mess!' 'That station was two ruddy miles away and we had to hump that blasted piano every inch of the way, mugs wanted!'.

There was a series of thuds from the German lines and someone yelled 'Look out, mortars!' as we fell flat in the bottom of the trench. The mortars made an unearthly howl as they soared in the air and then they came down to explode with a nerve racking crash. We feared and hated them. The German artillery joined in and by nightfall we had 3 officers and 20 men killed, 2 officers and 42 men wounded. The place was a shambles of dead, dying, and wounded, with men buried in dugouts and trenches wrecked, no relief and no food could reach us and the wounded just had to lie and hope. The following day it continued and we had another 2 officers and 27 men killed and 39 were wounded while the rest of us manned the parapet and waited for the expected attack to develop. It didn't come, and that night through the hours of darkness we were relieved and crawled back wearily to Armentieres and rest. Passing through Houplines we saw at the side of the road the still figures in grey blankets of 50 of our comrades and cold deserted wrecked Houplines was to be their resting-place.

'That's what we get when some old bugger with red tabs says 'Look here old boy its time we had a jolly old raid, what,' growled Spud as he tramped along beside me.

'Be a good thing if the brass hats had the job to do,' said Ron.

Jacky Barratt marching behind us burst out laughing 'What the hell's the joke Jacky?' asked Spud turning his head.

'Oh Christ can't you see it Spud,' answered Jacky, 'just imagine us lying on the parapet giving covering fire for a bunch of fat arsed brass hats going over No Man's Land!' It was certainly a picture worth dwelling on!

> Now when we take the cobbled road
> We often took before,
> Our thoughts are with the cheery boys
> Who tread that road no more.
>
> Oh boys upon the stricken fields
> If you could call to mind,
> The wine of Cafe,' Pierre Le Blanc
> You wouldn't stay behind.
>
> But when we leave that trench at night
> And stagger 'neath our load,
> Grey silent ghosts as light as air
> Come with us down that road.
>
> And when we sit us down to drink
> You sit beside us too.
> And drink at Cafe Pierre Le Blanc
> As once you used to do.

As I sat in my billet cleaning my equipment Company Sergeant Major Pyburn stamped in and stood in front of me 'How about a second tape?' he asked.

I looked up at him wearily 'Look here Sergeant Major,' I replied 'you can have this one free gratis, and for nothing, I don't want it'.

He shook his head glumly 'I know how you feel boy, but the point is we're damned short of N.C.O.'s, you're up on orders for your second stripe so get it sewn on and don't argue!'

'I don't bloody well want it,' I growled.

'Maybe not, but the battalion want N.C.O.'s, and don't forget we're on active service my lad, get that second tape up'.

As he left us Spud grinned across at me and said 'Its no use Tommy, they've got you by the short hairs now all right'.

'You've soldiered all your blinking life Spud, why the hell don't you have a go?'

'Oh, I've had plenty of tapes in my time boy,' he replied.

'And where the hell are they now?' I asked looking at his tunic.

'I ditched them when I got fed up with the bull,' he laughed 'if you have a long read at my crime sheet you'll see where my stripes went'.

There was no way out of it that I could see so I got Viccy to stitch on my second stripe and I found that I was tied up more than ever with regimental duties. Fresh drafts of men came out from England to replace the losses and early in February in a heavy snow storm we marched out of Armentieres, but not towards Houplines, this time we crossed the railway through Chapelle Armentieres and carried out a relief on the right flank in a sector known as the mushroom. It deprived this name from a huge mine crater that had erupted there, hundreds of tons of earth had gone skywards and come down again in a maze of blackened rubble. It was an ugly, forbidding locality of broken down trenches but the snow continued to fall steadily, soft white snow that soon covered the man created ugliness in a carpet of white. Patrols went out at night with their khaki covered in white sheeting; and it was in these trenches standing to at dawn I stood on the fire step looking over the parapet through our barbed wire across the white wilderness of No Man's Land.

I caught sight of a flicker of movement behind a stunted bush beyond the German wire. My eyes popped and focused on that bush about 120 yards away, I had been thinking more of breakfast than Germans, and again I caught a slight movement. There was a Jerry there, but I couldn't see him from my position. I scrambled along the trench about 25 yards easing off the safety catch of my rifle as I went. I mounted the fire step and carefully peered over the top. I could see him all right now, a Jerry on his knees behind the bush looking through field glasses towards his left flank, and on his head he wore the spiked pickelhaube helmet of the German officer class of that time. Slowly I eased my rifle forward and cuddled the butt into my shoulder muttering to myself 'I'll get you, you cheeky bugger, I'll get you'.

There he was, his chest dead in my sights, 'keep calm now,' just a gentle squeeze on the trigger like they taught you on the range!

The rifle kicked suddenly and I saw the Jerry flop in the snow his helmet rolling a yard or two away. 'Got you, you bastard,' I growled as I jumped down off the fire step and reported to Sergeant Brodwick.

The Sergeant and Major Babbage were soon peering over the parapet and Major Babbage exclaimed 'I can see him now, good shooting Corporal. Sergeant, get a lewis gun lined up on that spot and if they try to get him in give them a burst'.

'Yes sir,' and as the Sergeant went off Major Babbage still peered over the top with interest and I sat on the fire step smoking a cigarette.

'That's one blighter who won't go back across the Rhine anyway,' remarked Major Babbage and then he nearly fell on top of me as a burst of machine gun fire swept our parapet.

We spent a week in the line and a week in reserve at the mushroom and we thought it fairly cushy, we only lost 1 officer and 3 men killed, 4 N.C.O.'s and 7 men wounded, but it was a bitterly cold spell and we were pleased to get back to Armentieres. New faces appeared daily and weekly as replacements joined us, sometimes a handful of men and sometimes a good sized draft, sometimes men fresh out from England and sometimes men who had been wounded or sick, returning from hospitals in France to be absorbed into the ranks of the fighting battalions. The front was stagnant, locked in the miserable grip of winter weather, but every day some stiff, blanketed forms were lowered into their last resting place, and every day on every road leading to the front the ambulances trundled along, carrying their broken burdens back to the hospitals. Men and more men, food for the hungry guns, more men, more men! Two chaps had been posted to my section and I was pleased when I found they had been with the 8th battalion, both wounded at Ypres and sent to us from the base as replacements. It was good to get chaps with front line experience, but they were a strange pair and needed careful handling. Tug Wilson was a poor soldier and a real lead swinger but he was an amazing rifle shot and proved his value in the mushroom when he sniped a German at 500 yards range in poor visibility. According to him, he had been born in the London docks area and had to fend for himself at an early age. He had worked on barges on the river, went to sea on tramps, jumped ship in a Canadian port and worked on farms and lumber camps all over that country, going as far as fur hunting in the far North. He had done quite a bit of boxing and had won the 9 stone title with the 8th battalion. Paddy Finnigan was a different type, he was a typical Irish boy and when he was in the mood he would soldier with the best, but he was as stubborn and obstinate as a mule at times. He was gifted with a golden tenor voice and it was a treat to hear him sing his native songs. Huddled up to the sandbags at night, cold and wet and miserable, you would sometimes hear 'When Irish Eyes are Smiling' or 'Danny Boy' and you knew that Paddy was in the mood for singing in spite of everything.

Spud, Ron, and I made our way to our little cafe and on entering we found a good company of the boys already there including Tug and Paddy, all clamouring for chips and eggs. Viccy and her mother were busy and as we seated ourselves Viccy caught sight of us and gave us a wave and a quick smile.

'This is getting quite a busy little nest,' said Spud.

'Well you can expect that,' said Ron 'the boys soon get to know where they get a decent meal, hope we don't have to wait too long'.

We sat smoking and talking watching the proceedings with interest, and feeling at peace with the world when suddenly that peace was rudely shattered. Viccy was spitting and a mixture of French and English with a very red face and it was directed at Tug, who sat on a form beside Paddy, grinning at her.

'What the hell's Tug been up to?' muttered Spud.

'Dunno, but she's giving him a mouthful,' I replied.

Viccy went on serving and then I saw what the trouble was, the next time she was at a table near Tug he ran his hand down her spine and laughed, 'Just made for the troops eh!' Viccy flushed and spun on her heel the back of her right hand catching Tug a resounding crack on the cheek, she swiftly recovered her balance and swung again, a full blooded right that landed like a pistol shot on Tug's other cheek and toppled him backwards off the form.

'Why, you dirty little French bitch,' he spluttered as he scrambled to his feet but already half a dozen chaps stood between them and I stepped across, 'That will be enough Wilson, get out of here'.

Tug stared at me both sides of his face showing scarlet patches 'She hit me, Corporal!' he exclaimed.

'I know she did and you damn well asked for it, this happens to be a decent joint, now get out quick!'.

His eyes glinted, 'You thinking of starting something Corporal?'

That was something I had to avoid, as much as I would have liked to take off my coat, trouble in these places usually finished up with the premises closed down by the military authority.

'Listen Wilson,' I said 'I'm ordering you out of this cafe, if you don't obey that order I'll put you under arrest and have you taken to the guard room, and I'll charge you'.

'What with, I wasn't doing any harm!'

'I'll charge you with insulting behaviour to this girl, creating a disturbance, and disobeying an order; you'll get plenty for that'.

'Aw come on Tug,' said Paddy 'You'll land in the clink for a bloody year'.

'All right,' growled Tug as he pulled on his hat 'plenty other places in this bloody town for a feed and a bit of fun, come on'.

The door opened and they were gone and I sat down feeling a bit weary and fed up 'As if there wasn't enough trouble up the line without starting it here!' I grumbled.

Tommy Lowery came over to us 'Why the hell didn't you slug him?'

I shrugged 'I couldn't do that Tommy, it would have meant trouble for Viccy and her mother'.

'Oh I see, I never thought of that'.

Viccy came over pale now and smiling, 'Merci Tommee, that man no good, no?'

Spud grinned at her 'Listen kid, next time you swing one just close your fist like that, see, and make it a K.O.'

'Kay-ooh,' she stared at him 'I no compree that one'.

'Never mind, Viccy,' said Ron 'What about some feed?'

Viccy bustled away to supply us and then the door opened and Sergeant Lockhart from battalion headquarters stood there looking around. He got his eye on me and beckoned me over to him, 'What the hell's on now?' I growled as I rose from the table.

'You're to report to the Adjutant at H.Q. right away Corporal,' he informed me.

'Why, what's this about Sergeant?' I asked.

'I don't know, I was just told to find you and give you the message'.

'I was just going to have a decent feed,' I moaned.

'Well you'd better skip it and get along'.

I went back to our table to get my hat.

'What's up now Tommy?' asked Spud.

'I don't know, I've got to report to H.Q. right away'.

Spud chuckled 'Good old N.C.O.'s, get on with the job Tommy, we'll see to your eggs and chips for you'.

'You can go to hell Spud, and I hope the food chokes you,' I replied.

I soon reached battalion H.Q. and reported to the Adjutant in his office. 'I've a job for you Corporal,' he said as I stood before his table 'I believe you have a pretty sound knowledge of the Houplines sector?'

'Yes sir'.

'Well, I've just had a message from brigade that Lieutenant General Whitelock wishes to tour that sector and I'm sending you with him to act as a guide. Get your rifle and equipment and go to the White Chateau in Houplines. Wait there for the General and I suggest you take him in by Cambridge Avenue, cover the front line to the canal and return via Buttercup Lane, clear?'

'Clear enough sir,' I replied staring at him Cambridge Avenue is sound enough, but Buttercup Lane was a bit of a mess the last time I was that way'.

The Adjutant sighed wearily 'I know Corporal, but the orders are that you cover the sector and that's the only way to do it'.

'Very good sir,' I saluted and went off for my equipment cursing my luck and the brass hats who were taking me back into the line while the rest of the battalion were out of it. I tramped wearily along the cobbled road out of Armentieres towards Houplines in a drizzle of sleet with visions of the boys in the cafe snug and warm with their eggs and chips and coffee, what a life! I reached the White Chateau and scrounged a mug of tea from the East Yorks while informing them of the visit of the brass hats.

'How are they coming up?' asked a Sergeant of the East Yorks.

'I don't know, in a ruddy Rolls I expect,' I replied shortly, 'I know how I had to come, on my two flat feet'.

About an hour later they appeared, not in a Rolls but on horseback, the Lieutenant General and a Staff Captain resplendent in gold braided hats, red tabbed tunics and shining Sam Browne belts and leggings. As they dismounted and their horses were led away by an East Yorks Corporal I stepped up smartly and saluted 'Guide, at your service sir'.

'Oh yes, well Corporal there are two ways into this sector I understand and I want to cover both of them'.

'Very good sir'.

'Right, you lead on and we will follow you'.

I made my way to Durham Castle, a broken down factory chimney stack, and into Cambridge Avenue, the trench that led into the reserve trenches and then on to the front line. Things seemed pretty quiet, just the usual occasional burst of rifle and machine gun fire and the trench was only ankle deep in mud so we were soon in the reserve trenches where we found the East Yorks H.Q. dug out and the brass hats went in for a conference with their Commanding Officer. I sat outside with a mug of tea while they, no doubt, had a snort of the C.O.'s whiskey. After a time a worried looking R.S.M. appeared at the entrance of the dug out and glared up and down the trench, catching sight of me sitting on some sandbags he crooked his finger at me and I put down my mug of tea and joined him. 'I suppose you are acting as guide to those two blokes in there,' he said looking at my cap badge and jerking his thumb towards the dug out.

'That's right sir,' I replied.

'They say they're going in by Cambridge and coming out by Buttercup?'

'Right again sir'.

'Do you know this sector Corporal?'

'Should do sir, I've been in and out all the winter,' I replied.

He glared at me 'Then why in hell's name Buttercup Lane, it's a bloody death trap?'

'Now look here Sir, they've picked the route, not me. I know all about Buttercup Lane; I was in the line when Jerry blasted it and I know its been wrecked ever since. I wouldn't use Buttercup Lane in daylight, but what the hell can I do about it?'

'But there's no cover for half its length,' snorted the R.S.M. 'and Jerry is watching it, he's got it taped!'

'I know that too sir,' I replied 'tell you what to do, you tell those two geezers to come out by Cambridge Avenue and you'll make me feel a lot happier, I'm not looking forward to this'.

The R.S.M. threw up his hands in disgust and dived back into the dugout leaving me to hope for the best. The two brass hats soon appeared followed by a worried looking Adjutant, and as I stood waiting I heard the Adjutant say 'I wish you would change your route sir and avoid Buttercup Lane'. The

General snorted 'rubbish sir, Buttercup Lane is part of this sector and I'm here to inspect the lot, anyway the front is quiet so I'll do the show properly, lead off Corporal'. I led the way along the trench leading to the firing line, stopping every now and again while the officers discussed the conditions of the sand bags and the floor of the trench. 'Must have better drainage,' grumbled the General as we trudged through a stretch of knee deep mud and water 'make a note of that Captain, more work on drainage, blast this mud'. 'Yes sir,' replied the Staff Captain entering it in a notebook, and I grinned happily to myself as I noted the sorry mess their nice shining leggings were now in. Soon we entered the firing line and turned left and now a Company Commander joined us and pointed out to the General his machine gun posts, H.Q. dugouts, signal arrangements and everything of interest to the old boy. The chaps on duty stood at their posts looking into periscopes or peering occasionally over the top and taking no notice of us as we trudged along the trench. Suddenly there were three sharp explosions ahead of us and I pulled up sharp.

'What was that Corporal?' asked the General, standing beside me.

'Rifle grenades sir,' I replied 'we'd better wait a few minutes, Jerry usually sends a few over to find the range and then follows up with a shower of them'.

I sat on the fire step, the Staff Captain leaned against the sandbags, but the General paced up and down in the mud.

'Make a note Captain,' he barked 'I've seen match sticks and even pieces of paper lying around, it won't do, we must have the trenches clean'.

I gaped at him, the trenches clean, Ye Gods!

A machine gun stuttered a few rounds, here and there a rifle cracked, the dull boom of guns came from Ypres way, but no more grenades came over so we moved on our way until we came to the end of the sector where the trench was up against the River Lys. I pointed to a narrow cut leading from the trench, 'That's the way to Buttercup Lane sir'.

'Good, that's the way we go back,' said the General and the Captain of the East Yorks in command of the company flanking the river looked at him aghast, 'I wouldn't advise that sir, the place is in an awful mess'.

'Look here Captain, I take it your men use this Buttercup Lane?'.

'Yes sir, but only in emergency and at night'.

'Well then, I'll damn well use it by day, raise the morale of the troops my dear chap, you're all windy of Buttercup Lane'.

Sadly I led the way into the narrow cut where there was just room to move along and soon we came to the section that had been battered by shell fire, broken sandbags were strewn everywhere. Deep waterlogged holes had to be carefully crossed on sagging duckboards, the drainage was destroyed and soon we were up to the thighs in muddy water. A bullet cracked into a sandbag only a foot or so away and I turned to the brass hats puffing behind me, 'Better keep your heads well down sir, Jerry's got this lot well marked'.

The Staff Captain was looking a bit pale about the gills, but the General just snorted, push on Corporal, push on'. Slowly I trudged along, each step forward meant pulling your foot out of the glue like mud under the water and I had the uneasy feeling that someone was watching us, another bullet hissed by very, very near, and then a quick burst of machine gun fire made us crouch low in the broken down trench.

The Staff Captain crouched beside me 'Is it all as bad as this Corporal?'

'The worst bit is a bit further along sir,' I replied, 'the parapet is all down and the trench is impassable, there's only a stretch of sacking for cover and you have to double across the duck boards fast! If you slip off the duck boards you'll be overhead in the mud'.

A gun boomed and a shell howled overhead to explode with a roar about 50 yards away. The General grinned 'By gad sir, they're sniping us with their artillery now!'

Very funny, for those who like it, I didn't!

'Perhaps we should go the other way sir after all,' said the Staff Captain.

The General stared at him 'What! Go back now, not on your life sir, we'd be the laughing stock of the army, push on Corporal'.

Slowly we made headway until we came to the sticky patch I had mentioned and I stopped under cover of some sandbags. Forty yards of broken down trench filled with muddy stinking water and forty yards of one-foot wide slimy duckboard erected above it as the only means of getting across. The only cover when crossing was a stretch of hessian sacking that was riddled with bullet holes.

'There it is sir,' I said 'we've got to double over that and don't forget there's craters under that water 10 feet deep, and for God's sake keep your heads down'.

The General looked at it doubtfully 'Is there no other way?'.

'No other way in daylight sir'.

'All right Corporal you go first and we'll follow your example'.

I slung my rifle over my back so as to have both hands free and I pulled the sling tight to keep the rifle from bouncing, and then I wiped the soles of my boots on a piece of sand bag sacking. I moved forward crouching low and with my eyes fastened on the duck boards I went over at a slow double and sank thankfully under cover at the other side. The Staff Captain came next and he hesitated as he put a foot on the duckboards, hell, didn't he know he was exposed!

'Come on double over,' I shouted at him.

He looked up and then started to run, good show. Half way over and a machine gun started to chatter and I heard the hiss of bullets as they whipped through the sacking. Jerry was wide-awake and he had seen the movement. The Staff Captain looked startled then threw caution to the winds; he straightened up and finished the course like a track runner.

'Oh my God,' he gasped as he sank down beside me, 'this is just a bit too thick, those blighters nearly got me'.

The gun continued to chatter in short bursts and I saw the sacking fluttering as the bullets passed through it. I made a downward movement with my hand to the General and called out 'Not yet sir, wait until he stops firing'.

'Its no use you telling old 'spit and polish,' what to do,' said the Staff Captain 'he'll just do as he damn well pleases!'

However old 'spit and polish,' had enough savvy to stay put and after a short interval the firing died away.

'Here I come,' he called and he doubled on the duckboards but he was a tall chap and he didn't crouch half enough. Just over half way and the vicious burst of firing started again, the general looked up and that was his undoing, he slipped on the duckboards and fell his full length.

'My God, he's hit,' gasped the Staff Captain.

Fortunately he didn't fall into the water but he stayed flat on the duckboards and crawled the rest of the way to join us.

'Are you wounded sir?' asked the Staff Captain.

'Wounded be damned! No I'm not wounded, but I've lost my bloody hat!' snorted the General.

True enough, that lovely hat with the red band and the bright gold peak was slowly sinking into the mud. The rest of the journey was easy and I breathed a sigh of relief when I reported at the White Chateau in Houplines with two wet, muddy, bedraggled brass hats, better a General without a hat than a hat without a General. I had some hot tea and biscuits and told the East Yorks my story in front of a hot cook house fire, the story went down well and someone said, 'Well the old bugger made it anyway'.

Dusk was drawing in but I was lucky enough to get a lift on a transport back to Armentieres where I had to report on the trip to our own Adjutant. He laughed at the story of the General's hat in Buttercup Lane, and then shook his head.

'It was a damn silly thing to do coming back that way, but he wouldn't be told'.

I was thankful to get my clothes off and roll into bed; there's no joy in being in the trenches when your pals are miles behind.

'Hell to pop over Plug Street way,' said Spud and I cocked an ear to the thunder of the guns away on the left flank.

'Someone's copping it Spud,' I replied, 'But I'm going to sleep'.

All next day the roar of the artillery went on and that evening we had just sat down to chips and eggs in the cafe when the alarm was sounded. I got up from the table 'What a bloody war,' I moaned, 'not even time to eat, come on get a move on'.

'On parade! Full marching order'.

Swiftly we got into our equipment and soon we were marching out of Armentieres, moving towards the left flank and the thunder of the guns.

'What the hell's doing mate?'

'Jerry's building up an attack at Plug Street'.

In the darkness under the flash of the guns we took up reserve positions to act as reinforcements and waited for the attack to come, but after two days and nights the firing gradually died away and nothing developed. Back to Armentieres once more. The weather was beginning to improve a little now and we began to hear rumours that battalions were on the move.

'Have you heard anything Tommy?' asked Ron, 'where we are likely to be going?'

I shook my head 'Not a thing Ron, I thought we were here for the duration,'

'Some hopes you've got,' said Spud 'I bet its Ypres or that lousy Loos front for us before long'.

'Sure I heard we were going to Egypt,' said Paddy Finnigan 'that's where they've got the harems'.

'In that case they might give us some leave,' remarked Ron hopefully.

'Yes they might,' replied Spud 'in about twenty years from now'.

Viccy dropped a bombshell when she said one day 'You soon depart Tomee, you all depart eh?'

I shook my head; 'I haven't heard anything Viccy!'

'Ah mon cheri, it's always like that, you come, you go'.

'Honestly Viccy, its all just talk'.

She shook her head and turned away 'I'm sorry, Tommee'.

Spud sucked his pipe and looked after her 'I think she's right all the same Tommy, we won't be here much longer'.

'Oh well if we do go we'll likely land back here before long'.

Spud shook his head 'I wouldn't like to bet on that, when you've been in the army as long as me you'll know it doesn't do to forecast where you'll be a week ahead'.

Sergeant Milner came over to our table on his way out of the cafe and said 'You blokes seen battalion orders for tomorrow?'

I shook my head 'No Sergeant, what's doing?'

'Parade of full battalion at 9am in full kit for delousing and baths, all blankets to be rolled and handed in, nobody will be excused parade'.

Spud grinned and scratched himself 'These poor little lice will be sorry to part with me, they've been feeding on me all the winter'.

Ron laughed 'don't mourn for them Spud, you'll soon have some new ones, with claws and ruddy sharp teeth'.

The next morning blankets were rolled and piled on transports, billets were cleaned and inspected and then I noticed that cook house gear, signals gear, cases of ammunition, first aid kit etc. was also being stowed on to transport.

'What do you think about it?' I asked Spud.

'If ever I saw a unit pulling out its happening now,' replied Spud.

Then we fell in on parade and I saw that even the cooks, orderlies, and batmen were in the ranks, this was it! We moved off, not on the road towards Houplines, but down the street where our little cafe stood and I saw Viccy and her mother standing at the door watching the troops march by. As our company moved along I saw her mother speak to Viccy and point. Viccy's hand went to her mouth as her eye caught mine and I smiled and waved to her. She waved back to me and I heard her call out 'Bonne chance, Tommee, Bonne chance!' Then we were past and tramping along the cobbled road that led out of Armentieres towards Hazelbrouck and the back areas. I looked back a few times at dull drab Armentieres and I wondered what the future had in store, and as a farewell note the boys began to sing a farewell ditty.

'Mademoiselle from Armentieres parlez vous,
Mademoiselle from Armentieres parlez vous
Mademoiselle from Armentieres hasn't been kissed for twenty years
Hinky pinky parlez vous'

'Landlord have you a daughter fair, parlez vous,
Landlord have you a daughter fair parlez vous
Landlord have you a daughter fair, with bright blue eyes and curly hair
Hinky pinky parlez vous'

On and on it went to the monotonous tramp of boots and my thoughts went back to Viccy and the cosy little cafe that had brought a little pleasure into our miserable lives, back to Houplines and Plug Street and the Mushroom where we had lived in the valley of the shadow in cold and wet and hunger, back to the many little wooden crosses we were leaving behind us.

'Well I'm pleased to be out of that lot,' said Jacky Barratt as we tramped along 'I feel choked with mud'

'It might have been worse boy,' replied Spud 'it could have been worse!'

'Wait till you blokes get to Ypres,' said Tug Wilson; 'you don't know nothing till you've been in that lot'.

'To hell with that,' growled Spud 'we were in Loos before you joined us and I'll take your bloody Ypres any time before that lot'.

'Time we had some leave boys,' said Ron 'we've done our bit'.

'Wonder where we are heading for now,' I remarked.

'Nobody cares, so long as its miles and miles away from the front line, I'm all for a quiet life now,' said Tommy Lowery 'Come on Paddy, give us a good old Irish song'.

4. BACK INSIDE THE ROPES

Late in the evening we reached a camp of huts at Oatterstene and bedded down wearily for the night, a winter in the trenches made marching hard work and we were far from fit. The following day we were bathed and deloused for the second time in six months of active service, and for a week we lolled around taking things easy while the M.O. carried out inoculation and medical inspections, and old worn kit was replaced. Then once more we were on the march and arrived at a railway siding where a train of cattle trucks awaited us. 'Ah, this is more like it,' said Spud as we climbed aboard and he removed his equipment 'all that bloody marching is bad for my corns'. The train chugged along with many stops and we noticed the boom of the gunfire was getting fainter and fainter, speculation was rife with regard to our destination, and then someone cried out, 'Look over there, that's the sea'. We looked, and true enough it was, the North Sea glittering in the pale sunlight, and a few miles across it lay England, our England!

'I told you so,' cried Ron excitedly 'they're taking us back to Blighty for leave'.

Spud squinted at him 'I'll believe that when I'm on the bloody boat'.

'Even then the boat might not head for England,' I said.

'Where the hell else would it head for?'

'Oh, anywhere Ron, Dardanelles, Mespot, Italy, its a big world and there's a war on,' I replied.

'Why should we be sent to Italy?' asked Jacky.

'The Austrians are pushing the Italians back and I hear that British reinforcements are being sent out there'.

'Aw to hell, let them fight their own war'.

The sea disappeared and still the train chugged on, darkness came on and we settled down for an uneasy sleep to awake at daybreak and find ourselves at a railway siding outside Amiens. We climbed stiffly out of the cattle trucks and found the cooks had been busy getting a hasty breakfast ready for which we were truly thankful. Then it was packs on and once more we were tramping the cobbled roads. Mile after weary mile until the pack straps were biting into my shoulders, my haversack was rubbing a sore on my hip, my rifle felt like a lump of lead and my feet were just moving up and down, up and down as I tramped on staring at the neck of the man in front of me and seeing nothing. At the end of each hour we collapsed at the roadside for 10 minutes rest, soon too weary even to remove the burden from our backs. Mile after mile until it became a nightmare through which you moved in a daze, the rigour of a winter in the trenches in Flanders was taking its toll. A winter spent sloshing around in icy water up to the knees, up to the thighs, sometimes up to the armpits, sleeping in wet dripping dugouts with only a waterproof cape, one blanket and your greatcoat for a bed did not tend to keep you marching fit.

Left, right, left, right, boots moving up and down, up and down, shoulders humped with the weight of the pack and eyes staring vacantly ahead at nothing, how much longer!

'What price the bloody trenches now?' groaned Spud.

Late in the afternoon we halted beside some houses on the outskirts of a place called La Neuville and as I dropped to the ground beside the wall of a house Paddy groaned beside me 'Sheer bloody murder, how much more?'. I was too far-gone to reply, all I wanted to do was lie with my eyes closed for hours and days and weeks. There was a lot of growling among the ranks and a nasty feeling seemed to be developing as someone said, 'To hell with them, I'm not marching another bloody step!'

Tug Wilson took it up 'Not another bloody step, I'd sooner be in clink,' and he tugged at his bootlaces.

'For God's sake Tug don't take your boots off,' cried Spud, 'you'll never get them on again'

'Don't want them on again,' said Tug savagely, 'My bloody feet are bleeding'.

An officer came along and announced that the halt would be for half an hour instead of the usual 10 minutes and someone shouted 'And let us rejoice!'. The officers,' face went red and he beat a hasty retreat and then word was passed along that our billets were at the other side of La Neuville, just through the town and we would be at the end of our journey.

'Got anything in your water bottle Corporal?' asked Paddy huskily.

'Might be a drop or two, help yourself,' I answered wearily. He helped himself, and that was the end of that.

'Anyone got a fag,' asked Paddy and there was no reply. I fished in my tunic pocket and pulled out the little tin box in which I carried my cigarettes; opening the lid I exposed one solitary cigarette. I looked at it and I looked at Paddy, then I broke the cigarette in half and handed him a half. He took it and said gratefully 'You're all right Corporal, I won't forget'

'All right Paddy, now shut up and lets have some peace'.

I closed my eyes and lay back beside the wall of the house, too weary to care about what went on around me. I only knew that, somehow, when the time came I would have to show an example.

'Would Anglais soldat like drink?'

Startled I opened my eyes to the sound of that voice which seemed to come from far away; standing beside me was a tall dark girl with a jug in her hand. I stared at her and she smiled and stooped to hand me the jug, in a dream I took it from her and in a dream I took a drink of its contents, good strong coffee. God, that was good!

'Come on boys, coffee for the troops,' I roused my section with the words 'and make it go round, play fair'.

They each had a little and the jug came back to me empty. I handed it to the girl saying 'Merci Mademoiselle, you're an angel'.

Then it was packs on and fall in and as we shuffled into position and marched away she stood in the doorway of the house smiling and called out 'Bonne chance m'siur - vive Anglais'.

'Give the lassie a cheer boys,' croaked Spud and she got a husky cheer and a wave from the section, she deserved it!

Our troubles were nearly over, we marched through La Neuville and found our billets in farm buildings on the outskirts of the town, and we soon got settled in the cowsheds for rest and peace. Things were pretty easy for us for a time, the weather was now turning good and we were getting decent food regularly, there was a river near by where we could swim and keep reasonably clean and we had money to spend in La Neuville and Corbie. In the distance we could hear the rumble of gunfire but we were out of range so that didn't bother us and in the blue sky we would at time see aircraft with woolly burst of shrapnel around them, but the war seemed a long way from us. Everyone was happy and the general feeling was that we could stick this kind of soldiering for a long time.

It was early in September, Sunday evening I remember
We'd been marching all the day long an,' our skins was sweatin,' salt,
We were weary with the marching an,' our tongues was dry an,' parching
When we fell out by the roadside for the old ten minutes halt.

She was tall and she was slender and her smile was sweet an,' tender
As she stood there by the roadside a-lookin,' down at me,
I lay a minute dozing - and I gazed at her supposing
She was just the sort of dream stuff that a weary Tommy would see.

She stood a minute waiting - smiling still an,' hesitating
An,' then she spoke up softly 'Would le Anglais soldat care to drink?'
Oh I was parched God! I was thirsty - huskily I murmured :Merci,'
As I took the jug she held an,' pressed my lips against its brink.

Then it was 'Packs on! Fall in! an,' I heard her voice a'calling
As we tramped along that dreary road –
'Bonne chance M'sieu, Bonne chance'.
Now I ain't a chap that's flighty - I've a wife an,' kids in Blighty
But I shan't forget that girl - that demoiselle of France!

Time was spent in a general overhaul of weapons and equipment and a fresh interest began to develop throughout the battalion in sport, a sure sign that the men were getting back on their mettle. Physical training was the order of the day and in the warming sunshine of spring it was good to feel that we were shaking off the ill effects of the winter now behind us. A rumour went round that as a preliminary to Divisional sports we had to hold battalion sports competitions. Lieutenant Stuart Walker rejoined us after a long spell in hospital and he seemed pleased to see us all, he carried a nasty scar down one side of his face as a momentum of the battle of Loos.

'How's the boxing Corporal?' he asked me when we met.

'I don't know sir,' I replied 'we've been waterlogged and ice bound all the winter so I don't think we'll be much good now'.

'I've heard all about it,' he answered 'but you've got to snap out of it now and get some training in, we want you up for the divisional sports, if you're still good enough'.

'I feel fairly good sir and I've been doing light training'.

'That's good, I can't box any more myself, I got a bullet through my arm as well as this,' he stroked the scar on his face 'I hear there's a chap called Wilson in the company who is pretty good, know him?'

'Yes sir, he's in my section'.

'He boxes at 9 stone, what's your weight Corporal?'

'Eight stone six pounds limit sir'.

'Will you box him in the battalion sports?'

'I'll box him if he makes eight stone nine pounds sir, I don't feel like giving weight away at present'.

'That's fair enough Corporal, I'll arrange it,' said Lieutenant Stuart Walker and he left me at that.

Everyone got busy at their own particular line of sport, rifle shooting, football, putting the weight, running, jumping and boxing and I was soon as busy as the rest with Ron, Tommy Lowery, and a good chap called Corporal Brewer from 'B,' company to assist me. One day when I was training Paddy Finnigan came along and watched me at work for a bit and as I took a breather he said, 'How about a couple of rounds with me Corporal?'

I eyed him; he would be about a stone the better of me 'Right you are Paddy,' I replied 'when you're ready'.

Spud whispered to me 'Watch your step Tommy, he's been sparring with Tug Wilson don't give anything away'.

I nodded and waited for Paddy and then Spud called time.

The Irish boy was on me like a hurricane slinging them in from all angles and I bobbed and weaved and back peddled swiftly using a straight left to try to keep him away. He took not the slightest notice of it and kept on tearing in until after a hectic minute his right cracked on my chin and brought me down on one knee.

'All right Corporal?' gulped Paddy.

I grinned up at him and nodded, 'Nice punching Paddy, here we go,' and I was on my feet again.

He tore in again slinging lefts and rights, his Irish blood was up and he wanted a fight, not a spar. I met him this time, instead of going back, with a straight left to the throat and a sound right under the heart and then we were together and I was pounding away to the body. His head was on my shoulder and I heard him gasping for breath. As we broke I said 'Too many fags Paddy'. His mouth was open and he swung a wild right that I slipped under and drove my own right hard to the solar plexus. Paddy dropped his arms 'That's enough,' he croaked and his face turned a nasty colour.

I shrugged, 'Right you are Paddy, if you're going to be sick go over to those bushes; I don't want to see it'.

He went, and he was! When he came back the Irish was subdued and his face was white but he grinned at me and said 'I'm all right now Corporal'

'What was the big idea of the rough stuff Paddy?' I asked him.

'Aw hell Corporal, sure I didn't mean nothing, I can't box, I can only fight, bedad its the Irish in me but I'll tell you something'.

'What is it Paddy?'

'I'm telling you now that Tug Wilson is just about twice as fast as you are, but he can't hit'.

I had never seen Tug box so this was news for me to digest. The following day the Lance Corporal of my section Tommy Lowery came to me and said 'The section want to see you Corporal in the billet'.

I went over to the cowshed expecting some kind of complaint and found the boys gathered in a group.

'Well, what's the trouble?' I asked.

Spud acted as spokesman 'Its like this Corporal, you remember that French wench that gave us the jug of coffee the day we were flaked out on her doorstep?'

I nodded, 'Not likely to forget it Spud'.

'Well the boys have been talking it over see, and we thought it would be nice if we gave her a little present so we had a whip round and we've collected 40 francs, would you like to put something in?'

'Sure, here's ten francs Spud,' I replied handing him the money.

'And that's just the price of the bracelet, 50 francs,' said Ron.

I stared at him 'What bracelet?' I asked.

'There's a little jeweller's shop in Corbie where Ron saw this bracelet thing, its got little enamel gadgets hanging on it,' said Spud 'the enamel gadgets are the Union Jack and the tricolour, and we reckon its just the thing for a souvenir for that wench'.

'Right you are,' I agreed 'Buy it and take it along to her'.

Spud shook his head 'No Corporal, you're the bloke she gave the coffee too, so you're the bloke to handle this little job'.

In the end I agreed and the following day Spud, Ron, Paddy and I wandered off to buy the bracelet. It was a pretty little trinket and we ambled along through La Neuville until we came to the house where we had been handed that jug of coffee.

'Listen you blokes,' I said as we approached the door 'has it occurred to you that she might be married and her husband at home. What do we say if a six-foot froggie answers the door?'

'Aw hell we don't say nothing,' grinned Spud 'we just run!'

I knocked on the door and it soon opened. She stood there with a look of enquiry in her eyes that changed swiftly to a look of recognition and a smile 'le Anglais soldat!'

I held out the little box 'Souvenir pour mademoiselle,' I stammered waving a hand to the others 'from the troops'.

She opened the box and gave a little cry of delight when she saw the bracelet 'Oh tris bon - entre m'siuer - Marie, Marie'.

Another girl joined her as we trooped into the house, later I learnt that they were sisters, and they chattered away in French while admiring our little gift. Soon the coffee was on the table and we found out that the two girls lived with their mother, the father was listed as missing at Verdun and their brother had been killed. The girl who had given us the coffee was named Yvonne and I called to see them a few times later when we were back from the line but their knowledge of English was scantly and it was rather difficult. However there was always a welcome for us and it made a change to enter a civilised house now and again. Paddy was their constant visitor and he and Marie soon became great friends. We were all pleased Yvonne accepted our little gift.

Two days later we were on the march once more heading for the front, we passed through Méaulte and marched past Albert where the first time we saw the hanging figure of the Virgin with Christ in her arms. The figure hung from the top of the church tower at an alarming angle and the troops said when that figure fell the war would end. We took over the reserve trenches at Becordel-Becourt from French troops. Becordel-Becourt had been a village but it was now just a notice board, a pile of battered rubble where not one brick stood on another. After four days in reserve we moved up and took over the front line to spend a fairly quiet week. What a change from Flanders, the trenches were deep and the soil chalky, the weather was fine and the whole area was dry. After our spell of duty we marched back to Méaulte for one night there and the following day we marched back to La Neuville with word that the battalion sports would be held within a day or two. While we were in the trenches Tug Wilson asked me if he could come at 9 stone but I told him I wouldn't concede more than 5lbs.

'No Tug you'll make the weight or back down'.

'I'm having a hell of a job making 8 stone 9lbs Corporal,' he said.

'8 stone 6lbs is the official weight Tug,' I replied 'why the hell didn't you stick to the 9 stone class where you belong?'

His eyes glinted 'Well you see Corporal I've been wanting to have a go at you ever since that affair in Armentieres'.

So that was it, Tug was bearing me a grudge. The sports field was being fitted up and the day was fixed for the various events. The boxing programme was pretty good as it ranged from bantamweight to light heavyweight and the whole battalion was looking forward to a good time. The day came fine and warm and as I stripped off in the tent beside the ring that had been erected I felt pretty good. As Spud fussed around like an old hen Lieutenant Stuart Walker said 'What's your plan Corporal?'

'I hear he's pretty fast sir but he hasn't much of a punch. He's had trouble making the weight so I aim to crowd him all I can'.

The officer nodded 'That sounds good enough, oh by the way, I notice he has a few old scars around his eyes'.

He looked at me meaningly and I nodded, 'I get it sir'.

I was in the ring and the sun was warm on my body, birds were singing in the blue sky overhead, a sea of faces wavered around the ring and I felt very much alone in the world, alone except for the chap in the opposite corner with whom I was going to spend twelve hectic minutes, not long as time goes but it can be a hell of a long time inside the roped square.

'Time'. And we were off.

Tug came out fast, moving lightly on his feet and crouching. I led with a left and he swerved, I missed. I led again and he blocked it and sent in a left that I took on the glove. We circled and again I led with a left which he slipped and suddenly an avalanche of gloves seemed to be falling on me, they were coming from every angle and they were landing everywhere, head, face, chest, ribs, neck and back. I weaved and went back fast but I couldn't get clear of that storm of leather until I went into a clinch. Hell! He was more than fast, he was lightning, but true enough he wasn't hurting me, he was hitting with the open glove. As we broke I hooked a nice left to the eye and tried a right to the body that Tug blocked with a grin. I hooked a left to his ribs and missed with another left to the face, then once more the storm broke and I was smothered in flying gloves. The gong went and I made for my corner where Spud awaited me. As he sponged me he said 'How do you find him Tommy?'

'Bloody awkward to handle, he's fast'.

Spud nodded 'Take your time boy, don't let him fluster you, set yourself for one good punch'.

'Time'. One good punch! One good punch! As we weaved around for the second round it hammered in my head. One good punch! I feinted with the left and followed in with a good left to the mouth, ducked under his right and got home with my own right to the stomach. Once more the storm started but this time I was expecting it and I saw his chin exposed about a foot from me as I shot a short right through his gloves. It landed smack on the point and to my surprise his whirling arms dropped to his sides, for a split second he just stood flat-footed staring at me and then he moved again. Too late I realized I had missed a golden opportunity. I landed a left to his eye and saw a trickle of blood as I went in close and belted away to the body and as we broke he crowded me with a flurry of blows but through it I hooked a hard short left to the chin and once again his arms dropped and he stood staring at me as the gong went. Hell! Another chance gone.

'You've got him boy,' cried Spud as I sat on the stool 'follow it up, damn you'.

'Time'. We met in the centre with a rush and I started slinging them, lefts and rights, to hell with the boxing, lefts and rights. Back went Tug on the ropes and I crowded him, lefts and rights, I felt my punches landing and I knew I was hurting. Tug tried to grab me into a clinch but a nice uppercut brought blood from his nose I belted him hard round the body and ribs and kept crowding him all the time. He came out of the corner to try something and I swung a left that started from the floor and landed under his jaw. As I moved in I saw his eyes waver and his knees sag and my following right cracked home on the other side of his chin. His arms dropped and as he fell forward a left hook went in to his chin and Tug lay sprawled on his face out to the world. He never looked like getting on his feet again. I stood in my corner to the count of ten and Spud jumped into the ring when it was all over. 'They're carrying him out,' he cried as he unlaced my gloves; I looked across and saw them carrying Tug into his tent with the M.O. following. Then I made my way through the usual backslapping crowd to my own tent for a rub down and during the process Sergeant Brodwick came in.

'Good fight Corporal,' he said shaking my hand.

'How's Wilson, Sergeant,' I asked.

'He's coming round all right now,' he replied 'the M.O. had the wind up for a bit, but he'll be all right'.

Lieutenant Stuart Walker came in, his wounded face twisted in a grin, as I was dressing.

'Well you're back in form again Corporal,' he said 'but you were a bit slow, why didn't you finish it earlier when you had the chance?'

'I don't know sir, I thought he might be kidding'.

'Well you finished it with three knockout punches instead of one, you've got everyone scared stiff in case Wilson didn't come round'.

'How is he sir'.

'He's come round all right but the M.O. suspects a damaged jaw, Wilson will be going to hospital for an X-ray'

'Can I see him before he goes?'

'Yes of course, Sergeant take him along to the other dressing tent'.

Sergeant Brodwick and I made our way to the tent where we found Wilson lying on a camp bed with his jaw bandaged.

'Sorry Tug,' I said as I held out my hand 'I hope you'll be all right old man'.

He shook hands with me and as I leaned close to him he mumbled 'The weight beat me'.

As I left the tent Paddy Finnigan said to me 'That's the first time Tug has even hit the deck and you've belted him clean into hospital'.

However things didn't turn out so bad for Tug after all, he spent a cushy week in hospital where he had three broken teeth removed and then he returned to us for duty. We moved back up the line again but this time we didn't go into the front line, we spent a week digging gun positions for the artillery behind the reserve lines. This didn't go down too well.

'Why the hell can't the bloody artillery dig their own bleeding positions?'

'If a job has to be done give it to the poor bloody infantry!'

'Wonder how the gunners would like digging our trenches for us!'

'We might be pleased to have those guns behind us,' I remarked.

'To hell with the guns, we're better without them!' grunted Ron.

After a week of digging we marched to Bois de Tailles where we billeted in tents in some woods and there spent a cushy eight days under good conditions alongside some Indian cavalry troops. They looked pretty good with clean uniforms and polished leathers, but seeing that their work was behind the fighting line, they lived in a different world to the infantry.

It was here that I saw a chap doing 28 days No. 1 field punishment. He was spread-eagled to the wheel of a stationary transport, wrists and ankles strapped to the spokes of the wheel for two-hour periods day and night with military police in attendance to see that no one approached him. He had been court-martialled for desertion.

Then we marched away from Bois De Tailles and took over the trenches from French troops at Bray where we had a comfortable time. The French seemed to be happy in leaving Jerry in peace and we were inclined to do the same until we got to know the locality better. But it was noticeable that more and more troops were on the roads in the Somme area, more and more guns were on the move and we knew that something was brewing. After a couple of weeks at Bray we marched back to La Neuville to our old billets, a weary march on a hot day along the straight cobbled roads of France.

Sport once more held sway and I met a new draft man called Ken Franklin in the ring but he gave me no trouble and I beat him on points. Three days later the brigade sports were held and I was in with Tuffy Jones of the West Yorks. He was a rough tough handful with wild swinging punches that came from nowhere and landed anywhere. He dropped me in a heap in the first round when I made the mistake of swaying away from his swings but I was ticked off by my seconds in the corner and the second round saw me going inside his swings. Then I found it pretty easy and had most of it my own way, he was on the floor when the final gong went and I ran out an easy winner on points with a nice black eye to show for it, I was now in line for the divisional finals.

We were issued with steel helmets and orders that they must be worn at all times in the trenches but we didn't take kindly to them.

'More bloody lumber for us to hump around,' growled Spud.

Away we went, once more tramping the road to shell stricken Albert, now choked with the dust of guns, transports and marching men on the busy roads leading to the front.

'Dunno what the hell's being cooked up, but it looks like we've landed right in the middle of it,' remarked Ron, 'Give us a song Paddy old boy'.

'There's a long, long trail Paddy,' someone suggested but Paddy tramped on eyes to the ground and made no response.

'What's up with Finnigan, Tug,' I asked Wilson 'he's been like a bear with a sore head these last few days'.

'Women trouble,' replied Tug with a grin 'you ask him yourself'.

I stepped into the blank file alongside Paddy and said 'What's biting you Paddy, trouble with the boys?'

'No, the boys are all right Corporal'

'Trouble at home?'

He looked at me with hot fierce eyes as we marched along.

'None of your bloody business,' he growled.

'That's right Paddy, but I don't like it, see a chap like you down in the dumps,' I replied. 'Keep it to yourself if you like and brood on it, but it sometimes pays you to get it off your chest you know'.

'Left, right, left, right,' we tramped along another mile in silence and then Paddy humped up his pack and said 'Aw hell! I got a letter the other day, from my girl in Andover; I was stationed there before I came to France'.

'Not just a passing fancy Paddy?' I asked.

'Oh hell no, sure and we got engaged when I was on embarkation leave, it was the real thing for me'.

'And I suppose she's written to chuck you Paddy,' I said.

Paddy laughed bitterly 'Chuck me - hell! Its more than that, she's written to say its all off because she's in the family way to some blasted Canadian soldier'.

'Sorry Paddy, that's rotten, but why mope over it now'.

'Why, bloody hell, the dirty little bitch has been writing loving letters to me for months and lying in the arms of some lousy Canadian at the same time, if I was over there I'd put a bullet through the pair of them!'

'Do you reckon that would make things better?' I asked him.

He glared at me 'Yes, better for those two rotten bastards, I'm fighting out here and that's what goes on behind my back'.

'Do you really think she's worth it Paddy?' I asked.

'Yes, she was worth it, aw, go to hell Corporal and leave me alone, I'd swing for the bitch if I was in Andover now'.

It was no use saying any more so I left Paddy to his misery as we tramped through the ruined streets of Albert and I gazed up at the hanging virgin and wondered why God allowed the agony to be piled on men who already had enough to bear. Into the reserve trenches in front of Albert we went and we soon discovered that things were warming up. The Germans were very active with trench mortars in this sector and his snipers were on the alert. I found this out the first day in the trenches when Lieutenant Walker and I were looking over the sandbags checking on the lay of the land. A bullet whizzed between us, a very near miss and as we ducked two more followed it. We looked at each other and Lieutenant Walker shook his head, 'Pretty good shooting, this reserve trench is 500 yards from Jerry's front line, we can't take many chances here'. The Germans were worried by the movement of guns and troops and they made our life a misery with mortar and shell fire by day and night and after four days in the reserve lines we took over the firing line. Our own artillery was hitting back hard at the enemy lines but still Jerry kept plugging away and soon we saw the sorry picture of stretcher bearers carrying away broken or still figures of comrades. We had been warned about enemy snipers and soon it was noted that the enemy was carrying out dangerous sniping from a mine crater that lay in No Mans Land. Apparently they were getting into the crater before dawn, sniping during the day and retiring to their own trenches as darkness came on. The order came through 'A fighting patrol will clean up the crater,' and Lieutenant Blackett of B Company took on the job.

Tommy Lowery and Paddy Finnigan of my section volunteered and were accepted for the patrol, consisting of one officer, one N.C.O. and four men. The drill was that a stream of bullets would be kept skimming the brim of the crater before daybreak to allow our patrol to approach unseen, then a shower of flares would go up over the crater and the patrol would go in for the kill. I saw the patrol as they made ready to leave our trenches and I noticed that Paddy's face looked white and drawn and his eyes were wild.

'Good luck Paddy,' I murmured softly 'it'll soon be over'.

Paddy nodded his head 'Yes, for those bastards,' he replied.

As they crawled away into No Man's Land we mounted the fire steps and opened out with steady rifle fire into the darkness.

'Hope they're not twigged before they get there,' I said as I reloaded a fresh clip into my rifle.

Spud grunted 'This is going to stir up another hornets nest, damn funny thing, we come into a quiet sector and before we know where we are merry hell start's popping'.

'Unlucky regiment, that's what we are,' said Ron.

Rifle fire came back at us from the German trenches and occasionally a machine gun burst out viciously traversing the sandbags behind which we ducked for safety and out there in the darkness six men were slowly crawling forward to their destiny.

'Hell, they must be there by now,' growled Tug Wilson 'either there or ....'

'Shut up Tug, blast you,' cried Spud.

'They're working to a timetable,' I said 'they have to be in position ready before the flares go up, and as soon as they are up we turn our fire from the crater to the German trenches'.

Suddenly to right and left of us we heard the thud of Very pistols and saw the trail of flares as they soared into the dark sky to burst in a blaze of white light over the crater.

'There they are,' cried Tug 'they're over the rim and in'.

Out there someone shouted hoarsely, rifles cracked and then there was the crash of hand grenades. The Germans were alerted and a stream of crossfire from machine guns swept back and forth across No Man's Land.

'Rapid fire on the German trenches,' I called to my section 'and you, Tug, watch for the flash of the machine guns and try to place your bullets there'.

'Got one marked right now,' replied Tug cuddling his rifle butt.

'Eyes like a bleeding hawk,' exclaimed Spud.

'How the devil are those poor sods going to get back in this?' asked Ron.

It certainly looked a bit of a problem, a storm of bullets were sweeping No Man's Land in both directions, and dawn would soon be breaking.

'There they are over to the left,' cried Tug suddenly.

'Can't see anything Tug,' said Ron.

'Over there, look, they're getting to their feet now,' said Tug.

A hoarse voice called out in the darkness 'Blackett's patrol here, for Christ's sake cease fire and help us in'.

We saw shadowy movement to our left and then our own private little war was over, the patrol had returned. I heard the word passed for stretcher-bearers and we soon knew that some of the patrol had been wounded.

'Wounded,' said Ron 'I don't know how the lot ain't riddled with bullets'.

I moved along the trench and as daylight was breaking over the land I saw Paddy lying on a blanket on the floor of the trench with first aid men working on him.

'Is he hit bad?' I asked Tommy Lowery who sat on the fire step staring at nothing.

'Afraid so Corporal, ask them, I'm not sure,' he replied.

'What's the trouble?' I asked a Lance Corporal with a Red Cross on his sleeve.

He looked up 'Chest and hip, doesn't look too good, when the hell is that stretcher coming!'

The stretcher party came along and Paddy was gently lifted on to it, he groaned and his opened eyes rested on me, I leaned over him.

'You'll be all right now Paddy, they'll soon get you to Blighty'.

A slow smile came to his white face and he shook his head 'I got two of them Corporal, it was great, but, but I wish that Andover bitch had been there'.

Paddy died in the field dressing station in Albert the next day, bitter to the end at the girl who had let him down. Lieutenant Blackett had a clean bullet wound in the shoulder and Private Mercer of A company had a badly shattered finger; and they left behind them five dead enemy snipers to rot in the crater in No Man's Land. Later, when the wounded were got away and things quietened down, I heard the story of the fight at the crater. The patrol had reached the edge of the crater without incident and lay there peering into the black hole without seeing or hearing anything until the flares burst overhead flooding the locality with light. Then they saw the German snipers; spread out too much apart for grenades to be effective and Lieutenant Blackett shouted 'Charge!'. The patrol jumped down into the crater as the enemy turned to meet them with a burst of wild firing, and for a few minutes chaos reigned in that huge dirty hole in the ground. It was definitely stated in Lieutenant Blacketts report that Paddy Finnigan shot one German at point blank range and then rushed a second and killed him with a bayonet thrust before he went down himself. When they picked Paddy up they saw that his bayonet was right through the German and sticking out of his back, he was very, very dead. Tommy Lowery was the boy who picked Paddy up and he carried and dragged him across that bullet swept No Man's Land to get him back to his own trenches. As Tommy said 'I just couldn't leave that mad Irishman out there to die in that stinking hole'. The outcome of this action was a Military Cross for Lieutenant Blackett, a D.C.M. for Tommy Lowery, and a D.C.M. for poor old Paddy, but Paddy was gone without knowing of this.

Jerry was a very uneasy animal for the rest of our time in the trenches, he kept up incessant mortar fire and his artillery sent over some pretty accurate shelling that kept us on the move for cover. However, the increase of guns behind us gave him plenty in return and the enemy was also having a rough passage. After another three days we were relieved and we marched back through Albert spent three days at Méaulte and then headed back for La Neuville, one officer killed and two wounded, eight men killed and twenty-seven wounded.

Men and guns, the roads behind the front were congested with traffic and it was on the move day and night. It was now an open secret that a battle was pending on the Somme, and we were in the middle of it. Lectures were being given on behaviour in battle and training was stepped up; once more sport came to the forefront and the divisional sports were to be held soon in Corbie. I was told that I was due to meet a chap called Clem Davies of the Royal Welsh Fusiliers in a semi-final bout and I got busy with my training but before anything developed we were once more on the march and once more into the trenches facing the village of Fricourt. This was a pretty hot spot, one part of the line called the Tambour jutted out into No Man's Land and the German trench was only 40 yards from ours. Once you were in there you spent most of your time close to the ground, ever on the alert for grenades that were constantly being lobbed back and forth. Saps and mines were being dug both ways underground and at night, if things quietened down a bit and you put your ear to the ground you could hear the tap, tap of picks as German Sappers dug away under your trench. As Spud said, 'One of these days all this bloody landscape, and us, will go up in smoke'.

It was here that Tommy Lowery, now a full Corporal in D company went out with a raiding party 20 strong one night to capture a German if possible. They ran into trouble in the enemy trench and only 12 of them got back, with two prisoners, Tommy Lowery was killed. Two nights later a strong German raiding party on my right flank was seen as it approached our wire and a storm of rifle and machine gun fire broke it up. At dawn a group of bodies in field grey lay in No Man's Land. We came out of the Fricourt sector after a hectic week, weary and bleary eyed for want of sleep. Two officers killed and two wounded, 16 men killed, 3 missing assumed killed, and 32 wounded.

Back to Méaulte once more and after a day of rest the battalion was set the task of humping ammunition and grenades up to the reserve trenches where it was packed into dugouts ready for the coming battle. The men who were representing the battalion in the divisional sports were excused this duty and we stayed in Méaulte and carried on with our training. Never had I had so many offers of sparring partners; I picked out four good ones and that was enough. The weather had now turned hot and we didn't envy the boys lugging heavy boxes from Méaulte to the trenches. After a week of this we marched back to Corbie and quite a number of us now slept out in the open fields instead of crowding into lousy cowsheds. The sports day was on, in the morning an overcast sky made things doubtful but the sun broke through and everyone was happy. As I sat in my tent waiting for my turn a chap came to see me and introduced himself as Johnny Basham 'I'm over to second Clem,' he said 'lets have a look at your bandages son'. I held out my hands and he felt the bandages on my fists. As he did so I looked at him, Johnny Basham, welter and middleweight champion and holder of the Lonsdale Belt.

His bright blue eyes twinkled as he grinned at me 'Well good luck son, I hope you enjoy Clem's company, see you later'.

He was in the same Regiment as Clem Davies so it was understandable that he would be on the job, but Spud looked a bit worried.

'Don't let that worry you Tommy, he can't throw punches for Clem'.

'Good job he can't,' I replied 'I'm not bothered'.

The doctor gave me the once over and then I was in my corner.

Clem climbed in after me and came over to shake hands; he was a chunky sort of chap with a big chin, red hair, and a mass of freckles around his nose and cheekbones. The freckles fascinated me.

'Time'. And we were off. Clem came out fast and light and we started pumping lefts at each other, in the first minute I discovered my left lead was just a fraction faster than his. Then suddenly I saw that big chin exposed and I slammed home a good solid right. Clem grinned and held his chin out again. Again I cracked it with a good right but it was like hitting a stone wall and when I had a third shot at it I took a snorting right to the stomach in return. Clem grinned and weaved away and we circled the ring with left hands busy. Again the jaw came out and I cracked in a good left hook that knocked his head round but he just grinned and came in close for a spell of body fighting. As I sat on my stool at the end of the round Spud said 'How do you find him Tommy?'

'He's got a cast iron chin,' I muttered.

'Leave his chin alone, use your left hand, box him'.

Out we came for the second and again that chin was stuck out for me. I ignored it, I had my eyes fixed on that bunch of freckles and I lashed in a left and a right to the bridge of the nose. Clem went back but I followed up with two good lefts to the nose and a right to the body. As we weaved around I saw the blood trickling from his nose. Clem rushed and a straight left to the nose drove his head back and started a stream. I waded in then and we belted it out merrily along the ropes. A left from Clem split my lip and a right from me to the stomach had Clem gasping.

'You're ahead on points,' said Spud as I took my corner.

Up for the third and last and Clem stuck out his chin but I peppered him between the eyes with good lefts and once more the blood started to run. As we clinched he muttered 'Come on boyo, lets have a fight!' I knew then that boxing didn't suit him and I put all the speed I had into a stabbing left hand that found his eyes and nose repeatedly and I ran out a winner on points. It was a great moment for me when Johnny Basham walked into my tent as I was sponging down, a wide grin on his face.

'Good shooting kid,' he said as he shook hands with me 'that's a dandy left you've got'.

I smiled 'Thanks Johnny, but I couldn't bring Clem down'.

'Don't you worry about that, Clem isn't easy to bring down, he can take plenty of clouts on the chin and come back for more; in fact if you had kept on poking at his chin he would have licked you,' said Johnny. 'That's where you used your nut, Clem leads with his jaw until the other fellow gets tired hitting it and then he's on top, you didn't fall for it and that's how you won'.

'He can certainly take a punch,' I remarked.

'He can, and he knows it, good luck to you kid'.

Our own battalion heavyweight Peter Hague also won his bout with two smashing wallops in the first round, so that made two of us to box for the divisional titles, a great day for the battalion. I went over to the other tent to see Clem Davies and found them still applying cold water to his nose and eye; his eye was a nice purple colour and his nose was swollen all over his face.

He grinned at me and shook hands 'That left hand beat me, boyo'.

I smiled 'I just couldn't resist those freckles on your nose Clem'.

He pulled a face 'You've given me a hell of a conk, well good luck boyo'.

That evening a party was laid on by the officers of the battalion and the boys had a great time celebrating the events of the day, but I stuck to the grub and left the drink to those who could indulge, the final was too near for me to take any chances. My own section arrived back in billets with a good cargo of French beer and no complaints.

Two days later and we marched back into the front line in the Fricourt sector and on the way we noticed artillery everywhere, big guns and field guns their snouts poking out of gun pits pointing towards the enemy, and in the reserve trenches huge stocks of hand grenades, rifle and machine gun ammunition. In the air planes were on the increase and every time a German observation balloon went up behind their lines, down they went. As we sat by the roadside resting on the way in I overheard an artillery Captain say to Lieutenant Walker 'You won't have to worry this time old boy, we'll blast Jerry to hell before you blokes go over, for the first time since the war started the gunners are free to use all the shells they can'.

'Well, that's just great old chap,' replied Lieutenant Walker with a crooked grin, there's just one thing left to worry us!'

'And what's that?' asked the gunner.

'Lob them well over, we don't like shells up our backsides old boy'.

It was an uneasy spell for us. For the first time Jerry was in the unhappy position of being out-gunned and he didn't like it, he tried to take it out of the infantry in the trenches with mortar fire but an S.O.S. back to our gunners soon brought a storm of shells over and he liked that still less.

One evening at dusk I stood with Spud on the fire step looking over at the German trenches in front of Fricourt, every now and again a shell would whiz overhead to explode with a crash on the enemy lines.

'Jerry's fairly copping it now,' I remarked to Spud.

He nodded his head and soberly pointed the stem of his pipe to a cluster of blood-red poppies blooming in No Man's Land, 'See those flowers Corporal, they're not half so red as all this area will be before long'.

I laughed 'Cheerful old blighter you are Spud'.

Just then Lieutenant Walker came along the trench and stopped beside us.

'Bombing raid tonight Corporal and I'm taking it, any notion?'

'Right, if you want me sir,' I replied.

He pulled out a note book, 'I've got Sergeant Pyman of D company and four men, two men from A company, you, and I want you to get three volunteers from your lot, let me have the names as soon as you can'.

'That's eleven and yourself sir?'

'That's right, twelve good men and true eh!'

When he had passed along I turned to Spud, 'What about it Spud?'

'What about what?'

'Are you coming with us?'

'I've told you before, I'm not bloody well volunteering for anything in this army, but, I'll go with you all the same'.

'Good old Spud,' I replied, 'I'm away to find two more'.

I left him and went along the trench to contact some of the boys and Ron said he was willing to have a go. A newcomer to my section called Bert Miles stepped forward 'Count me in Corporal'.

I looked at him doubtfully. He was big enough and looked as though he might be useful in a roughhouse, but he was untried as yet.

'Think you can make it Bert?' I asked, 'you haven't been out long'.

He grinned 'I'll be scared stiff, but there's always got to be a first time'.

'Right, you're in, I'll let you have orders later on'.

Lieutenant Walker informed me that we would leave our trench at midnight under a barrage of shells our gunners would put on the enemy trench and we would occupy a ditch that ran in front of the German wire. There we would lie quiet until one o'clock and then right on the dot we would rush the enemy trench, just when Jerry thought the fun and games were over. 'Bomb dugouts and get one or two prisoners if we can'. At 2330 hrs we were collected and ready with blackened faces and hands, rifles and grenades, and at 2345 hrs our guns opened out on the sector we intended to attack. 'Right come on boys, follow me,' said Lieutenant Walker and we crawled into No Man's Land with the shells shrieking very close overhead to burst on the German wire and front line trench. I heard Spud whisper to Miles 'Listen you, keep your fat arse down, if you get one of those shells up your jacksy it'll carry you right to Berlin!'. The gunners were firing on a flat trajectory to hit the enemy trench and that meant the shells were whizzing past very near the ground. 'Hope to hell they don't fall short,' muttered someone, it was dark except for the gun and shell flashes and we kept contact by touch. German artillery was replying now but their shells were falling on our trenches behind us and that didn't worry us as we crawled on our way. The German machine guns started to traverse from left and right and being out in the open as we were wasn't so good.

'The bells of hell go ting-a-ling-a-ling, they've seen us,' muttered Spud. Sergeant Pyman murmured 'Twenty yards ahead, the ditch, make a run for it!' We jumped to our feet and bending double ran forward towards the German wire. I came to the ditch before I saw it, missed my footing and fell in. I felt my rifle butt hit something and heard a groan as I hit the bottom of the ditch. I groped around in the dark and felt a body and just then a flare went up to show me a German lying beside me his face a mass of blood where my rifle butt had hit him. 'Tell Lieutenant Walker we've got a prisoner,' I whispered to the chap next to me. Lieutenant Walker crawled over and by the light of a tiny torch he inspected the German in the bottom of the ditch.

'Look's like a broken nose and fractured jaw,' he whispered as we crowded around to keep the light from showing, 'get a man to take him back'.

'Here you are Spud, get him back to our lines,' I whispered.

'Yes, when those bloody machine guns stop,' whispered Spud.

Our artillery fire lifted and dropped their shells into the enemy reserve lines for a bit and then they gradually stopped firing, lying in the bottom of the ditch we had another twenty minutes to wait.

'I'm off with this bloody square head,' whispered Spud and they crawled away into the darkness, the German seemed to be more than willing, perhaps he had had all the fighting he wanted. Time dragged on with not a sound from the enemy trench just ahead of the ditch we were in, and then the guns started up again dropping their shells over on our left flank.

'Time gentlemen,' whispered Lieutenant Walker 'we'll risk crawling and if we're fired on make a rush for it, let's go!'.

He crawled ahead and we followed with Sergeant Pyman bringing up the rear of the party and we rolled thankfully into a battered and deserted German trench. 'We'll keep together and move right, come on'. Its a hair raising experience to be with a handful of men in an enemy trench never knowing what you're coming up against, and we stuck close together and moved along the battered trench. We came to an off shoot of the trench and Lieutenant Walker whispered 'I'll try this,' and moved into it along with the next man to him, grenades ready. I was next in the file and I moved cautiously along the main trench, the others tagging behind. Suddenly as I rounded the bay of the trench something hit me on the chest, I heard a gasp and as I staggered back a rifle shot exploded right beside me, there was a groan and somebody dropped.

'What the hell,' I gasped and I heard Ron chuckle beside me.

'You all right Corporal?' he asked. A flare burst overhead shedding a white light around and I saw the jackboots of a German soldier at the turn of the trench. 'That square head nearly got you with the bayonet said Ron, 'I've blown his guts out'.

Lieutenant Walker joined us as a machine gun started up close at hand 'I've found that machine gun post,' he whispered, 'We'll wipe it out and then get to hell out of this, come on'. We followed him down the narrow trench and he paused at the blanketed doorway of a dugout from which the thud of the machine gun was coming. He whipped aside the blanket and two grenades were thrown in, there was a shattering explosion and he dashed in with two men after him. Out they came pushing a scared looking German ahead of them and one of our chaps was lugging the machine gun, 'Come on lets get back,' called Lieutenant Walker prodding the German with his revolver. 'Here give me a hand with this bloody gun,' gasped the chap who was carrying it and we scrambled out of the trench and ran for the ditch through the broken German wire. We made the ditch all right and tumbled into it as bullets swept overhead, we had been seen, and it wasn't long before grenades began to shower over us. We lay flat for cover but we knew we were in a tight spot, a few yards from the German wire and a hell of a long way from our own little trenches. There was a brief spell of silence, and beside me Lieutenant Walker and Sergeant Pyman held a hasty whispered consultation. I heard Sergeant Pyman say 'The main party and the prisoner are your responsibility sir, leave me all the grenades and two men and we'll cover your retreat to our own lines'.

'What do you think Jerry will do Sergeant?' asked Lieutenant Walker.

'He'll try to wipe us out with grenades and rush us,' said the Sergeant, 'You get back, we'll hold Jerry down'.

Two men of D company stayed behind with their Sergeant while the rest of us crawled, slithered, and finally ran for our own lines and behind us we could hear the burst of grenades and the crack of rifles as the three held the enemy at bay. After a short lapse of time things grew quiet over at the German wire and we knew that the hopeless task of the three had been completed. Orders came along for a sharp lookout to be kept during the hours of darkness in case any of the three had got clear, but there was no sign of them until at the crack of dawn a sentry reported movement at a shell hole about thirty yards across No Man's Land. Tug Wilson reported seeing an arm waving at the edge of the shell hole and two men of D company crawled out to find one of the three who had covered our withdrawal during the night. He was badly wounded with grenade splinters but they dragged him back to our lines and he reported Sergeant Pyman and his pal Tony Chadwick both killed in the ditch. How he got away himself he didn't know, he had a dozen wounds from splinters in the head, body and legs. Distinguished Conduct Medals were awarded to Sergeant Pyman, Tony Chadwick, and the one who got back Tom Hartley, but we heard a week later that Hartley had died in hospital. D company got the credit for the captured German machine gun and the two prisoners were got back to our lines; the two who brought Hartley in were awarded Military Medals and Lieutenant Stuart Walker was awarded the Military Cross.

I had to report to the Adjutant on how the injured prisoner came by his injuries, I rather gathered that he had complained that he was struck after being taken prisoner.

'I didn't strike him sir,' I reported 'He was in the ditch and I fell on him, it was bad luck for him that his face was in the way of my rifle butt'.

'Well, he's in a bit of a mess Corporal,' said the Adjutant with a smile. 'Not much use for talking at present, but after all, he's lucky to be alive and in hospital'.

I discovered that the Jerry who had half-heartedly lunged at me in the trench had pierced my tin box of cigarettes and a prayer book in my tunic pocket, so I was lucky his thrust was feeble. The following night a German raiding party got into A Company sector killed two of A Company and captured two. They were caught by machine gun crossfire in No Man's Land and the report said they were wiped out, including our own two men on their way back to the enemy lines. We were relieved and made our way back to Méaulte, two officers killed one wounded, 16 men killed 22 wounded and 5 men missing believed killed. 'That Fricourt sector is becoming a hell of a place,' said Spud as we marched away 'I don't like the smell of things there at all'.

'Heard the news about Tug Wilson?' asked Jacky Barrett.

'No, what's he been up too,' I replied.

'A nice bit of good work, he nailed seven Jerries for certain during the seven days we were in the line, and he fought a sniping dual with one of them that lasted for an hour. Tug got him in the end, he's been mentioned in dispatches'.

'Good old Tug,' I exclaimed 'he can certainly shoot'.

Spud grinned 'Seven Jerries in seven days is good going'.

We settled down in Méaulte to take things easy, and although shells crashed into that deserted village we were happy to be among the ruins of the houses away from the trenches for a spell. Parcels and letters were arriving from England and in Méaulte we sat around and lazed in the hot sunshine watching the never ending stream of horse artillery and heavy mechanized guns passing through. Now and again shells disturbed us, but to us it was a world of peace in a world of war. Three days of this and we were on the march once more, not to Corbie as we expected, but through the ruins of Albert and into the trenches once more to the North of the battered town.

'This is a hell of a game,' grunted Bert Miles as he wiped the sweat away, 'thought you said we got a rest after being in the line, three days out and we're back in again!'

'They must be getting short of troops Bert,' grinned Spud.

'Aw to hell with that yarn, the place is lousy with troops'.

We soon got to know that something was doing in this sector and on our second night in the line our Sappers exploded a mine that wrecked a stretch of German advance trench and formed a huge crater in No Man's Land. Before the earth had settled a strong party rushed across to occupy the crater and a fierce fight developed before they returned to our trenches with four prisoners, the officer in charge, Lieutenant Middleton and Corporal Tommy Lowther were killed and five men were wounded in this fight in the crater. The Germans concentrated heavy mortar fire on our trenches and we were kept busy diving for cover, as I passed along the trench Jack Barratt said to me 'Joe Chapehow's got it, Tommy'.

I stared at him 'Killed?' I asked.

A young Tommy.

Tommy's mother.

Tommy's father, Squadron Sergeant, Hussars Regiment.

(Top to bottom) Tommy with brothers Charlie and Jack.

June 1915, Private Tommy Crawford, Durham Light Infantry.

Wounded in action, the Somme, 1916.

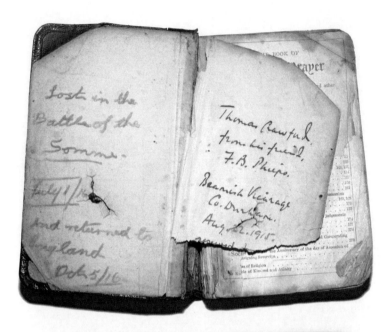
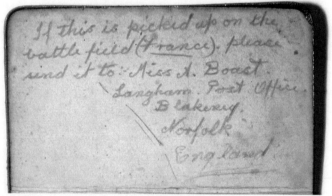

Tommy's prayer book, lost on the battlefield of the Somme but found and returned to Tommy's sweetheart, Amy Boast in England.
(Note the hole, made by a German bayonet that penetrated a cigarette tin before being stopped by the prayer book, which Tommy carried in the breast pocket of his tunic.)

LOGAN, EDWARD TOWNSHEND, D.S.O., Lieut.-Col., 3rd (Reserve) Battn. The Cheshire Regt., attd. 15th (Service) Battn. The Durham Light Infantry, eldest *s.* of the late Edward Logan, Merchant, by his wife, Emily Eliza (Upton Lawn, Manchester), dau. of Edward Townshend ; *b.* Valparaiso, South America, 6 Nov. 1865 ; educ. Westminster School ; gazetted 2nd Lieut. 3rd (Reserve)

Edward T. Logan.

Battn. The Cheshire Regt. 27 June, 1888 ; promoted Capt. 4 May, 1891, Major 1906, and Lieut.-Col. 6 April, 1912 ; served in the South African War 1900–2 ; took part in the operations in the Orange Free State Feb. to May, 1900, including actions at Karee Siding, Vet River (5–6 May), and Zand River, and those in the Transvaal in May and June, 1900, including actions near Johannesburg ; employed with the Mounted Infantry (twice mentioned in Despatches [London Gazettes, 23 April and 10 Sept. 1901] ; Queen's Medal with three clasps ; King's Medal with two clasps, and D.S.O.). On the termination of the war he joined the South African Constabulary, and from 1 April, 1904, was for three years District Commandant of Middelburg, during which time he showed great zeal in police work and all the necessary administrative work required for keeping a district in good working order from the point of interior economy ; returned to England in 1907, when he rejoined the 3rd Battn.

The Cheshire Regt. ; served in the European War 1914 ; was in command of the 3rd Cheshires at Birkenhead until he went to France in command of the 15th Durham Light Infantry 12 Sept. 1915, and was killed in action near Sailly Labourse during the Battle of Loos 26 Sept. On his return to England in 1907, General Sir Henry Rawlinson, Bart, C.B., M.V.O., wrote : " Major T. Logan, D.S.O., served as a Company Commander in the 8th M.I. under my command. During the latter part of the South African War—speaking from recollection— he was with me about 12 months, and I have every reason to send him this small token of my gratitude for the excellent service he rendered. His ready acceptance of responsibility, coupled with a remarkably good eye for country and a thoroughly sound knowledge of his professional duties, made him one of the best company leaders I had under my command. He was more than once somewhat highly tried in an independent position before a superior force of the Boers, and on each and every occasion he acquitted himself admirably. I cannot speak too highly of the manner in which he commanded the Cheshire Coy. of the 8th M.I. whilst they were with my column. I hold a high opinion of his capabilities as a soldier and a leader of men." For several years he was secretary of the National Service League in Cheshire and North Wales ; was a strenuous and constant advocate of Universal Military Training, and exerted his influence in that cause, being also a warm supporter of the Boy Scout movement. He *m.* at Rossett, co. Denbigh, 22 Jan. 1903, Hilda (Chorlton Hall, Chester), dau. of Carruthers Charles Johnston ; *s.p.*

Obituary of Edward Logan.

In memory of Captain Neville Field Smith
15th Battalion Durham Light Infantry
who died, aged 26, on 24 January 1916.
Son of George Henry and Agnes Mary Smith
of 12 Westbourne Avenue, Hull.

Remembered with honour
Cite Bon Jean Military Cemetery, Armentiers, France
commemorated in perpetuity by the
Commonwealth War Graves Commission

Private J. Barrett
7th Company, 17th Durham Light Infantry
killed in action on the Somme, 1916.

Tommy Crawford Jnr
Southern Rhodesian Air Force.

Jack Crawford
Royal Air Force.

1940 – Tommy teaches bayonet drill to Home Guard volunteers.

In the years when our Country
was in mortal danger

T. A. CRAWFORD.

who served from 16 Jul 40 to 31 Dec 44
gave generously of his time and
powers to make himself ready
for her defence by force of arms
and with his life if need be.

George R.I.

THE HOME GUARD

Tommy's Home Guard certificate.

Vera, Tommy, Colin and Brian.

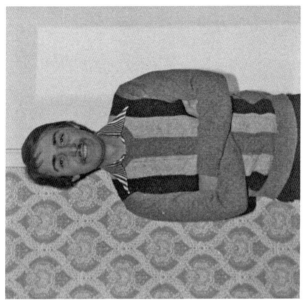

Colin.

Brian, Colin and Tommy.

Tommy and Vera, retired and at home in Harrogate.

Holt's Battlefield Tour, June 1978. Tommy returns to the Somme at 81 years of age. (He is fourth from right, next to Mrs Holt, with a bottle in his hand!)

Tommy and Brian Crawford – a proud son of a World War One veteran.

*Tommy's son Brian and Granddaughter, Jessica lay a wreath at
Crucifix Trench in memory of those who died in World War I.*

The War Memorial at Crucifix Trench.

Jacky grinned, 'No a lovely blighty one, he was dodging a mortar and tripped over a dixie of boiling stew, foot and leg scalded and he's away back on a bloody stretcher'.

'Some folk have all the luck,' said Ron, 'Show me a bloody dixie of hot stew and I'll trip over it any time'.

'Make way, stretcher party'.

We pushed back against the sandbags as the stretcher-bearers struggled along with their burden and I looked down on the white strained face of Dicky Knight, the chap who joined the battalion with me at Barnard Castle.

'Is it bad Dicky?' I asked as his eyes flickered.

'Its in the hip Corporal, hurts bloody awful,' he whispered.

'That's fine Dicky, you'll be in Blighty soon,' I replied.

He grinned feebly and then he was gone, gone on the long road back. Two more days and nights in the line and then we were relieved and marched back to Corbie, two officers killed and one wounded, eight men killed and twelve wounded, three men missing assumed killed.

'And they talk about Ypres!' growled Spud in disgust.

In Corbie duties were light for us and we did very little other than the overhaul of weapons and equipment, there was time for sport and bathing in the River Ancre and we had money to spend in the shops and cafes in the town. Ron suggested we should go along to La Neuville and see Yvonne and Marie and after cleaning up we walked over to pay our respects, Ron, Spud and myself. We were greeted with a warm smile of welcome and 'Comment allez vous monsieurs, entre, coffee yes!'

We sat at the table in the living room and drank their coffee and then Marie looked at us with wide eyes and struggling with the language she got out the question that had been on her face from the time we entered the house 'Paddy, he come, no?'

We looked at each other blankly and then Spud answered gruffly 'Paddy no come ma'mselle, not any more - he morti - fini - compree?'

Both girls burst into tears and we were pleased to leave that house, and that was my last visit there.

'War is hell,' said Ron as we tramped back to Corbie 'I never expected them to miss old Paddy'.

The next day we wandered along the bank of the river in the warm sunshine and sat down under the shade of a tree for a quiet chat and a smoke it was good to be alive and away from the thunder of the guns that we could hear in the distance. I was lying back on the grass with my eyes closed when a voice said 'Got a fag Corporal?' A fellow called Archie Howard of number 10 platoon stood beside me and I sat up and handed him a cigarette. He was a lanky thin-faced chap with black hair and large dark eyes that gave you the impression that his thoughts were always far away, a high strung nervous type. 'Thanks,' he said lighting up and drawing hard at the smoke and then he sat down beside us. For a while he gazed at the river gurgling by and then he said 'You been out here long Corporal?'

'About a year Howard, I came out with the battalion'.

'A year eh, and you're still alive, how long do you think you will stay alive?'

I stared at him 'A hell of a long time yet I hope'.

Spud rolled over and looked at Howard, 'What's the matter with you son, there's plenty of us been out here a year, and there's a lot more been here since Mons and that's two years ago'.

'I've been out three months,' muttered Howard 'And I'm going crazy, I can't stand this much longer, I just can't I tell you'.

Ron laughed shortly 'Tell that to the M.O. and see what it gets you'.

There was a short silence and then Howard turned to me 'Were you in the fight for the crater Corporal?'

'No,' I replied 'I wasn't in that'.

'I was in that,' said Howard 'and I killed a German, I killed him with my bayonet, he jumped over the rim nearly on top of me and my bayonet went through his stomach, he screamed his head off as I was pulling it out and he died lying there beside me'.

'Listen Howard you've got to pull yourself together,' said Spud 'there's many a man would give his back teeth to do what you did to that Jerry, the only good Jerry's are dead ones'

'Who started this war anyway?' muttered Howard.

'You know bloody well who started it, but that doesn't matter now,' said Ron 'the thing that matters is who'll finish it and who'll be left at the finish, and the more bloody Jerry's are killed the sooner we'll get home!'

'A very interesting conversation,' said a voice behind us and we turned to see the padre standing there 'I'd like to join you if I may,' and he sat down on the grass beside us.

'What's it all about?'

Spud grunted 'This blokes been out here three months and he thinks it's about time he got his ticket'.

'I don't like the war,' said Howard 'and I have nightmares'.

I laughed 'We all have nightmares, every time we go in the line it's a nightmare until we come out again'.

'None of us like the war son,' said the padre quietly 'we're just out here to get a horrible job over'.

'I wasn't brought into the world to live like this padre,' cried Howard 'Why should I be fighting the Germans?'

'Evil things must be destroyed my son,' replied the padre.

Howard looked at him with hot eyes 'You're a man of God sir, but you're a war-monger yourself!'

The padre stared 'And what do you mean by that remark?'

'You believe in your bible don't you?'

'Yes, of course I do'.

Howard's eyes glistened 'Right, now tell me of any book containing more fighting and warfare and ruthless cruelty than the bible that you preach from!'

'I dare say you are right,' replied the padre 'but don't forget that since the world began men have had two ways of living, good and evil, and those two ways have always clashed and always will'.

Howard sniffed 'Ours is the good way, and the Germans the evil way?'

'Invading other countries by force of arms cannot be right'.

Howard shrugged his shoulders 'If you care to read your British history padre I think you'll find we've done our share of that'.

'I grant you that Howard,' replied the padre 'but it doesn't apply in this war, we are fighting now for our liberty and freedom'.

'Liberty and freedom,' cried Howard with scorn, and what might that be, if I feel like getting drunk I land in prison, if I see a girl I fancy and speak to her and she complains I land in prison, if a chap insults me and I hit him I land in prison, there's a law that has something to say about liberty and freedom!'

The padre sighed 'I'm afraid we see things in a different light Howard, liberty and freedom does not mean doing what you feel like doing, it means doing what you ought to do, what you feel like doing can be evil, what you ought to do must be right'.

'All right padre support your war if you like,' said Howard 'but when I see men, moulded in God's image, lying out there with fat red-eyed rats gnawing the flesh off them and dainty little birds picking at the eyes of them I know that war is evil and there's no good or right in it for either side'.

He rose to his feet 'I've got to go now but I'll see you when hell's gates burst open up yonder, so-long'.

'He's a queer bloke,' said Ron 'I reckon he's daft'.

The padre shook his head 'No, he's not daft but he's very highly strung and I'm afraid his nerves might land him in trouble if he doesn't get a grip on himself'.

'I wonder what his nightmares are like,' I remarked.

'Poor chap, I feel sorry for him,' said the padre 'Oh, and that reminds me Corporal, the battalion orderly Sergeant was looking for you when I left headquarters'.

'No peace,' I groaned getting up 'see you chaps later'.

At battalion headquarters I met Orderly Sergeant Warren and he greeted me with 'Where the hell have you been, Corporal?'

'Along the river Sergeant,' I replied 'I'm off duty'.

'Oh, telling some French wench the story of your life I suppose'.

'No, listening to a sermon from the padre, check on that!'

'Aw hell, never mind, report at once to R.S.M. Shannon'.

I stepped into the orderly room and found a deputation awaiting me - Captain Dalton, Lieutenant Stuart Walker, R.S.M. Shannon, Sergeant Johnny Basham - Welsh Fusiliers, our heavyweight Peter Hague, and Tug Wilson. I saluted Captain Dalton and he motioned me to sit down with the others.

'Well now you're here I'll tell you all why you're here,' said Captain Dalton 'Divisional headquarters have got a boxing tournament laid on in Amiens between British and French troops in the area, and Sergeant Basham had the job in hand. Three men in his regiment, the Royal Welsh Fusiliers were taking part in it. Unfortunately his unit has been in action and these three men are out,' he picked up a sheet of paper and read from it 'Corporal Dai Davies heavyweight, killed in action; Sergeant Trevor Morgan wounded, featherweight; and Lance Corporal Clem Davies wounded, bantamweight'.

He paused and looked us over 'Divisional headquarters had instructed Sergeant Basham to find three substitutes to fill the bill and that's why he is here, now I leave it to you Sergeant'.

Sergeant Johnny Basham grinned at us 'Well boys what about it, I'll consider it a favour, and I'm boxing myself'.

Peter Hague stretched himself 'Count me in Sergeant, it'll be good training for me'

'Good, heavies are not easy to get fixed up,' said Basham.

'What's this tournament in aid of anyway?' asked Tug Wilson.

'Its in aid of French war widows,' replied Basham.

Tug grinned 'All right, I don't mind doing a bit for a French war widow, and I don't mean what you mean. I guess I'll scale at about nine stone five pounds'.

'The weight is nine stone two pounds,' said Basham 'but I don't think there'll be any trouble under the circumstances'.

'Right, I'll have a go, but I'm not making that weight now'.

'How's Clem, Sergeant?' I asked as Basham turned to me; he looked serious 'I'm afraid it's pretty bad for him, two machine gun bullets through one knee'.

I had visions of that red headed boy lying on a stretcher, his freckled face drawn with pain and I said 'Poor old Clem'.

'Are you willing to take his place boy?' asked Basham.

'Yes, I'll take his place Johnny,' I replied.

'Good!' exclaimed Basham jumping to his feet 'Can I use your phone sir, I want to report to divisional headquarters'.

Captain Dalton waved him to the phone and he spoke quickly for a few minutes, then putting down the receiver he said 'The show is on Saturday sir and transport will pick these chaps up on Saturday morning, they are to be excused all duties for four days commencing now, excepting for an emergency. Brigadier Aston Woodward will be sending you an official instruction to that effect'.

'Very good Sergeant,' replied Captain Dalton 'I'm pleased you've managed to get things settled, now you can all dismiss and I wish you all be best of luck in Amiens on Saturday'.

We trooped out of the orderly room and Lieutenant Stuart Walker said 'Get busy training boys, you've only got three days'.

On the Saturday morning a good party of us climbed on the transport, some of the boys having got leave to go with us and as we rolled along the road from Corbie to Amiens Spud leaned back in his seat and said 'We haven't much money but we do get around don't we?'

'We do that,' answered Ron 'but it's a wonder they didn't make us walk it'

'What's this Amiens place like?' asked Tug Wilson.

'According to what I hear you're a disgrace to the regiment if you haven't got a woman within half an hour,' laughed Peter Hague.

'Just my cup of tea, I'm starving!' replied Tug.

'Keep it until after the show Tug,' I remarked.

Soon we reached the outskirts of the largest town we had seen since coming to France and the only signs of a war showed in the troops moving along the streets with the civilians and the army transports on the roads. 'They don't know there's a bloody war on,' said Spud as he gazed at the shops and the people 'by hell, there's plenty of skirt and booze in this place'.

Ron grinned at him 'Plenty of ruddy redcaps too Spud, the place is lousy with them'. The transport pulled up outside a dingy looking building the entrance of which was bedecked with the lags of Britain and France and Johnny Basham met us with a cheerful grin on his face. 'Come on boys lets get you weighed in and then you can push off for an hour or two'. We stripped in a small dressing room and then stepped into the main hall where the boxing ring was erected and the weighing scales stood in the middle of the ring. Quite a number of people were about, a few of them in shorts and most of them in khaki or blue uniforms, British and French.

Tug Wilson scaled nine stone four and a half pounds and that raised a storm from the Frenchmen, but it soon calmed down, and Peter Hague raised a laugh when he brought the beam down at fifteen stone. I stepped on at a dead eight stone 6 pounds and my opponent scaled eight stone two pounds. He was a chunky black haired chap with a good pair of shoulders and as we shook hands I was told his name was Rene Brunet. He could speak no English but he seemed overjoyed at meeting me so I suppose he felt happy at his prospects. Soon we were dressed and Tug said 'Come on lets have a look at the ruddy town now we're here,' and we made our way to the entrance. However, it was not to be. At the entrance Lieutenant Stuart Walker met us and said 'Come on boys, there's a meal laid on for you, I'll show you the place'. He escorted us to a hotel a couple of streets away from the hall and we were soon tucking in to a first rate lunch.

'And now boys,' he said when we had finished the meal 'up the stairs we go and you can have a nice nap before the show starts'.

We stared at him 'Can't we have a look around the place now sir?' asked Peter Hague.

Sorry fellows, but the answer is no,' replied Lieutenant Walker.

'We're still in the ruddy army,' muttered Tug.

'Yes, we're still in the ruddy army,' said Lieutenant. Walker 'as a matter of fact there's a redcap at both the front and the back of this place now to see that you don't wander from the fold'.

Well, that was that, so up the stairs we went to the room allocated to us and made ourselves comfortable on the beds while Lieutenant Walker took the armchair. I was roused by someone shaking me and saying 'Come on boy, its time to go'. Back to the boxing hall and we pushed our way through the crowd of soldiers milling around the entrance and on arriving at our dressing room I heard that Johnny Basham was opening the show. I made my way into the main hall and took a seat at the ringside; this was something I must see. The place was well filled already with officers of both nations in the ringside seats and other ranks further back, and soon the officials were in their places and the show was on. Johnny Basham and his French opponent stepped through the ropes and took their stools, cool confident smiling Johnny Basham the welterweight champion of Great Britain and holder of a Lonsdale Belt. Soon the pair in the ring touched gloves and for three rounds I watched a delightful exhibition of dazzling brilliant boxing at its scientific best and Johnny left the ring at the end of the bout to a roar of applause, his blue eyes smiling and not a hair out of place. Tug Wilson stepped in next with his French opponent and I stayed to watch it. The Frenchman looked a useful customer but Tug sailed into him pumping punches with both hands and the Frenchman looked surprised as he was forced back around the ring under a barrage of fast hitting. Tug wouldn't let him get settled and he had it all his own way until near the end of the round when a desperate right swing thumped on his chin. Tug's hands dropped to his sides and he stood motionless for a split second, just as he had done with me, but the Frenchman kept away and Tug was belting away at the end of the round. Tug started the second like a whirlwind but once again a French right thudded home on his chin and this time the Frenchman stepped in with a battery of lefts and rights to the head and Tug came out of that with a split over his right eye that bled freely. After the round the referee examined the cut and stopped the bout in the Frenchman's favour, much to Tug's disgust.

Someone tapped me on the shoulder and looking round I saw Lieutenant Walker motioning me to the rear so I made my way to the dressing rooms and saw no more of the show. It wasn't my turn yet, but it was time to get ready and I was soon in my boxing kit and Spud wrapped the tapes around my hands.

~ Tommy ~

Lieutenant Stuart Walker came into the dressing room and I looked at me with his crooked smile 'Everything all right?' he asked 'you'll be on in a few minutes I think'.

'I'm just about ready now sir,' I replied 'A pity they had to stop Wilson's fight wasn't it'.

The officer laughed shortly 'Its better to lose a boxing bout than to have a sniper like Wilson with damaged eyes,' he retorted.

Spud laced on the gloves and as he was kneading the stuffing away from my knuckles the call came and I was soon climbing through the ropes to the usual buzz of noise. As I sat in my corner I looked around at the crowd of spectators, the khaki of Britain and the blue of France, men who had been fighting out of the trenches; its a strange life!

Another buzz of noise and Brunet jumped into the ring and ran across to shake hands with me, full of the joy of life. The usual announcement was made and the referee climbed in and called us to the middle, an English referee thank goodness I thought as Brunet and I touched gloves and returned to our corners. As I rubbed the soles of my boots in the resin and pulled at the ropes I once again had that feeling that I was in the loneliest place in the whole wide world, the boxing ring.

The gong clanged and we were off for three three-minute rounds. Brunet came out fast well covered up, and I met him fast, lefts flashed in and we both landed, we circled and again Brunet came fast but I pulled him up with a nice left to the mouth and he landed with a quick right to my ribs. Again we circled and I knew I had a stiff job in hand, this chap was fast and he was going to be hard to hit, he crouched and weaved and he carried both hands cocked and ready. I scored with a light left to his mouth and as he tore in I tried again but missed and he was slamming away with lefts and rights that had plenty of sting behind them. I slung a right that he slipped under and he drove me back to the ropes and never gave me a chance to get clear of his barrage of punches. By good luck I swerved clear of a vicious uppercut that only missed by a fraction and for a split second, with the ropes at my back, I caught sight of his exposed chin. I put all I had, including my prayers, into a left hook that smashed dead on the point of his chin and I felt the shock of the blow to my shoulder. I saw his eyes turn and I cocked the right to follow up but I was too late, he was on his knees with one hand holding the lower rope. The referee pushed me away and began the count while I leaned against the ropes and hoped Brunet would stay where he was. What a hope! He was on his feet at eight and tearing in at me like a wildcat when the gong sounded the end of the round.

Spuds eyes were shining as he sponged me in the corner 'Another one like that Tommy and its in the bag, box him off boy'. Good advice, but Brunet had something to say about it. The gong went and up we came for the second, that French boy started off like a bobbing weaving whirlwind and he never let up, no matter what I did or what I tried he took it all and hammered away with lefts and rights that had me dizzy. I was landing my share of blows but he didn't repeat his mistake of the first round and when I reached my corner at the end of the second round my lip was split and bleeding.

The gong went for the third and we touched gloves in the middle of the ring for the last round and the most hectic three minutes of my life. Brunet bounced in like a cyclone and hammered away with short jarring punches that hurt. I got him with a nice right that brought blood from his nose. A snorting right took me in the solar plexus and drove me into a corner where all I could do was cover up till my breath came back. He kept pounding them in and as I swerved along the ropes a sweeping right landed behind my ear and helped me on my way. I finished up on the seat of my pants and heard the referee counting but I was up at five and as that bundle of French fury came at me I side stepped and hooked a good left to his eye that drove him back on his heels. I tore into him then and we were pounding away in the corner when the gong went, and peace reigned once more.

Brunet was awarded the decision on points and he deserved it, he threw enough leather in nine minutes to sink a warship, he danced over to my corner, threw his arms around me and kissed my cheek. 'Tres bon, Tommee, tres bon,' he cried touching my left glove. As we left the ring General Dykes Brown presented Rene Brunet with a silver cup, and I received a silver medal from a French officer, later they told me it was General Chauveau. In the dressing room a French doctor examined my split lip and put a couple of stitches on the inside where it was split open.

'You box good,' he said as he worked.

'Not good enough,' I replied.

The doctor laughed 'Ah, our Rene is very good, he spar with all the best like Eugene Crique and Charles Ledoux'.

I stared at him - boxed with Eugene Crique - if I'd known that before I would have gone a long way to keep clear of that ring.

We heard a dull roar from the crowd and shortly afterwards Peter Hague burst into the dressing room carrying a silver cup.

'How did it go Peter?' asked Spud as he packed my gear.

'One round Spud, just one bloody round,' grinned Peter.

He had knocked the French opponent out in the first round.

Lieutenant Walker accompanied us back the hotel where we were staying the night, three battered boxers with one silver cup and two silver medals.

'I thought you had him in that first round,' he said to me.

I shook my head 'He came back as strong as ever, he was too strong, too fast, and too clever for me'.

'Well never mind boys, it was a hell of a good show, now there's supper laid out for you and then off you go to bed. The transport will be taking us back to Corbie tomorrow'

'Not giving us much chance to see Amiens sir,' said Tug.

'I'm afraid not this time, but that's orders'.

'What about the chaps who came with us sir?' I asked.

'They're free to fend for themselves, they'll stay somewhere for the night, and they know to catch the transport tomorrow'.

A good supper was laid on for us but I had to stick to slops on account of my lip and then we climbed wearily into bed.

'To hell with this game, I'm going to be a spectator next time,' said Tug 'Spud and Ron will be having a bloody good beano while we see sweet fanny adams of this gay city'.

'Aw shut up Tug,' I replied 'if I know anything of those two they'll wish they'd never seen the damn place by tomorrow'.

The next morning at ten o'clock the transport was ready to take us back to the battalion and we sat waiting for the others to turn up - myself with a lower lip like a sausage and Tug with a strip of sticking plaster over his damaged eye.

Lieutenant Walker counted us with a worried look 'Still two missing Baker and Delany, where the hell have they got too?'

We waited ten minutes while the boys grumbled 'Aw come on lets leave the silly bastards to stew'.

'Here they come,' cried someone, and looking along the street we saw Spud and Ron approaching with a redcap stalking at each side of them. 'Hell they're in trouble all right,' I exclaimed; their uniforms were untidy and Spud had his head bandaged. They halted beside the transport and Ron winked at me while the police Corporal made his report to Lieutenant Walker, then they were bundled on board and we were off.

'What the hell have you two been up to?' I asked them.

'We were done proper,' replied Ron 'after the show we went off and found a nice little pub to have a nice little drink, but was that enough for this silly old blighter, not on your bleeding life! He goes and gets in tow with a piece of skirt see and seeing that the pub was soon closing she offers to take us to a club she knows of where there's drinking all night and plenty of skirt'.

'She was a nice piece of stuff,' said Spud.

'Yes, like hell she was,' growled Ron 'anyway we landed at this club of hers, it was a private house but once you got inside everything was laid on all right. Men and women moving around and sitting at tables, drinks at double price being served, and everything free and easy so long as you paid for it'.

'You didn't expect it for nothing, did you?' asked Spud.

'Not in this bloody country I didn't,' replied Ron 'Anyway this wench of Spuds soon brings along a pal of hers for me to play with, and we got down to proper drinking and entertaining each other'.

He cadged a cigarette and pulled at it gloomily 'We were really knocking the booze back and the party grew merry and bright, Spud kept on suggesting bedtime to the wenches and they kept on trying to find out how much money we had left, which wasn't much because those drinks was really costing us something. In the end this daft old bugger grabs hold of his girl and starts carrying her up the stairs and she's yelling blue murder in French'.

'It was well past my bedtime,' said Spud.

'Well you got your sleep all right,' replied Ron 'I was laughing my head off when a couple of blokes dressed like waiters came out on the landing of the stairs and biff, one of them bust a bottle over Spuds nut and he rolled down those stairs like a dead man. I scrambled over to give a hand and as I bent over Spud to see if he was still with us somebody pulled the roof down on the back of my head, that's how it felt anyway, look at the bump'.

When he turned his head sure enough there was a nice egg shaped bump.

'Go on Ron,' I said grinning 'this is a nice love story'.

'We might have been killed,' moaned Spud.

'Yes and all your fault you bloody old tomcat,' retorted Ron 'anyway there's not much more that we know of. When we came round we were in a room with a bunch of redcaps, they reckoned they found us lying in a shop doorway in the Rue De Nationale and we are now faced with a charge of being drunk and incapable, a doctor patched us up and said we were lucky to be breathing'.

'They must have gone through our pockets after they beamed us,' said Spud 'we haven't got a bloody cent left between us, but you must admit Ron, they were a bit of all right!'

'Couple of bitches that's what they were,' grumbled Ron 'You'll do your courting on your own after this you old heathen'.

The following day saw them up at the orderly room and Ron got ten days while Spud got fourteen days defaulters, this meant all the dirty jobs that could be piled on them.

'Why did you get fourteen Spud, and Ron only ten,' I asked.

'Because I lost my bloody cap when I got crowned with that bottle,' growled Spud 'also these,' he pointed to his ribbons 'the C.O. says an old soldier like me should know better'.

The next day we marched away from Corbie and billeted once more in Méaulte and the battalion started more work on gun pits and carrying ammunition up to the reserve trenches, but Hague, Wilson and myself took no part in this. Lieutenant Walker came along to tell us that divisional sports would be held at Corbie during the weekend 'Hague and you had better get in a spot of training,' he advised.

I fingered my sore lip 'What about this sir,' I asked him.

The swelling had gone down but it still hurt a bit; he grinned as he looked at it 'That'll be all right Corporal, duck them instead of stopping them'.

That is something easier said than done and I wasn't feeling too happy as I started skipping, roadwork, and mauling around with Tug. I didn't do any boxing because I was afraid of getting my lip split again in sparring. Well, I was in this boxing racket now so I would have to see the job through. I knew whoever it was I had to meet would be no mug - he, like me, must have fought his way through battalion and brigade to reach the divisional final.

Back we tramped to Corbie in full marching order under a blazing sun and the sweat dripped from us as we swung along the cobbled roads, the boys in the ranks looked good and the troops we passed on the road looked good, there was a tenseness and an eagerness for the coming battle with the Germans. My mind was on my own coming battle. On the Saturday morning I stepped into the ring to meet Sergeant Paddy Carson of the Army Service Corps for the divisional title, and as I sat in my corner I had the feeling that I wasn't keen. I don't know if I was worried about my lip or if I had gone stale and needed a rest, but something was missing.

Carson was a good boxer and strong but in the first round I made him miss badly and I hurt him with a left to the stomach and a right uppercut that sent him to the ropes. In the second he got me with a right to the mouth that had me weaving to get out of trouble and it was ding-dong slugging to the bell. In the third round he out-boxed me and he was given the decision on points, he got the silver cup and I got another silver medal. Under different circumstances I should have beaten Carson. I wasn't half as good as on the night I boxed Rene Brunet in Amiens, but there it was and I couldn't make better of it. Peter Hague was also unlucky; he was knocked out in the third round of his heavyweight bout, so we didn't manage a divisional champion after all. 'I'm laying off boxing for a bit sir,' I told Lieutenant Walker 'I seem to have lost my form'.

'I'm afraid it was a mistake going to Amiens,' he replied 'but of course we didn't know this job would come so soon after, however there's a bigger fight coming soon so we'll give boxing a rest'. That suited me all right for the time being.

5.   THE SOMME

On June 24th we packed once more and marched to a place called Buire and that evening all hell broke loose as our artillery opened out with a concentrated bombardment of the German trenches. Large guns, small guns, and trench mortars hammered away unceasingly at the German trenches, by day throwing clouds of earth skywards and at night the bright flash of exploding shells went on hour after hour, Jerry was getting hell. We had an easy time in Buire, we were in the first assault and just awaiting the order and we watched the battalions tramping past to play their part. Men of the county regiments from Cornwall to Cumberland, men from Wales, Ireland and Scotland, gunners, fusiliers, riflemen and light infantry, civilians of yesterday soldiers of today. 'If you chaps have anything of value I advise you to send it home when you have the chance,' said Lieutenant Walker and someone sang out 'I've got sixpence jolly, jolly sixpence!' to roars of laughter. I obtained a green envelope (supposed to be safe in the post) and sent off my two silver medals, that was all I had of any value, and that was the last I ever saw of them, they never arrived.

In a last minute lecture we were told they had issued final orders 'We are going to advance and all movement will be forward, no unwounded men will be allowed to come back; if your pal is wounded leave him and push on, he will be attended too'. On June 28th our packs and blankets were stored in barns and we paraded in fighting order, each man was issued with an extra 100 rounds of rifle ammunition (that made 250 rounds per man) iron rations and hand grenades were issued and as we lined the street in Buire awaiting orders to move off the weather changed and the rain came pelting down. The move was cancelled and we dismissed with the information that the assault was postponed owing to the adverse weather conditions. It was lucky for me because the next morning I received a parcel from Amy containing fifty cigarettes, some block chocolate, a tin of boiled sweets and some sweet biscuits. I tucked this lot into my haversack along with my emergency rations and my grenades and it wasn't long before they were worth untold wealth to me.

So we waited and the bombardment of the enemy lines went on, gas and smoke shells adding to the inferno, and we hugged ourselves with the thought that men just couldn't live under that deluge of shellfire. On the evening of June 30th we once more lined the street of Buire in fighting order and this time there was no postponement, we were off; as we tramped the cobbled road the evening turned to night and it was dark when we entered the trenches and made our way slowly up to the front line to take over our assembly position. Considering the crowded state of the trenches casualties were few and by 3 a.m. we were settled down in position to await the dawn.

Cigarettes glowed fitfully in the trench as Lieutenant Walker told us 'We are to take the German first and second lines of trenches, there we consolidate and then attack the sunken road and Crucifix Trench between Birch Wood and Fricourt'.

'What time do we kick off sir?'

'Seven thirty is zero hour,' he looked at his watch 'its now five o'clock and looks like a lovely morning'.

'The beginning of a lovely day,' murmured Spud puffing at his pipe and fiddling at his tunic he unpinned his ribbons and slipped them in his pocket.

'What's the idea of that Spud?' I asked him.

'I'm using my brains son,' he replied 'when a German sniper sees ribbons or stripes or Sam Browne belts he just lines his sights on you thinking you're someone important and 'Bob's your uncle', see!'. And that was just cold hard logic.

It was a glorious morning with heat waves simmering in the air and the stream of shells whizzed and howled overhead to crash with an inferno of noise on the German trenches.

'Please Mister Gunner, leave a little one for me,' cried Bert Miles when at seven fifteen Sergeant Brodwick barked the order to 'fix bayonets'.

'Here we go gathering nuts in May,' sang Ron as his clicked home on the boss of his rifle.

'Its not May, its July,' grunted Spud 'July 1st'.

'Never mind Spud, we'll have nuts in July,' exclaimed Ron wiggling his bayonet.

Lieutenant Stuart Walker stood at the fire step his eyes on his watch 'five minutes to go boys,' he called and as he spoke the guns lifted and the shells began to pound the German second line.

'Forward my lucky lads,' he shouted and over the parapet we went into the smoke and stench of No Mans Land crouching and moving at the double. Looking right and left I saw the ragged line of khaki moving forward and here and there a man stumbled and fell. I heard the familiar hiss and crack of bullets and the 'rat-tat-tat,' of German machine guns opening up on us, the gunners hadn't wiped them all out after all. Just ahead of me I saw Sergeant Brodwick drop his rifle and roll to the ground his hands clawing at his stomach and Bert Miles fell back with blood on his face - on and on - there was no stopping this time. Ahead of us was Lieutenant Walker and a little to the left I saw Captain Dalton pressing forward and shouting but I couldn't hear his words. On and on - and at long last we were scrambling through the remnants of the German wire. I saw a white face in a scuttle helmet appear above the parapet, a blotch appeared on his forehead and he fell back.

'I got that bastard all right,' shouted Spud beside me 'Come on boys, into the trench'.

'There's a machine post to the left,' shouted Lieutenant Walker 'Get it with grenades'.

We dashed along the battered trench and tossed a couple of grenades into the entrance of the machine post 'Never mind about prisoners bombs into every dugout,' cried Lieutenant Walker and through an inferno of noise we moved shooting and bombing and bayoneting until the trench was cleared of the enemy.

Major Babbage stalked down the trench 'Forward, attack the second line,' he roared and over the top we went once more into the hiss and crack of rifle bullets.

I saw Lieutenant Walker stagger and fall to his knees and as I reached him his face was twisted with pain 'You all right?' I asked.

'Its just my foot, and that won't stop me, get on forward', and with blood pouring from his boot he got to his feet and pressed on.

Men were going down right and left now as the enemy fire increased and I saw Tug Wilson beside Lieutenant Walker when suddenly the officer pitched forward on his face. Tug dropped on one knee snapped his rifle up and fired, then he turned the officer over as I came up.

'He's finished,' he said 'and I got the bugger that done it, come on I'll show you'.

Forward we went, about twenty yards to a shell crater, and there a German lay with arms outstretched his face shattered with the bullet from Tug's rifle.

Into the German trench we jumped and plunged right and left to clear it of the enemy. I came to the entrance of a dugout and saw a khaki figure hanging on to the barrel of a rifle 'help, help,' he croaked. 'Out of the bloody way,' I cried, I lunged past him and felt my bayonet strike something and go in, it was too dark to see but there was a yell and the thump of someone falling. I pulled the pin out of a grenade and flung it into the dugout grabbing the chap in khaki and pulling him clear.

'What the hell do you think you're doing,' I yelled at him 'bomb the bloody dugouts don't go into them'.

Then I saw he was a young officer and he replied 'I wanted to take one or two prisoners'.

'Prisoners be buggered, kill them,' something thudded in the trench 'look out!' I yelled and fell flat on my face behind a couple of sandbags. It was a German stick grenade and it exploded with a shattering roar. When I got to my feet the young officer was dead. The German second line was soon cleared and for a short time we rested in it and tried to get ourselves organised but we found now that units were getting mixed up. Men picked the positions for themselves and got busy sniping at the enemy, and the bombing of enemy machine gun posts still went on, the German machine gunners firing to the end and dying at their guns.

The enemy gunners now seemed to have got over the shock of the attack, shells and mortar fire increased on our newly won positions and it looked like developing into a pretty hot party.

I said to Spud 'What about going forward a bit and squatting in shell holes, I reckon Jerry will knock hell out of this trench pretty soon'.

'Good idea,' replied Spud 'Hi, Ron, we're moving forward a bit'.

Ron stuck up a thumb to show he understood and I glanced back towards the old British front line, through the haze I could see men by the hundred moving forward and here and there a shell crashed among them.

'Bags of reinforcements behind us,' I called 'come on boys and find your own cover in the open'. We left the cover of the German trench and moved forward a good thirty yards to dive into a shell crater just as the bullets of a machine gun swept over us.

'That was a bit of luck,' gasped Ron as he stretched out amid the rubble.

Tug Wilson had come with us and as he sighted over the rim of the shell hole his rifle cracked out viciously.

'This is just my cup of tea boys,' he remarked 'I can see the whites of their eyes today'

'What's the score, Tug?' I asked him.

'Nine certs since we left our own trenches,' he replied 'how long ago is that?'

Spud laughed grimly 'Feels like about a week ago, how the hell will they get any rations up here to us?'

Mention of rations reminded me of hunger and I dived into my haversack for chocolate and biscuits to munch as a wave of men in khaki scrambled past us, moving forward. One of them stumbled and fell beside our shell hole and we dragged him under cover.

'Where are you hit mate?' asked Ron, and the reply came through clenched teeth 'In the back somewhere I think'.

We rolled him over and sure enough the blood was staining the back of his tunic. 'Rip that tunic with your knife Ron,' I said and when his back was exposed we saw a nasty wound in the small of the back low down just missing the spine. We did it up as best we could with a field dressing and part of the chaps,' shirt and I saw that his unit was the Tyneside Scottish.

'Queer where you get hit in this war,' said Spud 'that bloke was moving forward and he gets - Look out!'

We fell flat on our faces as the horrible moan of mortars filled the air, and then behind us the trench we had recently left erupted into the air as the shower of mortar shells scored a direct hit.

I gazed at Ron 'Good God, the rest of the section Ron?'

Ron stood up 'I'll go back and see if they got clear Corporal, but if they didn't our section is about wiped out'.

A storm of firing broke out in front and the wave of men who had advanced past us towards Fricourt dwindled away to nothing as though a giant hand had swept them away.

Ron came back with a rush and rolled into the cover of the shell hole as bullets flicked past him. I looked at him 'Well?' I asked.

He shook his head 'Not well at all Corporal,' he muttered 'This seems all you have left, in this shell hole'.

'What the hell happened?' I asked.

'I could only find one of them,' replied Ron 'Young Steadman, and he's got one leg off and the other broken, the place is just a bloody shambles of bits and pieces of men and gear, he says they were caught proper'.

My God - Jack Barrett, Wharton, Barson, Pringle and Lance Corporal Tyson, missing believed killed!

'And now Corporal, where do we go from here?' asked Tug, and my mind was brought back with a jerk to the present.

I saw men moving behind us and men moving in front and on the flanks, a crowded noisy battlefield in which I felt very much alone.

'Don't leave me,' groaned the wounded Tyneside Scot.

I felt the three pairs of weary eyes peering under the rim of steel helmet's from faces already grimy with sweat and dust 'where do we go from here?'

I saw a bunch of men in field grey with their hands shoulder high passing by our shell hole, prisoners moving briskly for the British lines and I yelled out at them and held up two fingers.

'Kamarad!' shouted one and they forged ahead for safety.

Tug jumped to his feet with a curse and cocked his rifle. 'Halt! You bastards halt!' he shouted and after casting one look at Tug they came to a sudden stop, hands higher than ever.

'What do you want them for?' asked Spud as the Germans approached.

'They're going back to our lines, get two of them to hump this chap back from here,' I replied.

The Germans were very willing and they were soon on their way once more carrying the wounded Tyneside Scot. Just then Captain Dalton strode over; a blood stained rag tied round his head and with him was Sergeant Plowden of A Company.

'Pretty grim show boys,' he exclaimed as they stepped into the shell hole.

'How many men have you Corporal?'

'They're all here sir,' I replied sadly.

'Hell, here have a drop of this,' and he passed us a water bottle that contained rum.

'There's another assault being built up and we've got to take the sunken road,' said Captain Dalton 'You see that mound over there Corporal, that's a German machine gun nest and its holding up the advance over this area, we've got to wipe it out and carry forward from there'.

The ground stretched away flat in front of us and it was swept with crossfire from Birch Tree Wood and Fricourt. Sergeant Plowden exclaimed 'There they go sir, the advance has started'. As we climbed out of the shell hole I saw the stumbling waves of men starting the advance once more and we moved forward into the storm of bullets. Twenty-five yards forward and we rolled into another shell hole for cover. Sergeant Plowden was hit and left behind, when we regained our breath Captain Dalton staggered to his feet 'Come on boys, forward, run or crawl blast you but get on, forward!'

We followed him once more and he turned his bandaged head to me 'Get your grenades ready, you'll ----!' he coughed harshly and went down, blood gushing from his throat.

'Come on,' I shouted as shells began to crash around 'we can't live here, we've got to reach that sunken road for cover'.

Ahead of us was the mound of upturned earth, the enemy machine gun nest, and thirty yards from it we rolled into a shell hole and lay gasping for breath.

'Looks as though we might do it,' gasped Ron 'The Jerries are firing towards the flank'

'I don't think the bastards saw us at all,' said Tug peering over the edge of the shell hole.

'Get your grenades ready, we're going in,' I ordered.

We waited ready, until the German machine gun opened up firing towards the flank, 'Right - come on!'

We ran fast, ten, twenty, twenty five yards 'grenades!' I yelled as I hurled my own grenade forward and the others followed my example. There was a satisfying crash as the grenades exploded over the machine gun post and we dived into a shallow trench. The gun crew of three were lying dead beside their gun.

Ron sat down heavily on the ground and turned a white face towards me 'Don't think I can do any more Corporal,' he said.

'What's up Ron?' I asked and then I saw the blood running down his hand from his arm. Swiftly while Tug kept watch we ripped away his tunic 'Christ! You don't half collect them Ron,' said Spud 'One through the shoulder and two through the arm'.

We patched him up as best we could with field dressings and waited for the wave of advancing troops to catch up with us, mostly strangers of different regiments.

Wave after wave of men in khaki were advancing from the captured German trench, stumbling forward over the bullet swept area, falling into shell holes for cover and falling to rise no more, the ground was strewn with hundreds who had paid the price.

A dixie of tea, hot and strong and sweet was carried into our shallow trench, bless the men who had carried it over, and sacks containing bread came with it. Major Babbage, haggard and dirty came along and said in a harsh voice 'Half of you feed, the rest watch the front, and get a move on we must get that sunken road'

'Dear Mother, sell the pig and buy me out,' groaned Spud.

A lewis gunner and his mate jumped into our trench and at once set up their gun in a firing position, two of the West Yorkshire Regiment.

Suddenly Tug shouted 'Look out boys, here they come!'

Tea was forgotten as we picked firing positions and peered through the battle haze to see a crowd of field grey figures moving at the double out of a small wood, roughly about 500 of them.

They spread out as we watched and headed for our position 'And this is going to be good,' growled Tug as he squeezed the trigger.

Machine guns and rifles opened out with rapid fire and the ranks of German infantry melted away leaving many on the ground.

'You'll have to do something better than that Jerry,' muttered Major Babbage as he lay watching.

I took a mug of tea to Ron and he looked pretty bad lying in the corner of the trench but he sipped the tea with a weak grin.

'How am I going to get back out of this Tommy?' he asked.

'I'll get some square heads to take you back Ron,' I replied 'You'll be all right'.

He smiled faintly 'We seem to have come a hell of a long way since this morning'.

I saw the Padre and a red cross man a short distance away and brought them over to attend to Ron, and Spud soon came along with a couple of Germans from the many who were making their way back. They soon understood what was required of them and with a few 'Yah! Yahs!' they picked Ron up and hastily departed from a place that was too hot for their liking.

Soon the order came to advance and forward we surged once more over the flat open ground and a storm of fire greeted us from the grey ruins of Fricourt on the right flank and Birch Tree Wood on the left flank while the enemy artillery found our range and their shells crashed over the area. We walked, we ran, we crawled, somehow we kept moving and at long last we tumbled into the cover afforded by the sunken road, the road from Fricourt to Contalmaison. The back area was once more strewn with heaps of khaki, wounded and dead, and those of us who reached the sunken road looked at each other in surprise, surprise to be still alive. We at once started digging with entrenching tools and making firing positions and word came to us to hang on until the flanks got lined up with us. If nothing else this gave us breathing space and a bit of time to get ourselves sorted out, but by now regiments were hopelessly mixed and sadly depleted. Major Babbage had been hit on the last advance and, being the only senior officer left, Lieutenant Colonel Fitzgerald now took over sole command.

I looked back, and away in the distance I saw the hanging Virgin of Albert; I looked forward and about 400 yards ahead I saw the Crucifix over Crucifix trench, and over the area between the two emblems of peace and goodwill lay thousands of figures in khaki and field-grey.

Tug Wilson patted his rifle butt and croaked 'Seventeen certs, all big fat juicy square heads, and that's not a bad days work'. I suppose some German sniper would be saying the same. Lieutenant Hyde and Sergeant Beasley came along with a small stone jar and issued to each man a tablespoon of rum. Spud's face was drawn and his eyes blood shot as he gulped his rum ration, 'My God, I needed that,' he gasped 'I'm getting too bloody old for this racket Tommy'. We huddled down in the holes we had scratched for ourselves, waiting for what we knew would come, and it did, a storm of mortar fire right on the sunken road. We could do nothing about it, just lie and take it and hope for the best, we sent up rockets for artillery support but none came. 'What's the matter with the blasted gunners,' growled Spud 'Hundreds of guns, thousands of shells, and not a single bloody round to help us out'. 'Look out, here they come,' someone yelled and peering ahead I saw the swarm of field grey figures rise from Crucifix trench and begin to stumble forward. Alongside me lay a lewis gunner of the Somerset Regiment and as rifle and machine fire opened out I noticed his gun was silent. The line of grey wavered and broke and then reformed and came on once more and when they were about two hundred yards away the lewis broke into a chattering roar beside me and great spaces were cut into the German ranks. The attack faltered and then died away and with it came the order 'Advance - forward for Crucifix trench!'.

A wave of khaki was climbing out of the sunken road and forward we went once more 'Come on Spud, this is our final objective,' I called as I moved forward. The storm of fire met us once more and I saw Lieutenant Hyde go down, halfway across and Lieutenant Colonel Fitzgerald was out in front and then he too went down but the advance went on. Weary and blinded with sweat we rolled into a ditch, we rolled into a shallow ditch a short distance from the enemy trench and thanked the lord it was there. A shower of rifle grenades came over and we sought cover among the dead Germans in the ditch. 'Come on,' I shouted 'We can't stop here, forward!'. Forward we went on the last lap, dimly I could see German helmets at the trench ahead, the crash of rifles firing directly in front of me, savagely I worked the bolt of my rifle firing from the hip as I ran, and then I saw him! Big and steady, right in front of me and his rifle aimed dead at me! With a heave I threw myself to one side and fell and I heard a shout as someone dashed past me and heaved himself into the enemy trench. I jumped to my feet and dived for the trench to find Spud looking at his blood stained bayonet and a German N.C.O. sprawled at his feet, two German soldiers stood with their hands raised.

'You all right Tommy?' Spud asked; and as I nodded he said 'I thought this bastard had got you, I pulled the trigger and found my magazine was empty so I had to go in with the bayonet'

'Thanks Spud,' I replied as more troops piled into the trench 'Get moving and bomb the dugouts!'

The enemy dugouts here went deep into the ground and grenades were the only answer, not many prisoners were taken because Jerry refused to come out so he just had to die below ground. Once the trench was captured we hastily made firing positions for ourselves and I found myself in charge of Spud and Tug, one chap belonging to the East Yorks, two Lancashire Fusiliers, one Tyneside Scottish, and two Kings Own Yorkshire Light Infantry.

'And we're here at last,' sighed Spud 'Now lets have some rest'.

An officer came hurrying down the trench and he called out 'Who's in charge here?' I raised my arm and he squatted down beside me.

'How many men have you Corporal?' he asked.

'Two of my own section sir and this other lot who have drifted,' I replied.

'Good, keep them on the look out, and watch that wood over there, that's where Jerry is concentrated, its Shelter Wood. By the way, I'm Captain Ethridge, West Kents, and I'm taking charge at present'

'Where are my own officers sir,' I asked.

'The only one I've contacted up to now is Lieutenant Ely,' he replied 'and he's further along the trench, anything you want?'

'We want grenades and grub,' I replied.

'I've already sent runners back for that,' said Captain Ethridge.

'Keep a good look out and good luck,' he moved away.

That Crucifix trench was a hard position to hold, it was swept from both flanks with rifle and machine gun fire as well as the fire from directly ahead of us; and the enemy artillery was now increasing its fire on the area behind us in an attempt to stop reinforcements getting up to us.

'Bad enough here,' said one of the Lancashire boys 'but it looks a bloody sight worse back there'.

'Well we can't go back yet boys,' I replied 'so dig for safety and watch out for Jerry'.

Tug snuggled down alongside a tree stump 'You do the bloody digging, I'll do the watching'.

Four men crawled up to the trench dragging a couple of cases of grenades and a sack containing four loaves of bread.

'Nice work boys, what's it like coming over?' I asked.

'Bloody murder Corporal,' one of them replied 'Make that lot last, might be a bit before you get any more'.

'Oh, here's something else Corporal,' said another of the ration party 'I damn near forgot it,' and he handed me a flask with a dirty piece of paper wrapped around it. As I unwrapped it I saw written in pencil 'With compliments - Ethridge (Captain) West Kents'.

I drew the cork and sniffed it 'Its whiskey boys,' I called to my makeshift section 'One tablespoon each for now and we'll make it last'.

'Hell, some of those officers can be nearly human at times!' sighed Spud smacking his lips.

Tug's rifle cracked out and he looked round with a grin 'and that brings it up to twenty three, what a ruddy birthday; I'll have mine now Corporal and mind you don't spill any!'

Men lay everywhere, dead, dying, and wounded but nothing much could be done about it, the stretcher bearers and Red Cross men were still busy away back where the advance had started; here and there a wounded man was pulled in over the bullet swept ground and taken down into a dugout out of harms way and many a wounded man was hit again and killed as he lay in the open. Above the din of the battle we could hear someone moaning and at times screaming with pain somewhere near our section of trench, but we couldn't place the sound for a time, although we watched for movement among the pitiful piles of khaki strewn around.

'Wish to hell that bloke would shut up,' growled the East York 'its getting on my bloody nerves'.

After a time Spud got to his feet 'Can't see that bloke from here, let's go out and find him,' he suggested.

'I'll go with you,' said the East York.

'Keep your heads down then,' I warned them and they nodded.

They climbed out of the trench and ambled off and I watched them searching among the fallen men. About twenty-five yards away they stopped and then Spud looked up and raised his arm. 'They've found him,' said one of the Lancashire men, and then I saw them lift their burden and then headed back towards us with bullets whistling and smacking ground. Ten yards from the trench and the East York man went down, the wounded man and Spud falling with him, God! They've been wiped out! I thought, and then Spud staggered to his feet grabbed the belt of the wounded man with one hand and started dragging him along the ground. Spuds other arm was hanging useless, dripping blood. 'Come on,' I said to the man next to me, the Tyneside Scot, and we jumped out and ran to meet Spud and relieve him of his burden. I saw then it was the Sam Browne belt of an officer he had hold of 'Let go Spud, we'll get him in,' and we lowered the officer into the trench. We jumped in after him and when I looked around I saw Spud on his knees at the edge of the trench a vacant look on his face, a look of shocked surprise.

'Jump Spud!' I yelled, but he didn't jump, he just toppled over into the trench and I was there to break his fall.

I lowered him to the floor of the trench and saw the blood on his sleeve, and more blood was showing at his breast pocket. With my knife I cut and ripped away his tunic and his shirt, he had two bullet wounds, his arm was broken with one and the second one had gone through his chest very near to the heart. The small hole in his chest showed dark coloured blood and the hole in his back where the bullet had come out was a ghastly mess. What the hell could I do about this, all we had was field dressings nothing to deal with wounds like this. I made pads with field dressings and ordered the two Lancashire Fusiliers to let me have their shirts that I ripped and used to tie the dressings in place. 'Get a couple of shirts off those chaps who are lying around,' I told the two Fusiliers and by the time I had finished the dressings I saw Spud's eyes were open and he was watching me.

'Pretty bad, that second one boy!' he stated weakly a trickle of blood coming from his mouth.

I grinned at him 'You'll be all right old timer, this time next week you'll have a nurse beside you'.

'Hell! My backs hurting me!' he coughed up more blood 'Prop me up Tommy, against the sandbags - ah, that's better, am I facing Jerry?'

'Yes Spud you're facing Jerry,' I replied 'now take it easy'.

He grinned weakly 'That's the idea boy, always face the enemy'.

As I sat beside him he closed his eyes and his face turned pale and old looking, a spasm of pain shook him and his eyes opened again.

'Got anything left in the bottle Tommy?' he whispered hoarsely.

'Yes Spud,' I replied 'but I don't think you should have any of that at present, wait till you see the doctor'.

He cocked an eyebrow 'Aw hell, and you call yourself a pal!'

Sadly I held the bottle to his mouth while he took a sip 'Ah! That's better,' he whispered and then out it came in bubbly bloody froth.

He sat quiet for a bit and then he said suddenly 'Well, Tommy I reckon this is where I hand in my kit eh?'

'Don't be daft Spud,' I retorted 'you'll be down in the old village pub in a few weeks time in good old Blighty'.

He shook his head slowly 'Seems a long time ago since we were at 'Barny', you remember Tommy?'

'I remember Spud, you still owe me five bob from those days,' I replied lightly but his eyes were closed again.

Tug called me over to his sniping position and said 'Get me some ammunition Corporal, I think I've got the bloke marked who got old Spud'.

I passed him a few clips of cartridges 'I'm certain the shots came from those rocks behind the Crucifix, I've been watching it ever since but he's crafty this one. How's Spud?'

'I'm afraid Spud's dying,' I replied.

'Hell! I'll get that bastard if I wait here a week,' growled Tug.

I returned to Spud and found him still sitting up but looking grey and his features seemed to be falling in.

'Feeling better Spud?' I asked and he smiled.

'A lot better, boy,' he replied 'remember that march to Mandalay, it was as hot as in the Sudan, I'm feeling pretty cold'.

I got some old sandbags and covered him as best I could as another spasm shook him and blood ran down his chin.

'You haven't taken my boots off, have you?' he asked.

'No Spud your boots are on your feet'

'Right, I'm going to die like a soldier, with my boots on, boots, boots, boots, moving up and down again - where are you Tommy?'

'I'm here with you Spud'.

'Feel, in my tunic pocket boy, you'll find my ribbons there'.

I picked up his ripped tunic and found the medal ribbons now sticky and stained with his blood 'Here you are Spud'.

He took them and a feeble smile lit up his face 'Got to be properly dressed when we parade for Saint Peter'.

There was a shout from Tug 'Look out, he's starting something!' and I jumped to the parapet to see a crowd of Germans coming out of Shelter Wood. They started to advance slowly and then broke into a run. 'Hold your fire,' I ordered my section and just then a heavy burst of machine gun fire burst out from the flank and swept the enemy ranks away. One of the Koyli's (Kings Own Yorkshire Light Infantry) beside me swore 'Aw hell, I want a crack at them,' and he squinted along his rifle and fired. Suddenly he yelped and fell into the trench and I saw the blood on his shoulder. Tug squinted round 'That shot came from the bloke I'm after, he's by the Crucifix all right'

'Can't you get him Tug?'

'I'll get him,' growled Tug 'but you blokes keep your nuts down'.

I made my way back to Spud, but Spud was dead, still propped up against the sandbags facing the enemy, his service ribbons clenched in his hand and old sacking wrapped around him.

I suddenly felt horribly deflated and very much alone, one after another the boys were going, how much longer, Oh God how much longer?

I sat beside Spud and scribbled a report for Captain Ethridge. A report about how Spud had brought a wounded officer in at the cost of his own life and I got one of the Fusiliers to sign it under my name.

'Find Captain Ethridge and give him that paper,' I ordered.

'Where will I find him Corporal?'

'God knows, but inquire along the trench until you do,' I retorted.

One of the Koyli's came up to me. 'My pals comfy Corporal, nice blighty one through the shoulder, and by the way, that officer bloke has snuffed it'.

I had been so busy with poor old Spud I hadn't given a thought to the officer he had dragged out of danger.

'Where is he?' I asked. The Koyli pointed to a bend in the trench 'Just round there, we couldn't do anything for him'.

I went round the bay and there he lay on a German overcoat, a fair-haired youngster who should still have been at school.

His wounds were ghastly, one hip was smashed to pulp, his privates were shattered and part of his stomach lay open, no wonder he moaned and shrieked while waiting to die. I left him and I was sick in a corner of the trench when Captain Ethridge came along.

'I got your message Corporal,' he said looking at me keenly 'here sit down, steady old chap, have a drop of this rum and a fag with me, and tell me about it'. I took a swig of his rum and as we sat and smoked I told him how Spud had behaved.

'And it was no use sir, the officer has died,' I finished brokenly.

He left me to have a look at the dead officer and when he returned his face was grave 'That was 2nd Lieutenant Fitzmaurice of my regiment,' he said 'What a mess he's in, now where is the chap who brought him in?'

Sadly I took him to where Spud still sat and Captain Ethridge stood for a moment looking at the old soldier and then his hand went to his helmet in a salute of respect.

'Put them together Corporal and I'll see if I can arrange for them to be buried together, your report will go forward to headquarters. What men have you got left here?'

'Five men and myself sir, two killed and one wounded'

'Right, I'll send you four more men and a lewis gun, you need a lewis in this position, we're waiting for the flanks to line up with us and then I believe we are having a go at Shelter Wood'.

I stared after him as he moved away, Shelter Wood next, we had done everything asked of us and still they were shouting for more, never mind the losses - forward - forward!

Spud and the officer were gently laid side by side in the entrance of a dugout and I turned back to my duty with weary eyes.

I pulled myself up beside Tug, without moving Tug muttered 'Be careful, this bastards isn't missing much!'

'Spud's gone West, Tug,' I told him and I saw his eyes harden.

'Poor old Spud,' he whispered 'now there's only you and me left Tommy!'

I didn't reply for a minute and then I said 'How's this job going?'

'I've seen his rifle flash twice, you'll notice the sun is making a shadow there now, but I haven't got a shot at him yet, I will'.

An aircraft approached high overhead with shrapnel bursting around it and as I turned to watch it a bullet smacked into a sandbag beside me knocking sand into my face. 'That's him,' growled Tug 'Get to hell out of this Tommy, you're only a bloody target for that chap'.

I dropped back into the trench and met the four West Kents who had arrived with lewis gun and ammunition and told them to find a firing position to cover our right flank. I came across the sack containing the bread and decided to break it into chunks and issue it to the men, and as I was doing so Tug's rifle cracked out viciously. 'Got him!' yelled Tug 'Got him! And the lousy bastard's got me, help me down someone'. We lifted him down from the parapet where he had lain so long behind the tree trunk and found the snipers bullet had entered the shoulder and come out near the elbow, a nasty would but it could have been worse. He winced with pain and gloried in the fact that he had got his twenty fifth German that day.

'Have a squint over Corporal,' he exclaimed 'he rolled over when I hit him, we must have fired together'.

I peered carefully over in the direction of the Crucifix and there lay the outstretched field grey figure at its base.

'Spud will have company to the pearly gates,' I muttered.

The enemy had mortars in Shelter Wood and they now directed their fire on us, adding to the unearthly din of shellfire and machine guns. A couple of chaps staggered down the trench with a dixie of hot soup, God knows where it came from but we were ready for it. I told Tug and the Koyli, the wounded men with me, that they could please themselves what they did; they were both walking cases so they could take a chance and go back now or wait for darkness. They looked at the shells crashing to the rear and decided to wait so I told them to get into the dugout where Spud and the officer were lying. A Lieutenant Morley and Sergeant Rees came along to join us, I knew Sergeant Rees, he was a B company man, but the officer was new to me. However they were my own unit and I was pleased to see them.

'How are you managing Corporal?' asked Sergeant Rees and I shrugged my shoulders. 'I'm the last of my section Sergeant, these men are strays'.

'All right Corporal, keep them in hand, we're moving forward again soon'.

'Any of the old battalion along the trench?' I asked him.

'Yes they're still in action but all the regiments are mixed up now,' replied Lieutenant Morley 'can't do anything about it at present; I see you have a lewis gun here'.

'Yes Sir, West Kents'.

'Good, get them to watch Fricourt'.

'I've already seen to that sir,' I replied wearily.

'Right, well come on Sergeant,' said Lieutenant Morley 'and be ready to move forward Corporal when the time comes'.

The Tyneside Scot looked at their backs and grunted 'Forward be damned, its about time we were relieved and got back to hell out of this'.

'You heard what he said,' I replied 'so pipe down'.

But in my heart I knew the chap was right, the advance units in the attack had been torn to ribbons and the remnants were weary and disheartened at their losses; surely the army command must know.

It was late in the afternoon when the order came to advance and as we stumbled forward once more I passed Tug's victim lying stretched out by the Crucifix, face up to the sky. Tug's bullet had got him just over the right eye and he was very, very dead. If this was the bloke who shot poor old

Spud I could have almost wished him still alive so that I could have done the job myself. I looked at the dead German and I looked at the bullet chipped figure hanging above me on the cross, and as men have had reason to do through the ages, I wondered!

Then forward I went into the fury of the firing, but I only had strangers to keep my company. Shelter Wood, Shelter Wood standing ahead of us dark and sombre looking and for some reason our own artillery was not firing at it. There was something wrong here! The enemy fire increased and men were falling in increasing numbers. The Tyneside Scot went down, then the Koyli and one of the Lancashire boys went together, one of the West Kents fell on his face and the rest of my little section dived into a shell hole for cover. The same thing was happening everywhere and the advance was pinned down by intense fire that made further advance impossible. We were forty yards from Shelter Wood, which appeared to be swarming with enemy troops, and we lay in our shell holes and sniped away at them while behind us hundreds of khaki figures lay sprawled on the ground, mute evidence of our futile attempt.

Soon the sun set in a red blaze of glory and with the coming of darkness some of the tenseness eased from us although bullets still swept the area and the guns boomed and shells crashed and every man crouched in his hole in the ground and waited.

> *I see across the shrapnel seeded meadows*
> *The jagged rubble heap of La Boiselle -*
> *Blood guilty Fricourt brooding in the shadows*
> *And Thiepvals Chateau empty as a shell.*
> *Down Albert's riven streets the moon is leering -*
> *The Hanging Virgin takes its bitter ray,*
> *And all the road from Hamel I am hearing*
> *The echo of Death's Trumpets over Bray.*
>
> *Oh, spacious days of glory and of grieving*
> *Oh, sounding hours of lustre and of loss.*
> *Let us be glad we lived you - still believing*
> *The God who made the cannon - made the Cross!*

My lewis gunner was hit and killed in the darkness, just one of those bullets that came from anywhere and landed anywhere, and as the night dragged on I lay and dozed fitfully for odd minutes at a stretch. My thoughts were not on the enemy prowling in Shelter Wood, they were with the comrades I had left by the wayside, Lieutenant Stuart Walker, Corporal Cowley, Nobby Clark, Dusty Miller, Sergeant Brodwick, Paddy Finnigan, Jacky Barrett, Tommy Lowery, Spud Baker, and the others wounded and gone, perhaps to recover, perhaps not.

My head was weary as I lay stretched on the ground in the shell hole and gazed at the stars overhead, what was it all for, when would it all end? The spirits of the thousands dead seemed to whisper on the cool breeze that blew over that stricken battlefield, according to later reports that bitter day of fighting cost us 60,000 men and it cost the enemy 40,000 men and there would be sad hearts beating somewhere in 100,000 homes.

Twice during the night we beat back enemy attempts to drive us out of our positions, and in the early hours word came that relief was on its way to us. Then just before dawn all hell broke loose, the enemy artillery away on our left flank opened out on us and shells came crashing down where we lay in front of Shelter Wood. We crouched and waited while shrapnel howled and splinters of shells tore men apart 'Oh my God, hurry up that relief,' someone moaned.

And then it happened, a direct hit on my shell hole, my head seemed to be filled with the thunder of the blast and I felt as though a giants hammer had hit me, a brilliant white flash and then I knew no more. How long I was out I don't know but when I recovered I opened my eyes to candlelight and heard the tap-tap of a signals set working in morse. I stirred and someone bent over me 'How do you feel now old man?'

'Bloody awful,' I moaned 'where am I?'

'Battalion Headquarters, here have a drink of char'.

Then, as I made to reach for the mug I found my right hand was tied up in a mass of bandages so I tried the left hand and found it worked.

'Your mitts in a bit of a mess,' said the chap who handed me the tea, 'And you've got a smack on the nut, your forehead was bleeding, but you're all right boy, Blighty next week'.

'What part of the line is this,' I asked him.

'This is the old German front line, and we are the Middlesex, you're halfway home already, now shut up and go to sleep'.

I lay with closed eyes and throbbing head, feeling sick and weary, listening to the thud of guns hammering away at the enemy and the crash of shells that shook the dugout where I lay, and I must have dozed off to sleep. I felt someone gently shake me and I opened my eyes to see a Sergeant of the Middlesex Regiment beside me.

'You feeling all right son?' he inquired and I grinned and nodded my head.

'Right, well we're moving forward out of this, so you can either stay here a bit or try to make your way back,' he said 'here's a mug of tea and some bully and bread and I'll leave you a couple of candles. If I was you I'd get to hell out of this but please yourself'.

The signaller had packed up his kit and as he moved out he said 'Blighty for you chum, here's a couple of fags, so long'.

'Good luck,' I replied and I was alone in the dugout.

I stuck it for a time, and then the loneliness got the better of me. I had visions of a direct hit and the dugout crashing on top of me, buried alive and no one the wiser! To hell with this. I climbed to my feet and mounted the dugout steps for the open air of the trench where troops were bustling along loaded with gear and ammunition. 'Where's the dressing station chum?' I asked a sweating Tommy as he passed me. He jerked a thumb towards the old British line 'Only one I know of is back there,' he replied. A Tommy, sitting smoking on the fire step, his shoulder tied up with blood stained bandages grinned at me.

'You going to chance it pal?' he asked.

'Yes,' I replied 'I want to get to hell out of this'.

He stood up 'right, we'll go back together,' he said.

We helped each other over the parapet and headed across the original No Mans Land, strewn with the sorry harvest of the British advance, dead men lay thick everywhere and shell holes were full of khaki figures, wounded men who couldn't walk; and still the enemy shells crashed around and stray bullets whipped through the air.

'You think we'll make it pal?' asked my companion as we picked our way along.

'I hope so,' I replied looking at him.

He was pale and trembling slightly and fear showed in his face, a fear that he might be hit again and left among those piles of dead.

And I felt the same fear in myself as we hurried along.

At long last we reached the old British front line and willing hands helped us into the trench where we sat down exhausted, and in the trench I saw Lieutenant Ely of my own regiment having his foot bandaged up with field dressings.

'What have you got, Corporal?' he asked looking at my club like bandaged hand and my bandaged head.

I grinned at him 'I'm afraid I don't know sir,' I replied 'this is how I found myself done up when I came round, heads not so bad but my hand is giving me hell'.

He looked at the hand bandages stained red 'Its still bleeding,' he said 'you'd better keep it up, tuck it in your tunic'.

'Where's the battalion sir?' I asked him.

'We were relieved at Shelter Wood and they're back here now,' he replied.

'I got this one in the foot but managed to stick with them until they got sorted out a bit, Jerry chewed us up somewhat'.

I nodded my head 'We had a lot of men hit,' I replied.

'Ten officers killed,' he said softly 'and 450 other ranks, there's more than half the battalion lying out there Corporal'.

'Well, you've got a Blighty one sir,' I said pointing to his foot.

He shook his head slowly 'Not yet Corporal, when this chap finishes tying that up I'm rejoining the boys, you see there are no officers left with them and very few N.C.O.'s. Can't leave it all to you N.C.O.'s you know'.

Later I saw his name in the papers, killed in action. [2]

A stretcher party staggered along the trench with their groaning burden and I asked the chap with a Red Cross on his arm 'Where's the dressing station chum?'

'In the reserve trench,' he replied, wiping the sweat from his face 'you hurt bad mate?'

'I don't know, I haven't seen it,' I replied 'but I seem to be losing a bit of blood from this hand'.

He looked at the blood soaked bandages and nodded 'You'd better follow us mate, we're heading for the dressing station'.

It was slow work following that stretcher along the crowded trenches, fit men going in, broken men coming out, and the God of war trampling and breaking and blasting whichever way you turned. The trench where the dressing station dugout was situated was packed to overflowing, stretcher cases lay everywhere and bandaged men, both British and German, were packed together awaiting their turn to enter the large dugout where doctors and orderlies sweated it out in appalling conditions trying to hold back the hand of death.

'Looks like we might wait here a bloody week,' grumbled a Corporal of the Kings Royal Rifles with his arm in a bandolier sling 'why the hell don't they attend to us and to hell with the Jerry's'.

'I suppose we'll have to take our turn,' I said wearily.

'While the bloody square heads get attended to, to hell with that,' retorted the rifleman 'Up where we advanced these bloody wounded square heads picked up rifles and fired into our backs after we passed them, dozens of blokes shot in the back'.

'The dirty bastards!' growled a Black Watch soldier with a bandaged head and leg 'What did you do about it mate?'

'Didn't leave any more wounded Jerry's, killed the swine as we went along'.

After an hours wait I got fed up and said 'To hell with this racket, I'm going back, anyone coming?'

'Where are you going mate?' asked the rifleman.

'Anywhere out of these bloody trenches,' I replied 'back to Albert or Méaulte or Corbie, somewhere to find a doctor'.

'I'm coming with you,' said the rifleman 'what about you Jock?'.

The Black Watch man pointed to his bandaged leg 'I can no walk chum'.

---

[2] Captain Denis Herbert James Ely died 1st July 1916. Thiepval Memorial Pier and Face 14A and 15C.

We set off down the trench, the two of us, and soon found it was hard going, the trench was packed with laden troops making their way up to the slaughter we were leaving behind.

'What about over the top chum,' said the rifleman.

'Right, we'll chance it,' I replied and we climbed out of the trench and headed for the back area, bullets whizzed past us but we made better time and on reaching Becordel-Becourt where the trenches started we sat down to rest and have a smoke, watching the troops marching up the road and entering the trenches.

A Corporal with an M.P. armband came over to us 'What are you two chaps doing?'

The rifleman looked at him 'Just enjoying the sunshine, copper,' he said.

'Where do you think you're going?' asked the military policeman.

'Just as far away from this bloody place as we can get, compree?'

'You can't go back without a permit, nobody is allowed back!'

'Is that so?' retorted the rifleman, drawing a bloody bandaged arm out of its sling 'Well there's my bloody permit see, and the same applies to my mate here, we've done our job of fighting copper, now why the hell don't you join those boys going up the line and have a go at Jerry yourself instead of scrounging in a trench 3 miles behind the fighting, you can go to hell copper, we don't like you'.

A big chap walked across to where we were sitting, his company was waiting its turn to enter the trenches, and I saw from his shoulder badges he belonged to the Irish Guards. He looked at me 'you been wounded chum, and on your way out eh?'

'That's right,' I replied.

He pointed to my steel helmet strung by the chinstrap to the left shoulder strap of my tunic.

'You won't be needing that tin hat anymore will you now?' he asked.

'What are you getting at?'

'We packed up in a rush and I couldn't find my tin hat, I don't fancy going into this bloody lot without one, what about it chum?'

'Take the bloody thing and welcome,' I replied and he grinned as he unbuttoned my shoulder strap 'That's your good deed for today,' he said.

'Have you got a woollen cap comforter?' I asked him, and he dived into his haversack and handed me the grey woollen comforter.

'Level swap mate, and thanks,' he said.

'Look here, you can't go swapping Government property around like that!' said the M.P. who had been watching us.

The Guardsman pulled himself up 'Just you try and stop us and see what happens,' he said viciously and the M.P. tramped away.

'What's it like up there?' asked the Guardsman.

'You'll bloody soon find out,' replied the rifleman 'Anyway good luck'.

'Do you want that comforter on?' asked the Guardsman 'the sun is pretty hot - here, I'll roll it for you'.

He rolled it like a turban and put it on my head 'Got your cap badge?' I fumbled in my tunic pocket and pulled out my badge, which he fixed in the front of the comforter.

'There,' he said 'You look like a bloody Cossack, so long mate'.

'Come on chum lets start hoofing it,' said the rifleman and we tramped along the road toward Méaulte, feeling sick and weary and stopping many times to rest by the roadside.

It was late in the afternoon when a horse drawn artillery wagon picked us up and carried us to the casualty clearing station beyond Méaulte and I only had a dim recollection of a cluster of big tents when I passed out and knew no more.

I woke up to find an orderly beside me with a mug of hot tea 'How do you feel this morning chum, here's a mug of char for you'. I drank the tea gratefully and saw I was lying in the open on a pile of straw with a blanket over me, and around me lay hundreds of others. 'Have I been here all night?' I asked the orderly.

He nodded his head 'the tents are packed with stretcher cases, arms and legs off, belly and chest wounds, bloody awful,' he replied.

'When will I see a doctor?' I asked him and he shook his head.

'You're going back to Corbie, the doctors here are about beat handling the bad cases'.

I lit my last cigarette and lay smoking moodily while my head throbbed and my arm gave me hell, I looked at the bandages on my hand and saw a blood soaked pulp. This was July 3rd and I had been wounded on the night of July 1st, that period without proper attention didn't seem too good to me.

'Give me a draw chum,' a voice said hoarsely and I looked round at the chap beside me his face heavily bandaged, only one eye and his mouth showing. I handed the cigarette over and he drew on it eagerly 'Thanks chum,' he said and handed it back 'Shrapnel got me, I've lost a bloody eye, Norfolk Regiment. Wonder how long we're going to be left here, hundreds here and hundreds more coming'.

'They reckon we're going back to Corbie,' I replied.

I must have dozed off to sleep again and I opened my eyes to hear someone say 'One load for Corbie', I threw aside my blanket and got to my feet to see a horse drawn transport beside me. I scrambled on board with a crowd of other chaps and soon we were on our way and arrived at Corbie casualty clearing station. This was much bigger than Méaulte but it also was packed with wounded and again we had to be bedded down outside the tents, thank the lord it didn't rain. We got hot soup and tea and an orderly issued us with cigarettes and we settled down to wait. Late afternoon and I was startled out a doze by hearing an English female voice say 'What about this one orderly?' The first female voice speaking in English I had heard for twelve moths, it sounded good.

I opened my eyes and found a nursing sister looking down at me 'Can you sit up while we see your dressings?'.

I sat up and the dressing was removed from my head 'Good, that's doing fine, clean it up orderly and fix a new dressing. Now lets have a look at that hand'.

She tried to unwind the bandages on my hand but the blood had clotted solid and she said 'What's the wound like, when did you get hit?'

'Haven't seen it sister,' I replied ' I was hit in a shell hole up by Shelter Wood and someone must have bandaged me up and got me back, the night of July 1st.

'And it hasn't been uncovered since, how did you get here?'

'Walked most of the way'.

'You poor boy, orderly take him to Doctor Shaw at once!'

We walked slowly over to a large tent and I sat down with a batch of bandaged men, by now I felt just about all in, but I was still conscious of the burdens being carried out of that tent, some completely covered by an army blanket, and many with missing limbs. When my turn came I entered the big tent to find inside a number of white-coated figures working at various tables and the smell of blood and antiseptics was rather over-powering. I was handed over to a black bearded figure in a white coat, he looked more like an artist than a doctor and he talked as he worked on me. He gave me an injection and then directed his nurses to remove the bandages 'And how far at the front did you manage to get son?' he asked.

'Shelter Wood sir', I replied, groaning at the agony that was my hand.

'My word you were well up in the thick of it, they are still fighting for that place, steady sister, it's not coming easy'.

The agony seemed to be unending and sweat rolled down my face. I had a dim view of my exposed discoloured hand being plunged into a bowl of liquid, it felt like liquid fire, and then I passed out.

When I came round I was laid out on a bunk and the clatter of wheels told me I was on a train, my head was swathed in bandages and felt a lot easier and a chap with a red cross on his arm grinned at me and said 'How do you feel now, fancy a cup of char?'. I sat up in the bunk and replied 'I could do with a drink, where are we heading for now?' He handed me a cup of strong tea, 'We'll be in Rouen shortly chum, then its hospital for you'. Soon the train slowed down and stopped and orderlies got busy getting us disembarked. Stretcher cases were carried away and walking cases like myself hung around awaiting further orders. An R.A.M.C. officer hurried over to me 'Name, rank, regiment, nature of wounds?' he barked at me and as I gave him the details he wrote them down on a label which he tied to a button on my tunic. A Sergeant took charge of a crowd of us 'Come on boys, get on that train over on that other platform'. We climbed aboard once more and soon we were off, to arrive at dusk at Le Havre docks. 'Walking cases up this gang-way,' someone shouted and we shuffled along the dockside to the gangway of the ship with the huge Red Cross painted on its side. Wearily I leaned on the rail and watched the busy scene on the dock as the wounded were herded on board and suddenly it came home to me, for me it was all over and I was on my way back to Blighty and I looked at the dark shadow that was France and my thoughts were back with the boys who were staying behind at Loos, and Armentieres and on the Somme.

Soon the hospital ship was on its way out into the darkness of the open sea, and still I stood by the rail and wondered if I was as contented as I should be to be returning home. Everything I possessed was gone, my rifle, my equipment, all I had was my dirty bloodstained uniform and a few cigarettes.

6.   BACK TO BLIGHTY

As dawn broke over the sea we could dimly see the outlines of England and soon we were steaming up the approaches to Southampton harbour and we saw the flags run up on the rigging of a training ship and heard faintly across the water the cheers of the boys to welcome us home.

Soon the ship was berthed and we stepped ashore to find tea and meat sandwiches ready for us, issued by smiling girls in strange uniforms, and it wasn't long before an officer collected about twenty of us and saw us on board a train bound for Cheltenham in Gloucestershire.

It was a slow weary journey during which I saw the blood was once more soaking through my bandages, so I decided to sleep most of the way and sometime during the afternoon I was awakened and told we had arrived. On Cheltenham station people looked at us with wide eyes. I suppose we must have looked pretty ghastly, and an elderly chap came up to me and held out a twenty packet of cigarettes.

'Here's some smokes for you,' he said 'just back from the front eh?'.

I took the fags but I didn't reply to his silly remark.

'My word you chaps have been knocking the stuffing out of the Germans! We've got them on the run all right now eh?'

'Don't kid yourself,' I replied 'there's hell going on over there and believe me there's a lot more to come'.

We were loaded on to a waiting bus and taken to a hospital on the outskirts of the town where we found every bed was occupied. The hospital staff did what they could but beds had to be made up for us to sleep that night on the floor, and after breakfast the next morning we were once more on our way, to arrive at last at a place called Moreton-in-Marsh where accommodation awaited us. Our dirty lousy clothing was removed and we were given hot baths, a decent meal, a suit of pyjamas and then off to bed, peace at last, peace to sleep and rest, away from the thunder of the guns and all the misery of war.

> *I stood upon the troopship deck*
> *when the job was through,*
> *And I saw the coast of England*
> *come rising through the blue.*
> *But I'm just a common soldier man*
> *God! can't you see its true?*
> *That 'home sweet home,' means more to me*
> *Than it ever meant to you!*

The sun was shining; a soft breeze was blowing through the open window of the ward bringing with it the soft rustle of leaves and the song of the birds. When I opened my eyes after a prolonged sleep and stretched myself to the forgotten comfort of a real bed with white clean sheets and a quiet that seemed unreal. No greater pleasure had ever come my way and what more could a wounded war weary soldier ask for. Added to my feeling of contentment was the low voice that greeted me with 'Come on soldier, you can't go on sleeping all day'.

I looked up into a pair of dark smiling eyes in a happy face it was good to look at and I sighed 'If you're the angel detailed to show me round I'm happy to be here'. A laugh answered me 'Where do you think you are?'.

'I know where I am,' I replied 'I've arrived in heaven and I'm satisfied with everything I see'.

Another laugh and she said 'If you can sit up I've brought you some tea and toast, don't you feel like it?'

I sat up in the bed 'Lady, now that I've seen you I could dance round the barrack square'

'Now cut out the blarney, you're in Kitebrook Hospital and I'm the nurse in this ward; get that tea and toast, the doctor is coming this morning'.

As I drank the tea I saw the ward I was in was just a nice large sized room containing four occupied beds and I said 'Nurse, is this a military hospital?'

'No, its a V.A.D.,' she replied 'the upkeep and the nursing staff is voluntary but the sisters are from military hospitals; that hand of yours is still bleeding I see!'.

I looked at the bundle of bandages 'Yes it's been like that for a week'.

'When was it looked at last?'

'Oh, I don't know, about three days ago I think'.

She turned back the bed covering 'There's blood on your pyjamas and on the sheets. I'll have to change that and give you a sponge down'.

'You'll what!' I gasped as she started to erect screens around my bed 'Haven't you any orderlies here nurse?'

'Yes, three orderlies but they are frightfully busy at present, I can manage this job all right'.

She trotted off and left me to worry about what was coming to me, my ideas about this heavenly place were undergoing a rapid change; and when she returned with a basin of water, sponge, towels etc. she was accompanied by another nurse carrying a waterproof sheet and bed sheets. This was getting worse; they were two of a kind, only about twenty years of age and good-looking wenches.

'Right, can you get out of bed on your own?'

'Oh yes,' I replied and then I made my last appeal 'Don't you think nurse we might wait for an orderly?'

Dark eyes looked into mine 'Don't be silly, there are about fifty wounded men to see too and some a lot worse than you, we can manage you all right, come on hop out'.

I had no doubt they could manage me but I felt I would prefer the trenches again as I crawled out of bed and to my surprise I staggered and would have fallen if one of the nurses hadn't caught hold of me.

'Not so good as you thought, we won't be a moment, just sit on that chair and keep quiet'.

They stripped the sheets from the bed and spread the waterproof for me to lie on and then one of them removed my pyjama jacket and they laid me on the waterproof.

I knew now how a chap felt when he stood on the scaffold awaiting the hangman to do his stuff; had I been a bit older or had the two nurses been older perhaps I wouldn't have minded so much. Anyway there was no escape so I shut my eyes and said to myself 'to hell with it, let them get on with the job'.

They sponged my chest and turned me over to sponge my back, then the upper half of my body was covered and they sponged my legs. Clean pyjamas were pulled on I was helped off the bed and clean sheets were spread. Then they helped me back into bed and rolled cotton wool and more bandages around my hand.

'How do you feel now?' asked the ward nurse as they folded away the screens.

'I feel just fine,' I replied with relief that the sponging business hadn't been carried too far 'what about the ham and eggs?'

'Sorry,' she replied 'no breakfast for you until after the doctors visit'.

'Aw have a heart nurse, I'm famished,' I moaned.

'Nothing doing soldier, Sister O'Brien was very definite, a cup of tea and a piece of toast'.

'And who's taking my name in vain this fine morning?' exclaimed a figure in grey nursing uniform at the door 'have you cleaned up this patient nurse Ranston?'

'Yes sister, he's ready for the doctor'.

'Good,' a pair of steel blue eyes glinted at me through glasses, eyes that would have bored a hole through the side of a warship.

'Young man we'll soon have you on top of the world again'.

'I'm there already sister,' I replied trying to catch nurse Ranston's eye. But that piece of charm had been at the nursing business long enough to be looking elsewhere and moving into top gear with a duster. Sister O'Brien was a thin middle aged type who had left her girlish curves behind her but she knew her job backwards. She looked a hard woman with her tight lips and gimlet eyes but I found out she was only hard where there was just reason.

'Get that table alongside the bed and lay his arm on it, put the screens around the bed, bring nurse Wharton and nurse Heslop along here and the usual in bandages, swabs, wool and water,' she ordered briskly, and as nurse Ranston hastened to obey, the gimlet eyes turned on me and the thin lips smiled 'Don't worry son, the doctors on his way here to attend to that hand of yours, he's a civilian and a good doctor'.

The sister and three nurses had everything ready when the doctor walked in carrying his bag of tricks and a white coat over his arm.

'So this is the youngster you mentioned sister,' he said eyeing me keenly as he put on the white coat 'what have you got in that bundle of bandages my lad?'

'It was a hand once,' I replied 'but I haven't seen it for a bit'.

'How old are you?' he asked as he started fiddling with the bandages and I noticed the nurses take up strategic positions around the bed.

'I'm nineteen sir,' I replied.

'And how long were you in France?'

'Twelve months,' I replied with a yelp as he cut through some clotted bandage.

'Bound to hurt a bit but you'll be the better afterwards,' said Sister O'Brien 'He's our youngest patient doctor'.

The doctor grunted 'Good lord I should think so, any younger than this and they'll have school boys when they arrive'.

I was beginning to lose interest in their talk; my whole world was taken up in the agony of my hand and arm. Sweat started to drip down my face and I felt a firm grip on my left arm and a weight on each of my legs. I groaned as pain shot up to my shoulder and I heard a voice whisper in my ear 'Stick it soldier, we're proud of you'.

I looked up to see a pair of dark smiling eyes and then I drifted away. I think it was pain that brought me round again and when I opened my eyes I knew the torture of the bandages was over. My hand lay like a lump of purple clay on the table and the doctor and sister were bending over it.

'Piece of something gone through the thumb but its all right, it missed the bone,' muttered the doctor 'this isn't a finger, its just pulp, can't do anything with that, you'll notice sister the whole hand is septic and its damned bad. I'm afraid he'll be without a hand'.

'I don't agree with that doctor,' answered Sister O'Brien 'take that finger off and give us a chance to save his hand'.

'Look woman, its nearly up to his elbow, you take a chance like that and the lad might lose an arm!'.

'Remove that finger doctor and we'll keep the wound open and drain it,' retorted the sister 'we might save the hand'.

'He won't thank you if his arm comes off instead of just the hand'.

'He won't thank you if his hand comes off instead of just the finger,' replied Sister O'Brien 'Don't be hasty doctor give the youngster a chance'.

The doctor shook his head 'Get him ready, I'm coming back at 5 o'clock and I'll operate on him then; I'll take the finger off sister but God help you if your chance doesn't come off'.

'God will help me doctor, and we'll pull him through!'.

I was bandaged up and the party broke up leaving nurse Ranston to tuck me up in bed and clear away the mess of dirty bandages.

'Doesn't sound so good nurse, does it?' I said as I stretched out.

'You heard them, did you?' she asked.

'Yes I heard them all right, that bloke sounds keen on chopping me up!'.

She smiled as she ran a cold sponge over my face 'No, he's not like that, whatever he does will be for the best, now what about a nice cup of tea and some buttered toast?'

'Now listen nurse, I can't live on tea and toast alone and the last meal I had was years ago, have a heart!'.

She smiled as she stood beside my bed 'I have a heart, and it aches for you but be a good boy and you'll get plenty to eat after tomorrow; I'll be back shortly'.

As she tripped away a voice said 'Don't tell me you're hungry, chum!'.

I turned my head and saw in the next bed a pair of twinkling blue eyes under a shock of ginger hair peering at me over the sheets. 'I could eat a stuffed mule, hide and all!' I replied 'what the hell is this place anyway, a hungry harem?'

Ginger laughed 'The grubs all right here chum once they get you settled down, judging by your 'harem,' remarks I take it you have weighed up the nursing staff?'

'Ours isn't so bad anyway,' I answered.

Ginger chuckled 'Hark at him 'not so bad,' and you haven't taken your blinkers off nurse Ranston since they brought you in'.

'Well you don't think I was going to improve my state of health by gazing at your ugly mug, do you?' I retorted.

'It might get you better results anyway,' replied Ginger.

'And what do you mean by that?' I asked.

'Well you're new here and I've been in residence for a month,' replied Ginger 'and I've spent most of that time trying to find a crack in the Ranston armour, and where's it got me, not anywhere, see. She's a nice wench with a heart of stone'.

'Well, at the moment I'm not interested,' I said 'but at the same time I don't think I agree with you'.

'Ah well, don't ever say I didn't give you warning,' said Ginger with a grin 'I'm telling you that our little nurse has either got ice in her bloodstream or she places a fantastic value on her virtue; go to it brother, it will be interesting to watch you perform'.

The subject of our conversation entered with a tray on which was a cup of tea and a couple of wafers of toast.

'Nothing more for you until after the doctor has been tonight,' she said.

'A strawberry for a starving elephant,' I moaned as I started on it.

'You're no elephant, you're not starving, and its not a strawberry, but its all you are allowed so make yourself happy,' she replied as she bustled around the beds 'The matron is on her rounds'.

When I had finished my snack she made me comfortable and left the ward with the tray as the matron walked in with the Sister.

'And here comes a real woman,' murmured Ginger.

'Good morning boys, I hope you are all comfortable!' boomed the matron as she swept into the ward, and I'm certain there was enough meat inside that maroon uniform to have made up four women. Her chest bulged out away ahead of her, in fact she appeared to lean backwards in order to keep herself balanced and at every movement you expected something to rip.

'This is the chap the doctor is dealing with this evening,' said Sister O'Brien and the matron breezed over to my bedside like a galleon under full sail.

'And how are you this morning, young man?'

'I'm fine thank you matron,' I replied 'but jolly hungry'.

Her smile was kindly as she said 'All right, we'll cure that after the doctor has seen you, you'll have some chicken soup before you sleep tonight and we'll start feeding you up tomorrow'.

She turned to Ginger 'and what about you Sims, how's the arm?'

Ginger grinned at her 'Better every day matron thank you'.

'Good, you'll be up in a day or two; and now keep quiet and let this boy rest, he's got a busy day ahead of him'.

They had a few words with the occupants of the other two beds; and after a talk with nurse Ranston they left us in peace.

'What couldn't I do with that!' sighed Ginger 'You can keep your young streamlined pieces for me'

'What's up with the arm Ginger?' I asked.

'Off at the elbow, the left one,' he replied.

'Get it on the Somme?'

'No, I wasn't in that, I got it at Bethune about five weeks ago'.

'Well, it doesn't seem to interfere with your love life,' I said.

'I'm making hay while the sun shines,' grinned Ginger 'Not much in that line for a common soldier before the war and not much for a discharged bloke with one arm, see? But at present I'm a ruddy wounded hero and believe me I'm out to make the most of the little darlings. What do you think of the matron?'

'She seems very nice,' I laughed 'the whole half ton of her'.

He glowered 'Trouble with you chaps is you'd sooner go chasing school kids, give me something mature, says I'.

'What's up with those blokes in the other beds?' I asked him.

'That chaps got a hole in his back, the other one has a leg off, they're not very sociable at present'.

Nurse Ranston came between our beds 'that will be enough talking from you Sims, I want this patient to go to sleep'.

'Listen nurse, when I came in here I had some cigarettes in my tunic,' I said 'where's my uniform?'

She smiled 'Where it ought to be, its in the incinerator, burnt,' she opened my bedside locker 'your cigarettes are here, want one?'

'Yes please nurse'.

'Right, here you are, I'll light it for you; only one mind you and then I want you to sleep'

'Why don't you hold his hand and croon him to sleep nurse?' said Ginger.

'That's the best thing you've said so far,' I retorted.

'If you don't shut up Sims I'll erect the screens,' said the nurse.

Sims laughed 'I bet he would like you to do just that'.

After my smoke I settled down to the comfort of the bed and soon the quiet of the place lulled me to sleep. I slept long and deep and felt wonderfully refreshed when a gentle shaking awakened me 'Come on boy, its time to go'.

I looked up to find Sister O'Brien beside my bed and nurse Ranston with an orderly wheeling in a stretcher 'We'll help you on to it'.

'I don't need that, I can walk,' I protested.

'Well, you're not going to, we'll drive you there in style,' grinned the orderly as they lifted me on to the stretcher and as we passed out of the ward I heard Ginger call out 'Bring him back alive nurse, he's worth preserving!' Good luck, chum!'.

'Tut! Tut! Keep quiet Sims!' snapped sister O'Brien.

The doctor and another man, along with two nurses, were in the room we entered and I burst out laughing as my stretcher was wheeled alongside the table. The doctor looked at me curiously 'What are you laughing at my lad?' he asked.

'This rather reminds me of the pictures in our books on 'Ancient History,' I replied. 'You remember doctor, Nero and party being carried in state by crowds of slaves'.

'All right,' said the doctor smiling, as I was lifted on to the table 'we'll soon have this little job cleaned up'.

There was a bustle of activity and as I lay looking at the ceiling nurse Ranston's face appeared above me 'Not worried are you?' she asked in a whisper.

'Are you staying on the job nurse?' I asked, and when she nodded her head I smiled at her; 'Then I have no need to worry have I? And by the way nurse, what's your name?'

'Nurse Ranston to you,' she replied, adjusting my head.

'Oh I don't mean that, I mean what's your Sunday name, what does your mother call you?'

Watching her face I saw her flush slightly, then she smiled and whispered 'My name is Ruby, Ruby Ranston, why?'

'Ruby Ranston, sounds good to me,' I replied 'and its something to hang on to when I'm drifting in the clouds'.

'When you're ready boy,' said a deep voice behind my head, and a rubber mask affair appeared in front of my face; I nodded my head and as the mask settled over my nose and mouth the voice said 'Count out aloud, and take deep breaths'.

'One, two, three, four,' I closed my eyes and feeling very very tired I knew it was time to go to sleep.

When I came back to this world I was in my own bed, back in my own ward and a cool hand was placed on my forehead. 'One thing I can give you full marks for, you're a good slow sleeper,' said nurse Ranston 'Heavens man I thought you were never coming out of it, how does it feel?'

'Great to be back with you Ruby, you can't get rid of me just like that; my hand feels as though it was in a vice, what's happened?'

'Your hands all right, just one finger gone, and please don't call me Ruby when I'm on duty'.

'But it might be ages before I see you off duty,' I protested.

'Well for goodness sake don't let the sister or the matron hear you'.

'Just as you like nurse, I'll keep it until we walk the country lanes of Gloucestershire together in the moonlight,' I replied.

'And I suppose this is the first chapter of a great romance,' came the voice of Ginger Sims from the next bed.

'Why doesn't someone gag you Sims!' exclaimed nurse Ranston as Ginger grinned at us over his blankets.

'All right Ruby darling, I'll turn my face to the wall,' said Ginger with a soft chuckle.

'Nurse to you Sims, and if I have any more of it I'll see that you are moved into the general ward,' replied nurse Ranston.

'Oh not that nurse, please, not that!' cried Ginger in dismay 'not a spot of sex appeal anywhere in that ward'.

'There's not a spot in this ward either so shut up!'

'If you could see what I can see nurse,' said Ginger with a solemn look on his face 'you wouldn't make such statements'.

She turned to me in despair 'He's just hopeless, now how do you feel about a little nourishment?'

'That would be a change for the better,' I replied 'but for goodness sake don't say tea and toast'.

'Well, what about a nice glass of milk with egg?' she asked.

'Now listen nurse,' I said severely 'orders are orders and the matron said a bowl of chicken soup!'.

'That's right nurse, I heard it,' said Ginger 'and leave the chicken in the soup, we'll see it off too!'.

'All right, if you think you can manage it, Tommy!' she said.
'And where did you get the 'Tommy,' from?' I inquired.

She laughed and pointed to the chart at the head of my bed 'Full name, rank, regimental number and religion,' she replied 'I'll be back shortly with your soup'.

As she left the ward Ginger Sims grinned at me and murmured 'Ruby and Tommy eh! Now that's what I call fast work; brother you're a man after my own heart, but watch your step!' I didn't answer I was drowsily contented.

'By the way chum,' I heard Ginger say 'that chap over there with the hole in his back says he thinks he knows you. Hi Fred, are you awake?'. A head in the far away bed turned towards us and a pair of eyes looked at me intently 'Were you on the Fricourt sector when the push started?' a North country voice asked me.

'Yes,' I replied 'but I can't place you!'.

The nurse and sister O'Brien came in with my bowl of chicken soup and they propped me up with pillows so that I could enjoy it properly. 'All right now?' asked Sister O'Brien.

'Better when I've had this sister,' I replied with a grin.

'Good, I like a hungry patient, I'll be back to see you shortly,' she said as she left the ward.

'Who's that chap over there nurse?' I asked ' he seems to think he knows me'.

'Private Fred Wake, Tyneside Scottish,' she replied.

I shook my head 'Doesn't mean anything to me'.

'Are you a Corporal?' asked Wake.

'Yes, but not in your lot'.

'Do you remember putting a dressing on the back wound of a chap in a shell hole in No Mans Land?'

My mind clicked back to July 1st. 'Good lord! Are you that bloke? I remember now,' I exclaimed.

He grinned 'Thanks Corporal, I was sure it was you, funny us landing in the same ward in Blighty eh!'.

'How's the back Fred?' I asked him and he pulled a face 'Pretty bad but it missed the spine, they're raking about in the hole for bits of buttons'.

'Your wound is doing fine Wake so don't grumble, you're a lucky man,' said nurse Ranston 'how are you getting along with the soup?'

'Its a treat nurse, a real treat,' I replied 'but I can't find any chicken in it'.

'You'll have the chicken tomorrow, Tommy'.

I finished the soup and lay back enjoying a cigarette when sister O'Brien entered the ward and along with her was the cutest piece of female beauty, done up in a uniform that seemed to be made to show off the charm of her curves. She was small and dainty, with dark hair and a happy smiling face, just the kind to make your bloodstream break into a gallop.

'This is sister Sutcliffe, night duty sister,' said Sister O'Brien. 'And if there's anything you want during the night she will see to it, this is today's operation case sister'.

I grinned at her and she smiled and said 'He looks in pretty good shape, I hope you won't give me a busy night'.

They moved around the beds and then the curtains were drawn and only one dim night-light left burning as the nurses left the ward with a cheery 'Goodnight boys'.

'Well what do you think of our little Shirley,' asked Ginger.

'Do you mean the night sister?' I said and he nodded.

'Yes,' Shirley Sutcliffe, the queen that walks the wards at night'.

'Gosh Ginger, this place is a bit breathtaking,' I replied 'is it a hospital or a beauty parlour?'

'Little Shirley takes us all like that, she's got everything, but she's a bit of a vixen,' said Ginger 'they're not all like that here, but most of them can be looked at twice; you'll see them when you get on your feet again and now go to sleep chum, and dream of your Ruby and Shirley'.

I snuggled down in my bed and dreamily thought, not of pretty nurses but of guns crashing out their salvoes of destruction and men desperately trying to push forward a few more yards and leaving behind them the pitiful bundles of khaki figures, and I drifted into sleep with a feeling of thankful peace. I woke bright and early to a cup of tea and a biscuit and after a wash I felt on top of the world and when nurse Ranston came back on duty and brought my breakfast, a boiled egg with thin bread and butter I greeted her with 'Good morning Ruby, its a lovely morning for a stroll'.

She smiled 'You're not strolling anywhere Tommy, the doctor will be round to see you'.

The doctor and sister O'Brien arrived after breakfast and the bandages were soon removed and my hand inspected. I could see the serious look on their faces and the doctor frowned and pursed his lips.

'I don't like it sister,' he exclaimed 'not one little bit, look at the veins of that arm, and feel here under the armpit, we're taking a risk with this case I tell you'.

Sister O'Brien's eyes glittered behind her glasses 'I know its septic doctor but we can beat it. I'm putting that arm in a bath and I'm detailing nurses to sit with him and work the poison out of the wound. He's young and healthy; if the wound stays open we can do it'.

The doctor shrugged his shoulders 'Carry on sister, I'll give my final word tomorrow, if its no better then I will have to take action; I admire you for what you are trying sister, but there is a limit, you understand that'.

An orderly brought a long narrow porcelain vessel containing a warm liquid and laid it in my bed, and my arm was gently laid in the liquid under the watchful eye of Sister O'Brien.

'Are you comfortable?' she asked me.

'I'm fine sister,' I replied looking up at her 'but I can't say I think much of my bed partner'.

For a moment the steel went out of her eyes and her lips twitched 'Sure and the boy's growing up, we'll make a man of you yet'.

Half a dozen nurses collected around my bed, wenches of different ages, size, and shape and they watched intently while sister O'Brien demonstrated how my arm should be massaged towards the wound of my hand 'You'll take turns of one hour each and you'll keep it up round the clock, if he goes to sleep you'll still carry on; nurse Ranston will supervise and relieve you if necessary, and I will accept no excuse for any break in this drill. I depend on you and so does this boy, don't fail us!'.

A kindly middle aged nurse started the monotonous drill and I was soon lulled into a drowsy state by the gentle stroking of her fingers on my arm. I opened my eyes hours later to the sound of soft voices and saw a young fair-haired nurse stroking my arm and staring into the bath with nurse Ranston beside her.

'What's up now nurse?' I asked.

Nurse Ranston smiled at me 'You're all right Tommy, the poison has started to drain from the wound, that's all'.

I looked in the bath and saw what looked like a dirty grey worm oozing sluggishly from my finger, and soon there were yards and yards of it and my arm bath had to be repeatedly changed. All that day and all through the night the nurses carried on with their job, and during the night sister Sutcliffe was a constant visitor. I was surprised when the doctor arrived before breakfast and entered the ward with Sister O'Brien and sister Sutcliffe.

'How are you feeling now my lad?' he asked me.

'Pretty good, doctor,' I replied.

'And so you jolly well should be,' he said 'wish I had a bunch of pretty nurses to keep me company all night, lets have a look at that arm'.

For a long time he probed and pressed and at last he stood erect and looked at sister O'Brien 'I came early sister because I felt uneasy, but damn it, you've done the trick. He's pretty well clear and out of danger, keep that bath going for another day or two and you can ease up a bit on the massage, he's going to be all right, young man you've a lot to thank the sister for'.

I looked at Sister O'Brien and I honestly think there was a trace of moisture in those eyes of hers.

'Sister,' I said solemnly 'I can't do much about it now but I'll kiss you when I get on my feet again bless you'.

She threw up her hands 'Listen to the boy, threatening me he is!' Sister Sutcliffe laughed 'What a lovely threat!'.

They left me in peace and nurse Ranston soon arrived with a cup of tea and a biscuit, a radiant look on her face.

'Isn't it great news Tommy, you'll soon be well again'.

'Of course I will Ruby,' I replied 'thoughts of that stroll down a country lane will soon have me up out of this'.

She tossed her head 'You might have lost your arm you know'.

'And he's only lost his blinkin,' heart murmured Ginger.

'You lost yours years ago, Sims!' retorted Ruby.

'I keep on losing it,' said Ginger 'but it always comes back for more'.

I lay for three weary days and nights with my arm in that bath and the only thing to break the monotony was an occasional chat with Ruby or one of the other nurses who looked after me. On the third night I was left without a nurse in attendance, and, what I had been rather expecting, happened in the still small hours. I had been asleep and must have attempted to turn over in my bed. The result being my movements upset the arm bath and I woke up to find myself soaked and the bed swimming with water.

'Hi Ginger wake up,' I called and his head poked out of the blankets 'What's up chum?' he asked.

'Ring that ruddy bell, I'm soaked,' I replied.

He reached for the bell with his good arm and peered at me in the dim night light 'Gee, you've made a bloody mess of things, little Shirley will be pleased!'.

Soon the neat little figure of sister Sutcliffe stood in the doorway.

'Who rang the bell?' she asked gazing round the room.

'Its him sister,' replied Ginger 'He's wet the bed'.

'He's what! Oh good heavens, everything's drenched, how in the world did this happen?'

'Sorry sister, I must have turned over in my sleep,' I murmured.

'Come on up you get, we'll have to change your bed, get those wet things off and wrap this blanket around you,' said the sister as she whipped a blanket off Ginger's bed 'off with those pyjamas, come on I won't bite you'. I fumbled with my left hand and let my pyjama trousers fall to the floor and she whipped the blanket around me 'That's better, now sit on that chair until I get a towel and we get your bed fixed up for you'.

She clicked away out of the ward and Ginger grinned at me and gave a wink 'I bet Shirley is laughing fit to bust after that eyeful!'

'Aw to hell Ginger, she never looked at me,' I protested.

'That's what you think!' laughed Ginger 'Her eyes were nearly coming out of their sockets, little Shirley don't miss much!'.

Two nurses came in with a load of bedding and got busy stripping my bed and making it up afresh, and sister Sutcliffe returned with a bath towel and some bandages.

'I'll do your hand up first,' she said 'and then we'll fix you up for the night, you are due to finish with that arm bath anyway but you needn't have used such drastic measures, you're a naughty boy disturbing us like this!'

'Sorry sister,' I mumbled as I watched her winding the bandage.

'Don't blame him sister,' said Ginger 'it was really your fault'.

'My fault!' Sister Sutcliffe stared at the smiling face in the bed 'What on earth are you talking about Sims?'

'Well you see sister, I happened to be awake at the time and just before the splash came I heard him say 'Oh Shirley,' and he turned over and threw his good arm around the bath, shows how your imagination can work in your sleep!'.

'Sims, you ruddy liar!' I gasped.

Sister Sutcliffe's face turned scarlet and her eyes sparkled as she said 'I think the best place for you Sims would be the military hospital in Gloucester, you're too frisky for a V.A.D.'

'Oh please sister I crave your forgiveness,' cried Ginger with a mournful look 'but you look so pretty when you're angry I just can't resist stirring you up a bit'.

'Oh keep quiet, I'll see you about this tomorrow,' said the sister, and I don't think she was as vexed as she pretended 'does that bandage feel all right?'

'Yes its fine sister, can I have a smoke?' I replied.

She shook her head and picked up the bath towel 'Not yet, stand up and drop that blanket, I've got to dry you'.

I stared at her and looked at the two nurses busy with the bed 'Aw sister, I can manage that myself,' I moaned as I rose to my feet. 'Manage nothing my lad, off with it!' and off came the blanket and she wrapped the bath towel around me, rubbing briskly at my damp body, she knew her job but she gave me an uncomfortable five minutes and I breathed a sigh of relief when I was once more in pyjamas and tucked into bed.

Before she left me Ginger got in his parting shot; 'Did you say he was finished with that arm bath sister?'

She nodded her head 'Yes, he won't need it any more'.

'Then I want to apply for it, for my arm'.

'Whatever for Sims, your arm is doing fine'.

'Ah, you don't understand, you see I could overturn it in the middle of the night, and then you would come running to give me the same treatment you've given him'.

She looked at him for a while, her pretty face rather solemn. 'And you would like that, Sims?' she said.

'Lady, I would willingly give my other arm for just that,' replied Ginger with quite a lot of feeling in his voice.

'I believe you would Sims, you're a rascal, but I believe you would,' said sister Sutcliffe 'now go to sleep and lets have no more trouble'.

As quiet reigned once more in the ward I murmured 'Ginger, I thought you said you liked them built like a battleship?'

He turned his head 'So I do brother, so I do, but I also like a change, think how grand it would be to have the matron one night and little Shirley the next, two heavenly extremes'.

Seeing that the matron would scale around sixteen stone and the sister around eight stone he was right when he talked about extremes.

'You're a queer cuss Ginger,' I said 'you'll land yourself in a heap of trouble one of these fine days'.

'I've been in and out of trouble all my blinkin,' life,' replied Ginger 'but I've never come across such sweet trouble as there is at this hospital and I'm meeting it halfway'.

'Well, its your trouble Ginger, goodnight'.

'You're not shaping so bad yourself, goodnight chum'.

The following day after dressings sister O'Brien broke the glad news that I could get out of bed and sit around in the ward, and with a dressing gown over my pyjamas and my heavily bandaged hand in a sling I was back on my feet once more.

'Don't overdo it, Tommy,' said nurse Ranston 'when you feel tired just hop back into bed'.

I looked at the bed 'I've had enough of that for a bit, nurse; when will I be able to get out into the grounds?'

'Another day or two, don't be so impatient,' she replied with a smile 'I'm getting your 'blues,' for you tomorrow'.

'Good, it will be nice to get dressed again, make sure you get me a good fit won't you?'

'I've got just your size put to one side in the store room,' she told me 'and I want you to look your best, you have a visitor tomorrow'.

I stared at her 'A visitor? What do you mean, Ruby?'.

She laughed 'Daddy is coming to see me, and he's sure to want to see my patients, he's going overseas this weekend'.

'In the army, is he?'

'Yes, he's in the Warwickshire Regiment, and my brother is in the navy,' she replied proudly, 'come and sit by the window and get some fresh air'.

As she bustled away about her duties I sat by the open window and idly glanced through the newspapers on the table beside me, the headlines hit me: 'Our gallant troops advance on the Somme,' 'Fighting against bitter resistance the British Army advances'. Nice reading I thought, when you're not mixed up in it! I turned the page and a face I knew looked up at me 'Lieutenant Colonel Fitzgerald, died of wounds, Westminster Hospital'. So they got the old boy home, but only to die![3]

My eyes ran over the list of casualties, two whole pages of the paper taken up with 'killed in action', 'died of wounds', 'missing, believed killed',

---

[3] Lieutenant Colonel A E Fitzgerald died 11th July 1916 and lies at Twyford (The Assumption) Churchyard

'wounded in action,' and I saw the names of many that I knew. Yes, the British Army was advancing, but at what a price!

At the bottom of the page 'awards for gallantry,' and I gulped as I read 'Private Herbert Baker, posthumous Distinguished Conduct Medal killed when bringing in a badly wounded officer'. Poor old Spud, another bit of coloured ribbon to show to St. Peter at the pearly gates, old soldier, old rascal, but all man! My thoughts drifted to that shattered trench, with an old man bloodstained and dying by the sandbags, his bloodstained service ribbons grasped in his hand, my eyes filled. I didn't hear her approach but I heard her voice beside me 'What is it Tommy, what's the matter?'

I looked up and saw Ruby gazing at me in concern and silently I pointed to the name in the paper.

'Did you know him, Tommy?' she asked as she read.

'I soldiered with him, right from the day I enlisted,' I replied 'and I was with him when he died - Ruby, he was true blue'.

Her arm slid round my shoulders 'Don't grieve Tommy, he died as he lived, a soldier!'.

And that, I think, was the complete answer. 'What I came to see you about was, have you written home to let your folk know where you are?' she asked me.

'Good Lord no,' I answered 'they sent a field card from a clearing station in France to say I was wounded, but I haven't tried writing with my left hand'.

'Well its time you did something about it Tommy, here's some writing paper and a pencil, have a go at it and if you can't manage I'll write it for you'.

I settled down to the task but I made heavy weather of it and when she returned I had pushed the paper and pencil aside.

'How are you getting on with it,' she asked.

'Awful,' I said showing her the scrawl. 'I can't read the stuff myself so it won't make sense to my mother'.

She pulled up a chair and sat down, picking up the pencil and selecting a clean sheet of paper.

'Now just you dictate and I'll write it for you,' she said 'and I'll sign on the bottom 'written by a friend,' because your mother will know its not your writing'.

'She'll also know my friend has delicate fingers and uses scent,' I remarked with a grin 'but that won't matter'.

I didn't find it easy to dictate my personal thoughts for someone else to put down on paper but with a struggle we got it finished and ready to post.

'Anyone else?' asked Ruby.

'No, I don't think so,' I replied with some hesitation.

She cocked a knowing eye at me 'What, no girlfriends, Tommy?'

'Well, yes, I think I should let Amy know,' I stammered, feeling a bit red in the face.

'I thought there must be someone,' said Ruby selecting another sheet of paper 'sweetheart I suppose?'

I shook my head 'No, not that Ruby, she's a girl I met just before going overseas and we've kept on writing ever since'.

'Did you like her, Tommy?'

'Oh yes, I liked her very much, she was different somehow, but I never had the chance to fall in love with her'.

'You'll see her again when you leave here I suppose?'

'I don't know, you see her home is in Norfolk and that's a long way from my home'

'All right, lets start a nice long letter to Amy,' said Ruby.

I staggered along with my dictation, but it wasn't a nice long letter, in fact it was very short and brief and Ruby looked at it with a critical eye 'Is that all? Well if a boyfriend wrote to me like that I wouldn't think much of his efforts'.

'Oh that's enough for now,' I answered her 'and have you any boyfriends Ruby?'

'Plenty,' she replied standing up 'but I'm not greatly interested, I'll get these posted for you'.

The matron and sister O'Brien paid me a visit and said they were pleased with my condition 'You'll get your hospital blues tomorrow and then you can walk in the grounds'

'I'm looking forward to that sister,' I replied.

Ginger was sitting up in bed talking to the Matron and I heard her say 'All right Sims I'll see to it myself shortly'.

After they had gone Ginger grinned across at me and said 'She's coming back to massage my shoulder'.

'What's the matter with it Ginger?'

'Oh, its stiff and aching. I'm sure the gentle touch of the matron will do it good and while that dame is busy you know what I'm going to do, I'm going to lay my head on her lily white breast!'

'Don't talk so daft, Ginger!'

'All right chum, like to make a bet on it?'

'You'll get chucked out of here you fat head!'

'Bet you twenty fags I do it!'

'You're crazy Ginger,' said Fred Wake 'She'll slaughter you'.

'Bet you the same Fred,' retorted Ginger 'and what about you Ross, you want to bet on it too?'

The chap with the leg off grinned at him 'I'm on Ginger but I'll be sorry to see you go'.

'Go where?'

'Off to some military hospital of course'.

'More likely to land in the blinking glass house,' I said.

'Right boys, the bets are on,' said Ginger 'leave the rest to me'.

Soon the matron returned carrying a towel and a jar of cream and she got Sims to sit up in bed with the pillows behind him. 'Are you quite comfy now?' she said as she sat on the edge of his bed 'Now just relax and tell me when it hurts'.

We watched with interest as she gently applied the cream to his shoulder and Ginger's blue eyes gazed at her in rapture. Then her fingers began to knead the flesh and after a few minutes Ginger let out a yelp 'Gosh! That's where it hurts matron'

'You poor boy. It will feel easier after this'.

Ginger's eyes closed and his head drooped forward, suddenly he seemed to go to pieces and his head fell forward onto the matron's ample bosom, her arm went round him and she cried out in alarm 'Heavens! The boys fainted, ring that bell quick!'

I pressed the button and nurse Ranston hurried into the ward 'A little brandy and some water nurse, he's fainted'.

Until the nurse returned Ginger remained nestled in the matron's arms and his head lay just where he wanted it to lie; a little brandy, a whiff of smelling salts and he opened his eyes with a sigh 'What's happened? Oh, matron I'm sorry,' he murmured.

'Don't worry, Sims, just rest and you'll be all right,' said the matron as they made him comfortable in bed 'Nurse will keep an eye on you, you're not very strong yet'.

When they had gone Ginger sat up in bed beaming 'Come on, me lucky lads, pay your bets'.

Sadly we parted with our precious cigarettes 'You did it Ginger,' I said 'but what about your shoulder?'

'Right as rain old boy,' he cried waving his stump 'Gosh! Did you see how she held me in her arms; it was like resting on a feather bed'.

'You're a hell of a good actor Ginger,' I replied 'but I wouldn't try that a second time if I was you'.

'Not on the matron, I won't,' he said with a sly grin 'but there's others here who might fall for it'.

The following morning I was supplied with hospital blues and a red tie. I managed to dress myself but with one hand the tie was beyond me and after breakfast I was allowed to walk around the hospital grounds accompanied by a nurse. Not nurse Ranston as I had hoped but a sweet little dumpy middle aged nurse who was good company. From the outside I saw that the hospital was a big country house with extensive grounds, wide lawns, and gravel paths and well away from the house was a huge vegetable garden and greenhouses with a number of gardeners employed to keep the place in trim and supply the kitchens. I liked everything I saw, I was going to be happy here.

After lunch I was sitting in the ward reading when the door opened and nurse Ranston bustled in with a tall man in khaki beside her 'This is my ward, daddy,' she exclaimed, and I hastily jumped to my feet as I saw the crown of a Major on his sleeve. He smiled and waved me back to my chair 'Sit down old chap'. Proudly she introduced us with 'This is my dad, Major Ranston of the Warwickshire Regiment, and these are my patients daddy'.

'Well I hope she's looking after you boys,' said the Major as he shook hands with each of us 'You certainly look comfy here'.

'No complaints sir,' said Ginger 'We're all doing fine'.

'This is the boy I wrote to you about daddy,' said nurse Ranston 'the one whose hand and arm we saved'.

He looked at me keenly 'Good work eh? You'll be pretty pleased about that I expect!'

'I'm both pleased and grateful sir,' I replied.

After a few minutes they left us and the Major left behind on the table a box of 100 cigarettes for the ward. 'There you are Tommy,' said Ginger 'Our little nurse is one of the nobs. Daddy second in command of a battalion, you'd better keep your nose clean when you mix with that lot'.

I grinned at him 'Did you know Ginger that the matron you were hugging so closely was the owner of this estate?'

He stared at me 'Who the hell told you that?'

'That little nurse who took me for a walk in the grounds'.

'Gosh! And I though she was just a woman!'

'So she is Ginger, but she's a big woman with a big purse'.

I was feeling a bit weary so I crawled into bed for the rest of the day but I was very contented with my lot.

> *We've billiards, bowls an,' tennis courts;*
> *we've teas an,' motor rides;*
> *an,' 'eaps o,' things besides;*
> *We've all the best of everything,*
> *As much as we can eat*
> *But my 'eart, my 'earts at 'ome in Bently Street*
>
> *I'm askin,' sister every day*
> *when I'll be fit to go;*
> *'We must 'ave used you bad,' she says,*
> *'You want to leave us so';*
> *I says 'I beg your pardon now,*
> *This place is hard to beat,*
> *But my 'eart, my 'earts at 'ome in Bently Street*
>
> *The chiffonier we saved to buy,*
> *the clock upon the wall,*
> *The pictures an,' the almanac,*

the china dogs an,' all,
I've thought about it many a time.
my little 'ome complete,
When in Flanders far away, from Bently Street

There's several things I sometimes want
which 'ere I never see,
I'd like some chipped potatoes
an,' a kipper for my tea;
An,' most of all I'd like to feel
the stones beneath my feet,
Of the road that takes me, back to Bently Street

They'll 'ave a little flag 'ung out,
they'll 'ave the parlour gay;
With crinkled paper 'ung about
the same as Christmas Day;
An,' out of all the neighbours doors
the 'eads will pop an,' greet
Me coming back there wounded, 'ome to Bently Street

My missus, she'll cry a bit
an,' laugh a bit between;
My kids'll climb upon my knees
there's one I've never seen;
An,' of all the days that I 'ave known
there won't be one so sweet
As the day when I go 'ome, 'ome to Bently Street

The following day sister O'Brien informed me, after inspecting my hand, that I was at liberty to wander beyond the grounds if I felt like it 'But don't overdo it for a day or two'. A couple of letters arrived from home, one containing a postal order from my mother, and another from Amy, full of joy that I was back in England once more. I spent the morning wandering around the grounds on my own and after lunch I had just settled down to a book when nurse Ranston approached me with rather a reproachful look.

'There's someone called to see you,' she informed me.

I stared at her 'To see me! Who is it?'

'I'm sure I don't know, but she certainly asked for you, she's waiting in the entrance hall'

'She, but I don't know anyone around here nurse!'

'Well it's a young lady, and she seems to know you, she's come from Moreton-in-Marsh to see you'.

I shook my head 'I don't know anyone in Moreton-in-Marsh, never heard of the place until I arrived here'.

Ginger was sitting up in bed with a wide grin on his face 'A young lady to see you! Oh boy, if I had a hat on I would raise it to you. At last I've met my master; I always thought I was a fast worker but you've got me licked. A young lady from Moreton and you've never been in the damned place. How the hell do you do it chum?'.

I was perplexed 'Aw shut up Ginger, it's a mystery to me'.

'Well you'd better go down and solve it,' said nurse Ranston firmly 'The young lady is awaiting your pleasure'.

I made my way down the wide staircase wondering what it was all about, it must be a mistake, this was the heart of Gloucestershire and I didn't know a soul within hundreds of miles.

A fair haired young lady rose from a chair in the hall greeted me with a smile and mentioned my name and regiment.

'Yes, that's right,' I replied 'but I'm afraid I don't understand, I don't know you and you can't know me'.

She laughed 'Did you know a Sergeant Coxhill in your battalion?'

'Sergeant Coxhill? Oh yes, he was on the transport at battalion headquarters,' I replied.

'That's my father,' she informed me smiling.

'But how did you know I was here?' I asked her.

'My brother works in the post office and when he saw a letter addressed to someone here who was in the same battalion as dad he rushed home to tell mum about it,' she explained 'Mum wouldn't come so she passed the job on to me, and she sent you this parcel'.

I accepted the parcel and smiled as I said 'I'm beginning to see daylight now, perhaps we had better walk in the grounds'.

As we strolled through the grounds she fired questions at me about her father but I couldn't tell her much. I didn't know him at all well because he was on the headquarters staff.

'And your name?' I asked her.

'My name is Flo, Flo Coxhill,' she replied 'I'm so pleased now that I came to see you, I didn't know what to expect'.

I smiled 'Its nice meeting you Flo, and I hope I'll see you again'.

'Oh yes, you must,' she said 'Mum wants to meet you so perhaps you'll come to tea?'

'I'd like that,' I replied 'but not for a day or two yet, how far is it to Moreton?'

'Three miles from here, say when and I'll meet you here'.

'We'll fix on Saturday after lunch, if that suits,' I suggested.

'That will be lovely,' she replied with an arch look under her picture hat and a pretty smile 'you and I are going to be friends'.

'I hope so Flo,' I replied as we reached the main gates.

'Won't you come with me down the road a bit?' she asked.

'I would like to but I'm afraid I can't at present,' I answered 'not long out of bed you know'.

She glanced at my arm in its sling 'Oh dear, I was forgetting you had been wounded, well don't forget, I'll be here at one o'clock on Saturday,' and with a wave of her gloved hand she was gone.

I wandered back through the hospital grounds in a thoughtful mood. I could see things getting a bit complicated if I didn't watch my step, Amy at home, Ruby in the ward, and now Flo. This Flo was smart and pretty and instinct told me that she liked what she had seen of me, well I liked what I had seen of her, but there was something there that didn't line up with Amy and Ruby. I couldn't quite place it and by the time I reached my ward I put it out of my mind with the usual soldiers outlook - live for today and to hell with tomorrow!

'Well?' said Ginger as I opened the parcel to disclose a box of sweets and a packet of cigarettes 'are you the father of her child?'

'Don't talk rot, Ginger, I never set eyes on the girl before,' I replied.

'Then how the hell did she know of you?' asked Fred.

'Her dad was in my battalion, that's all,' I replied.

'What's she like Tommy?' asked Ginger.

'Oh she's young, she's got a figure, she's fair, and she's got a pretty smile, her name is Flo,' I informed them.

'Is she coming again?'

'Yes, she's taking me out to tea on Saturday,' I answered.

Ginger rolled his eyes 'Will you do me a favour Tommy?'

'What do you want now?'

'We are likely to be here together for a month or two,' replied Ginger 'please teach me some lessons on how you operate!'.

Nurse Ranston came in to attend to Ross and she looked at me with a question in her eyes 'Who's the mystery lady Tommy?'

'His sins have found him out nurse,' burst in Ginger 'the poor girls been waiting for him returning from France'.

'That's a lot of tripe,' I exclaimed 'her father is in my battalion and she called to inquire about him, that's all'.

'But how on earth did she know about you?' inquired Ruby.

'Letters at the post office where her brother works,' I replied 'her dad is a Sergeant in my battalion'.

'She's rather pretty isn't she?'

I was getting a bit hot under the collar 'Oh I suppose she is but lets forget about her, when are you off duty Ruby?'

'She was only a Sergeants daughter,' sang Ginger and he ducked his head as I flung a book at him.

'That will do, no more rough stuff,' said nurse Ranston firmly, and then quietly she said 'at seven tonight, why?'

'At seven tonight I'll feel like a stroll down the road away from here, but I'm fed up with my own company'.

She smiled 'I always have a walk before retiring, I might see you if you're wandering around'.

I felt like climbing up the wall 'I won't be wandering, I'll be at the main gates at seven o'clock, here, have some of Flo's chocolates!' she laughed and was gone.

'Don't forget we lock up at nine o'clock,' chuckled Ginger.

I lingered at the main gate for half an hour, kicking the gravel and wondering if I was making a fool of myself but at about seven thirty she came down the drive and greeted me with a smile that was worth waiting for 'Goodness, I though you were never coming Ruby'.

'Sorry Tommy, I couldn't get away, which way are you going?'

'Lets go towards Moreton-in-Marsh,' I suggested.

She laughed 'We might meet your Flo that way'.

'I don't care if we meet the Queen of England Ruby, lets go'.

'Its nice to get away from the wards for a bit,' she remarked.

'Its nice to get away from blokes who listen to every word,' I replied.

'Tell me what made you join the army so young Tommy,' she said as we strolled along the road.

'Oh, I don't know, just wanted to have a go I suppose,' I replied.

'What were you doing before you joined up?'

'Nothing much I'm afraid, I was trying to be an engineer'.

'Will you go back to that?' she asked.

'I suppose so, but life's a bit muddled at present isn't it?'

The restraint of the wards was gone now, and, although still in uniform, Ruby was just a carefree girl enjoying a walk.

'Yes, I've been uprooted myself,' she said 'I was at school and mummy nearly had a fit when I packed it up to become a nurse. Daddy had quite a job making her see things our way'.

'Where do you live Ruby?' I asked.

'My home is at Reigate, its handy for daddy to get to the city,' she replied 'and we have a place at St. Leonards, that's by the sea beside Hastings, and a country cottage at Hemel Hempstead, mummy likes the country but my brother and I love the sea'.

My head was in a bit of a whirl as I looked at her and realized that I didn't rate very high in her social ideas, in fact I didn't rate at all. Class and good breeding was written all over this girl who walked by my side but there was no snobbery in her make-up, she was free and easy and full of the joy of life.

'Tell my about Amy, the girl at home,' she said.

'Oh, there's nothing much to tell, Ruby,' I answered lamely.

'Of course there is, silly,' she laughed 'you're a North country boy and she's a Norfolk girl, how did you meet and where, come on tell me!'

I told her the story and she listened with interest; when I had finished she said with a smile 'It could be a romance couldn't it?'

I shrugged my shoulders 'Anything could lead to that these days Ruby'.

She glanced at her watch 'Its time we were getting back,' she said and as we turned to retrace our footsteps a slight drizzle of rain started. 'I don't mind the rain,' she said 'but I hope it's not too heavy, I don't want my patient returning wet'.

The drizzle did increase and she pointed along the road to where some trees hung heavy with leaves at the roadside.

'I'll race you to shelter,' she cried with a laugh.

I grasped hold of her hand 'No Ruby, we'll run together'. And we did. Under the trees I looked at her as she shook the moisture that glittered like diamonds from her dark hair, her slightly tanned face was flushed with running and her white teeth gleamed as she laughed and said 'You're not wet are you Tommy? Goodness, where's your tie?'

I pulled the red tie out of my pocket 'I can't fasten the thing Ruby'.

'You're not properly dressed, I'll do it for you'.

As she tied it her face seemed to float in front of my eyes, nearer and nearer, until at last I could stand it no more and I leaned forward and kissed her, on the cheek.

For a moment we stood silent and her large dark eyes seemed to grow to twice their normal size, then said softly 'You shouldn't have done that, Tommy!'

'Why not Ruby, we're both free, and I wanted to!'

'Well!' she looked flustered 'If anyone had seen you what would they think, come on we must get back to the hospital'.

And two rather thoughtful people walked hand in hand to the hospital gates where the nurse said quietly 'Goodnight Tommy,' and the patient said shyly 'Goodnight - sweetheart!'

My mind was in a bit of a whirl as I walked back to my ward. I was pleased with myself at the way things had gone, just the way I had been hoping they would go, but I was also angry at myself because deep down in my heart I knew it just wouldn't work. I was allowing myself to be swept off my feet by this girl who belonged to a different world to me, and I was willing to be swept, but there was no future in it only a lot of pain for both of us. After all, I was only an infantry soldier with a couple of stripes and a crippled hand, and in civilian life I was nothing at all. I felt in a pretty grim mood as I entered the ward, and Ginger turned his head and put down his book with a grin 'Well chum, you don't look any the worse, sit down and tell us, does Ruby really play ball?'

I walked over to his bed 'Listen to me Ginger,' I said 'I can stand a bit of fun but any more of that from you and I'll pull you out of that bed by the ears and kick your spine through the top of your head'.

He sat up with a jerk 'You, and who else to help you?'

'Just me Ginger, just me,' I replied.

'Like hell you will!' he exploded, and then the voice of Ross intervened 'Half a mo,' you two, I've been thinking a lot lately and I reckon I've got things squared up now. I'm certain I've seen you before Tommy, so just to make sure I want to ask you a question: Do you know a chap called Clem Davies, Welsh Fusiliers?'

'Clem Davies!' I exclaimed, surprised at hearing that name 'Why yes, I knew a chap of that name'.

Ross smiled 'Thought I was right, I was there the day you licked Clem in the divisional sports; and I heard about you taking his place to fight a Frenchman in Amiens, I was in Clem's battalion'.

'Have you heard anything of Clem since he was wounded?' I asked eagerly but Ross shook his head and looking at Ginger with a smile he said 'I would lay off your kidding, Ginger, if I was you, this bloke might not see things your way'.

Ginger looked a bit deflated 'Didn't know you were a glove slinger, chum'.

'Aw, forget it Ginger,' I replied 'but quit kidding about nurse Ranston'.

I crawled into bed feeling a bit deflated myself, I wasn't even a glove slinger now, I was nothing at all!

The next morning the whole vexing problem was solved by fate. Nurse Ranston entered the ward in civilian dress with a strained look on her face and she came straight over to my bed.

'I'm leaving you this morning, Tommy,' she said in a broken voice.

'You're what!' I gasped sitting up in bed.

'I've had bad news from home,' she murmured 'My brother's ship has been sunk and he's believed killed. Mummy is ill with the news and I have to return home at once; daddy is on his way to France so I'm all she has left. I must go to her'.

I was silent; struck speechless at the sorrow that war had brought to her. 'I'm just leaving now,' she said.

I took her hand and found my voice 'Ruby, I'm dreadfully sorry, will you come back to us?'

'Say you'll come back nurse,' chimed in Ginger 'we need you here'.

Four pairs of eyes looked at her as she replied 'I hope to come back boys, I want to come back, but, oh, I can't promise'. Tears began to run down her cheeks and I threw all my overnight reasoning aside as I said 'Ruby, for my sake, please come back'.

She looked down at me and swiftly she bent and kissed me full on the lips 'Goodbye Tommy, goodbye boys and good luck!' and she was gone. Something seemed to have gone from our ward as we lay dumbly looking at the ceiling and we heard the crunch of the tyres of the car that carried her away, on the gravel of the drive outside.

'Poor kid, what bloody rotten luck,' mused Ginger.

'Do you think she'll come back, Tommy?' asked Fred Wake.

'God knows,' I replied 'She wouldn't promise!'

'You mean she couldn't,' said Ross 'She was a good kid'.

Another nurse came to take the place of nurse Ranston but she wasn't anything to dispel the gloom that settled on the ward; we soon realized that 'Hutch,' nurse Hutchinson was something different. She was tall, fair, and angular, if she had any curves they were well hidden by her uniform; she was efficient at her job and a very busy wench, her sole conversation seemed to be wrapped up in lint, splints and bandages, in fact, just a nurse.

Ginger shook his head sadly 'A poor exchange for our Ruby. I suppose 'Hutch,' has some of the female about her but it's hard to detect!'

'Well, I'm going out into the grounds,' I said 'this ruddy ward is a bit too morbid for me'.

'By the way, Tommy,' said Ginger as I was leaving 'I never for one moment imagined that you and Ruby were, well, just like that! I hope you'll forgive me for 'joshing,' you'.

I grabbed him by the hair and replied with a grin 'Just a bit of wishful thinking on my part chum, forget it!'

But as I wandered the grounds I knew it was no 'wishful thinking', I thought a mighty lot of Ruby and had she stayed on at Kitebrook I knew in my heart that things just couldn't have stood still. It was a week later that I received a postcard from Ruby and it said: 'Dear Tommy, sorry to say mummy is worse. Doctor has advised change and we leave Southampton today for America. Letter later. God bless you boys in ward 2. Love, Ruby!'

'Well that settles that blast it!' I exclaimed and chucked the card on the table 'that's from Ruby'.

Three pairs of eyes fastened on me 'Is she coming back?' asked Ross.

'Is she hell! Read the bloody thing,' I exclaimed and Ginger, who was now on his feet, picked up the card and read it aloud.

'That's torn it,' remarked Fred Wake with a sigh 'its 'Hutch,' for the duration'.

Never again did I hear from Ruby, although for many weeks I hoped. I never knew if they reached America; enemy submarines were creating havoc with our shipping and I wondered and feared the worst. Gradually her memory was pushed into the background, and it was always a memory worth having; but in wartime our destiny seems to be controlled by war and we have to take what comes. I met Flo as arranged for my visit to her home and as we walked along the country road towards Moreton-in-Marsh I found her a bright and cheery companion. At their little house in Moreton I was made to feel I was a very welcome visitor, although I couldn't tell her mother much and I spent a nice afternoon and evening with the family. When it was time to leave and return to the hospital Flo was ready to accompany me, and her mother pressed me to come again any time I felt like it. 'Just make this your home from home, Tommy,' she said.

As we started off I said to Flo 'Look here you can't walk all the way back to Kitebrook with me'.

'Why not?'

'Well damn it Flo, its three miles, you walked six miles this afternoon and now you're thinking of doing another six, that's twelve miles!'

Flo laughed 'There's a war on Tommy so what's twelve miles to entertain a wounded soldier. I'll do it every day if you want me to'.

'Do what, the twelve miles or the entertaining?'

'Both, for you Tommy,' she breathed and kissed me on the cheek 'I think you're a nice boy'. It was unexpected and a bit too sudden for my liking but that didn't stop me from kissing her goodnight at the main gate; Flo had caught me on a pretty fast rebound.

Ginger had just got in when I reached the ward and he grinned and said 'How did the tea party go Tommy?'

'Fine, I've had a good time in Moreton'.

'And what about the wench Tommy?'

'Oh, she's all right, she brought me safely home'.

'That's more than mine did, anyway'.

'Where have you been Ginger?'

'A place called Blackley in the Hollow or something,' replied Ginger 'and you know what chum, the widow at the village pub enjoyed stuffing me with beer and bread and onions, all free'.

I looked at him 'You're a bloody liar Ginger, blokes in hospital blue are not allowed in pubs'.

Ginger looked hurt 'I wasn't in the pub you mug, I was in the house that goes with the pub, smell my breath if you don't believe me'.

He expelled a mouthful of beer and onion fumes that nearly put me flat on my back and I cried in alarm 'For God's sake get into bed Ginger and keep turned to the wall. If 'Hutch,' smells that lot she'll have you in front of the firing party'.

I helped Ginger to undress as best I could and heaved a sigh of relief when he dropped straight off to sleep but during the night I was awakened by his voice 'Tommy - wake up, wake up'.

'What's the row about?' I grunted sitting up in bed.

'I'm going to be sick,' he groaned 'help me to the bathroom'.

'Well of all the bloody nuisances!' I moaned 'come on get up'.

We left the ward and prowled along the corridor to the bathroom where Ginger duly got rid of his burden, but our luck ran out as we were making our way back to the ward, we ran into sister Sutcliffe.

'And what may you two be doing wandering around in the middle of the night?' she inquired.

Ginger grinned feebly 'We were looking for the female ward sister!'

'Shut up you ass,' I said 'we've been to the bathroom sister, Sims was sick'.

'Then why didn't you call me?' she asked severely, looking at Ginger's white face 'what made you sick?'

Before Ginger could reply and make a mess of things I said hastily 'He was out this afternoon without a hat and you know how hot it was sister!'

'I don't, I was sleeping,' she replied 'well, if you're feeling all right now Sims get back to bed, and for your information, Sims, there is no female ward in this institution, its for wounded soldiers not maternity cases, off you go!'

As we climbed back into bed Ginger remarked 'I think there was a spot of acid in sister's last remark, don't you?'

'I think you're damned lucky she didn't tumble to you,' I answered.

'Well thanks for your help chum, and by the way, I've fixed a date for you next Thursday at 3 o'clock so keep it open'.

I sat up in bed 'What the hells this about Ginger?'

'Oh, this little widow with the pub has a young sister and I promised I'd bring a pal along with me on Thursday afternoon,' replied Ginger smoothly 'you'll have a good time chum'.

'Well it won't be on booze Ginger, I'm not playing,' I replied.

'Well never mind the booze Tommy, the females are all right'.

'You've got a bloody cheek Ginger, goodnight'.

Two days later I once more walked to Moreton with Flo by my side and I enjoyed her company, but she was inclined to be just a little more possessive and at her home I had the sneaking feeling that they were anticipating rapid developments. Perhaps it was just their country way of seeing things, goodness knows they made a fuss of me, but I had the feeling that Flo had cast her line and I was nicely hooked. Still, she was a nice girl and I was a lonely soldier (so called) so I could enjoy her company, but I had to watch my step.

Now that I had escaped the cauldron of the Somme I had no inclination to live like a hermit at Kitebrook; granted there were some high stepping nurses in that place but you had to weigh up the situation very carefully before you started fun and games in that direction; if they were willing to play well and good, if not they had the power in their hands to report you and make your life a misery. I only knew of one case where this actually happened, but one case is enough to warn you.

On the Thursday afternoon Ginger and I tramped off, heading for the place in the Hollow about 3 miles from the hospital. It was a scorching hot day and as we sweated along I said to Ginger 'I hope it's worth it, Ginger!'

He grinned at me 'Just think of the tankards of free beer at the end of this walk'.

'I told you, I'm not interested'.

'Well think of the dames'.

'Its too ruddy hot to think of them,' I replied.

~ Tommy ~

It was a tiny village at the bottom of a hill we tramped into and Ginger led me to the rear of the small public house. His knock on the door was answered by a large sized middle aged female who greeted him with a girlish squeal of delight, threw her arms around his neck and kissed him. I stood sheepishly to one side until Ginger came up for air and then he gasped 'This is Tommy, Daisy'. Daisy looked at me with a broad stile and as I held out my left hand she brushed it to one side and I too became submerged in the folds of her ample bosom. Some welcome!

'Come in boys and have a nice cool drink,' she boomed in a voice liked that of a Regimental Sergeant Major and as we passed the foot of a staircase she threw up her head and bellowed 'Come down Nancy, your boyfriend has arrived'. She cocked an eye at me and said 'Perhaps you'd like to go up for her, eh?' and as I flushed she burst into a roar of laughter and shook like a jelly. Nancy joined us in the parlour, a brown haired rosy cheeked country girl in a pretty summer dress that she filled; she was her elder sisters double in miniature, but it wouldn't be long before the 'miniature,' was crossed out, there was plenty of her!

'This is Tommy, Nancy,' boomed Daisy as she banged two huge tankards of ale on the table 'Ginger says he's a nice boy, go on give him a kiss!' Nancy wasn't slow at carrying out the order and once more I was buried in the folds of feminine charm - plus! I was rather staggered at the way things seemed to be going but Ginger was in his element 'What about one for your uncle Sims,' he cried and Nancy wasn't slow in obliging.

'Drink up your ale, boys, there's plenty more,' boomed Daisy and as I shook my head, Ginger said 'He's not a drinking bloke, Daisy'. She looked at me in pity 'A soldier and you don't drink ale, what is the army coming too!'

'I'd like a cider,' I replied and Nancy hurried off to get me one. I would have liked that tankard of beer but I wasn't use to it and the company was a bit too risky for me. Nancy returned with a pint glass of cider for me and two more tankards of ale that flowed down the gullets of Ginger and Daisy.

'What's that stuff you are drinking?' I asked Nancy.

'This is just for ladies,' she replied laughing, its called 'pop,' and its supposed to make you feel amorous! Isn't it a pity Ginger has lost an arm and Tommy only has one hand, it cramps their style with a lady!' and the rafters shook to the gales of laughter and bosoms danced a merry duet.

'Shall we stay here or go for a walk?' asked Daisy.

In desperation I cried 'Oh come on lets go for a walk, it's a lovely day for walking'.

'All right, we'll be ready in a jiffy,' and the two ladies left us.

Ginger looked at me mournfully 'What the hell did you want to say that for?'

I turned on him 'You bloody fool, Ginger, you've lowered three pints already, if we stay here you'll be blotto when we get back to the hospital'.

The two sisters came charging in on us like a pair of playful elephants and after Ginger had another for the road we set off arm in arm for our walk.

We climbed a stile to cross some fields and as Ginger perched on the top of the stile Daisy boomed 'Jump Ginger, I'll catch you!'

Ginger jumped and bounced off Daisy to fall flat on his back, Daisy grabbed him and they rolled over and over in the grass to peals of laughter.

Nancy looked at me and laughed 'Our Daisy is a one, isn't she, get up Daisy, you're showing all your legs!'

The pair climbed to their feet and as Daisy brushed down her dress she said 'You two take that path to the brook, Ginger and I are going through the wood, see you later Nancy'.

'Aw lets keep together,' I protested but that was turned down flat and Ginger ambled off with his mountain of joy.

Nancy grabbed my arm and said coyly 'Come on sweetheart!' looking at me with sparkling eyes and the expression of a hungry wolf that has cornered a rabbit, I was the rabbit!

'Where's this brook they're talking about, Nancy?' I asked.

'Over yonder in the hollow,' she replied pointing across the fields to where a line of trees stood 'its lovely by the brook'.

I looked round desperately for some distraction, but there was none, only two figures fading away into the shadow of the woods.

I felt it would have given me a lot of pleasure to go to work on Ginger with a heavy club, he had got me into this.

Nancy was becoming more and more amorous and she wasn't leaving much to the imagination, for a kid of eighteen she was packed as tight as a sausage skin with sex emotion.

'Come on Nancy, I'll race you to the brook,' I cried.

'Oh no, I can't run, really,' she squealed, but I pulled my arm free and started off shouting 'You've damned well got to!'

It was far to hot for running but I put all I had into a 'do or die effort,' and looking back I saw Nancy with her dress well up lumbering along behind me. I put all I had into a jump that only just carried me to the other side of the brook and sank down thankfully to wipe the sweat from my brow. Nancy thudded up to a stop at the waters edge and wailed 'I can't jump that Tommy, come back on this side!'

I looked at her and grinned, her face was like a big red sweaty beet and her bosom and tummy were heaving with her exertions.

'Come on Nancy,' I cried 'don't let a drop of water stop you!'

She looked at the knee-deep brook and she looked at me, and then she shouted 'All right then, I'm coming'.

With an air of determination she retreated twenty yards and then turned and broke into a lumbering gallop, taking off at the waters edge she missed her footing and with a squeal she landed flat in the water. What a sight, and what a glorious cascade of water rose from that little babbling brook. As the dripping figure rose to its feet and stood knee deep I was un-gracious enough to say to myself 'That'll cool your ardour for you, my beauty,' aloud I said 'I'm coming back to that side Nancy, I'll help you out'.

'Oh dear, I'm drenched,' she gasped.

Moving a little way along I jumped the brook and gave Nancy a hand to climb out of the water.

'Oh look at my dress, its ruined,,' she wailed and I agreed with her but judging by the way it clung to her bulging body I don't think she was wearing much else to spoil.

'What a shame,' I exclaimed 'come on Nancy we'll have to get back right away'.

'I can't go into the village with you looking like this,' she cried tears of vexation brimming in her eyes.

'That's right, you can't,' I replied with relief 'and you can't hang about here letting your clothes dry on you. Tell you what Nancy, you go back home on your own and I'll go back to the hospital, our day is spoilt but it can't be helped'.

Mournfully she squeezed some water out of her dress and then she shook me up by saying 'I could take my things off in the wood and they would soon dry in this sun Tommy!'

I gaped at her 'Not on your life Nancy, good God, supposing one of the villagers saw you, you'd never live it down'.

I bade her a sorrowful goodbye at the stile and headed along the road for Kitebrook with a song in my heart and I was chuckling to myself when I reached the crossroads and met Sister O'Brien out for a stroll. 'And what's making you so happy this hot day?' she asked as I greeted her with a smile.

'Sister, I've just been teaching a wench to swim, in her clothes!' I replied with a laugh.

Her sharp eyes glittered through her glasses. 'Now what on earth do you mean by that?' she asked as we walked along the road towards the hospital.

Solemnly I replied, 'I met a girl in that village back yonder and we went for a stroll together, it was hot and she was hotter and in the end she jumped into a brook to cool herself, clothes and all!'

Sister O'Brien burst out laughing and said 'I think you're a sweet liar boy, that's all blarney you're telling me'.

'No, honestly sister its the truth, you could hear the water sizzle when she hit it!'

'Well if that's the effect you have on the village girls I suggest we keep you in the hospital and make the villages out of bounds for you'.

'Won't that be a bit dangerous for your nurses, sister?' I asked.

'Something in that too,' she replied with a smile 'I might take you under my own personal wing for your moral welfare'.

'You might enjoy that sister,' I replied as we reached the gates and she laughed and said 'Away you go and don't try to kid me with your fancy tales'.

I hadn't mentioned the pub and I hadn't mentioned Ginger so I knew we were safe enough for the present, but I wouldn't have backed a penny on Ginger's future at that moment. I liked Sister O'Brien, she could enjoy a joke and she could be very nice and sociable but she could also pin your ears well back if you drifted away from her rules at the hospital.

Life at the hospital was good and sport was laid on in the grounds for those fit to indulge in it; also concert parties were given once a week indoors, but we didn't take kindly to any hard and fast arrangement of how we spent our time. Abiding by the rules of meal times, times for dressing of wounds, and times of freedom had to be obeyed of course, and the staff were kept busy with their sixty or so cases, all wounded cases, and some bad ones at that.

I was tucked up in bed when Ginger made his appearance and he scowled at me as he undressed for bed 'What the hell have you been up to with Nancy?' he asked 'she's in a hell of a stew about you?'

I grinned at him 'She looked cool enough when I left her, Ginger'.

'Well she wasn't very cool when we got back to the pub I can tell you,' he replied 'she says you slung her into a ditch!'

'That's a tale Ginger, I didn't sling her in, she jumped in!'

'I don't care what happened, but Daisy has jumped to the conclusion that you tried to assault her little sister,' replied Ginger 'and I left them talking of going to the local copper to lodge a complaint, and there's a pile of wet clothes to prove it'.

'Your Daisy can go and climb up a tree and take her little sister with her,' I answered shortly 'and no more jaunts with you Ginger!'

'What's been going on?' asked Fred Wake sitting up in bed.

Ginger grunted 'I fixed this bloke up for free beer and a girl and he goes and makes a complete balls of everything'.

Sister Sutcliffe entered the ward and looked around, then pointed a finger at me 'You're booked for an outing tomorrow, and you too,' pointing at Ginger 'there'll be a car calling for you two directly after lunch so don't wander away'.

'What kind of an outing sister?' I asked.

'Miss Audrey Hargreaves and Miss Alice Hargreaves request the pleasure of two quiet well behaved wounded soldiers to tea, and the matron has booked you two for the outing,' she replied.

'Did you say 'Miss'? Asked Ginger.

'I did, and mind you behave yourselves'.

'Sister, I always behave myself with a 'Miss',' grinned Ginger. 'This is right up my street, I wonder what they are like'.

I rolled over 'We'll see tomorrow Ginger, goodnight'.

After lunch the next day Ginger and I found the car awaiting us at the entrance, complete with elderly chauffeur in green uniform and bright buttons. He opened the door of the car for us to enter and as we settled back in the roomy seat Ginger said 'Where are you taking us, chum?'

'Hargrave Hall sir,' replied 'Buttons,' as he climbed into the front seat 'its about twelve miles on the Banbury Road'.

As the car rolled along Ginger mused 'Hargrave Hall, Miss Audrey and Miss Alice Hargraves, it looks as though this is something we could develop chum'.

'How do you mean Ginger?'

'We're moving up in the world chum, just supposing these two are a bit of all right, you case one lonely heart and I case the other, we might get ourselves fixed up for life'.

'Don't talk so daft Ginger, we haven't met them yet'.

'No, but we're going to, this might be our big chance and I'm warning you Tommy, lets have no more of this funny business of yours!'

'What funny business?'

'Slinging females into ditches, don't try any of that stuff here, if you don't want the one I leave for you just pack up in the proper way and leave me in peace with the other one, see!'

Presently 'Buttons,' exclaimed 'Here we are sir, Hargrave Hall,' and the car swung through an imposing gateway and swept along a curving gravel path lined with trees. Through the trees I caught glimpses of well cut lawns and masses of flowers and then the car pulled up at the steps leading to the entrance of an imposing building 'Looks like the ruddy town hall,' murmured Ginger as 'Buttons,' opened the car door.

Just go straight in, you're expected,' said 'Buttons'.

We mounted the steps and as we reached it the door swung open and an elderly gent who seemed to be all starched white shirt front greeted us 'Welcome sir's, to Hargrave Hall; step inside'. We stepped into a world of luxury and the butler said 'Your hats gentlemen, if you please'.

We handed over our hats and then he said 'This way gentlemen, perhaps you would like to wash your hands after your journey'.

Ginger got his breath back 'Well, we've only got one hand each but we'll do our best'.

When we rejoined him in the hall the butler said 'If you will follow me gentlemen, to the lounge'.

We followed and he tapped on a door, opened it, and said quietly 'Will you please enter'.

We entered a great room tastefully decorated in lavish style and from two basket chairs beside the French windows two little old ladies greeted us with charming smiles 'We're so pleased you have come to visit us; I am Miss Audrey and this is my sister Miss Alice, please sit down and make yourselves at home with us'.

Ginger had the look of a deflated balloon and I had to admit it was a bit of a shock, but it was a shock that soon left us because they were so nice in making us feel at home, they were two dear old souls who seemed to be living in another world, a world of peace and quiet tucked away in a corner of Gloucestershire untouched by war and pain.

The two old ladies rattled along with talk of our gallant troops fighting those 'awful Germans,' and the poor boys who were in hospital, and Ginger sat quiet twiddling his fingers until a picture book maid entered with a tray of coffee and biscuits. That brought him up with a jerk, she was something worth looking at, and Ginger gave her a load of the evil eye. After the coffee Ginger appeared restless, and then he made the suggestion that he would like a stroll through the grounds, oh no, he didn't want anyone to accompany him, he loved to be alone in a garden!

'I do hope he doesn't lose his way,' murmured Miss Alice 'we have quite a lot of ground'.

Ginger had not returned by the time the tea was laid out and in the end Miss Audrey rang for the butler. 'Would you mind looking in the grounds for the other soldier, James,' she said 'the poor man seems to have got lost'.

James sniffed and looked down his nose 'I think I will be able to find him Miss'.

It wasn't long before he returned with Ginger in tow and we settled down to a dainty meal that was never intended for the rank and file. 'Where did you get to Ginger?' I asked in an aside at the first opportunity.

'The conservatory with that wench,' he replied reaching for a wafer like ham sandwich 'everything was going fine when that butler bloke arrived and spoilt the whole show'.

After tea we departed for the hospital with the kindly wishes of two dear old souls in our ears and as the car sped down the drive a handkerchief waved from the upstairs window. 'That's her,' sighed Ginger waving back 'and I couldn't even make a date with her. I'll come back here one day'.

A day or two later as we sat quietly reading after lunch sister O'Brien entered the ward and announced 'There's a lady to see you Tommy, she's in the hall'.

Ginger looked at me over his book and moaned 'My God, not again!'

I stood up 'What do you mean, not again?' I asked.

'Is there no end to it chum, women are parading to call on you'.

'Who is it sister?' I asked.

'You go and see for yourself,' she replied with a smile.

I made my way down the stairs and entered the hall, wondering who it could be, to be greeted by my mother.

It was really great to see her once again and it brought a far distant home much nearer and soon I was talking of home and she was talking of the war, the wounds, and me. She stayed in Moreton for a few days and we had a nice time together, and after she met Flo she reminded me that Amy had left Norfolk and was now back in my home town.

'She's looking forward to your leave Tommy,' she told me.

'All right mum, you tell her it won't be long now, and I'm looking forward to seeing her'.

'She's a very nice girl Tommy,' mother murmured and I knew what she was thinking.

I think so too mum,' I replied 'but I didn't see a great deal of her before I went overseas'.

'Well, the more I see of her the better I like her and she's waiting for you to come home'.

'That's fine, its nice to know someone is waiting, I'll get ten days leave from here and I'll make the most of it'.

After my mother left Moreton I spent quite a lot of time with Flo, but the more I was with her the more I realized that she was shallow. The cards were thrown on the table one evening when she asked me to go with her on a trip to Stratford-on-Avon, the trip had been arranged for us by the people of Moreton-in-Marsh. I didn't feel like it so I declined, and despite her pleadings I refused to change my decision 'All right,' she said as we parted 'if you won't go someone else will!'

The day before the trip Ginger button-holed me with the remark 'Look here chum, are you serious with that wench in Moreton?'

'What are you getting at Ginger?'

He shrugged 'Well, I'd like to go with her on the trip, but I don't want to be treading on your corns, how about it?'

I grinned at him 'That's all right Ginger, help yourself'.

'Sure you don't mind chum?'

'Not one little bit Ginger, I hope you enjoy yourself'.

So Ginger took Flo on the trip to Stratford while I stayed at the hospital, he told me afterwards that he had a grand day, and I didn't feel in the least disturbed.

I knew then that Flo didn't mean a lot to me, a good friend yes, but nothing more than that.

And strange to relate Flo clung closer to me than ever after the episode of the trip to Stratford, I found her good company. It was shortly after this that something occurred between Ginger and sister Sutcliffe that seemed to create a spot of ill feeling. What the trouble was I could only guess, she could be a tantalising wench when she was in the mood and Ginger was the type who would jump to conclusions.

The climax came one night at about midnight when Ginger found himself locked out, and in making a valiant but noisy attempt to climb the ivy to the window of our ward he roused the hospital and nearly scared the night staff out of their wits. Why the silly ass attempted climbing the ivy with only one arm I never could understand but he was 'pegged,' by sister Sutcliffe and two days later he departed for a military hospital in Warwick.

Before he left he shook hands with me and said solemnly 'Don't try anything with that Sutcliffe wench Tommy!'

I laughed 'I don't intend to Ginger, what's up with her?'

'She's all cream and honey one minute and like a cat with a can tied to its tail the next. Someone should take that Red Cross off her chest and put in its place a label marked 'Danger''. A chap with a foot missing arrived to fill the vacant bed after Ginger had gone and a few days later Fred Wake was issued with khaki and left us for his ten days of leave. His place was taken by one of the Argylls with a badly shattered face and one eye gone, a difficult patient.

I had been in Kitebrook ten weeks, ten very happy weeks, when sister O'Brien informed me that I was due for discharge from hospital two days hence. 'You'd better come to the clothes store with me and get your uniform,' she instructed.

'My uniform was in a bit of a mess sister!' I replied.

She laughed 'That one was destroyed, we carry a stock of new uniforms, shirts and boots, it's just a matter of picking your proper size, come with me'.

We walked to the far end of the corridor and she pointed to a narrow staircase leading upward 'Our storeroom is up there in the false roof that's where we keep the uniforms'.

I was surprised when I saw the neat piles of khaki trousers and tunics, grey shirts and socks, hats and ammunition boots.

'Gosh, you seem to have everything sister,' I remarked.

She sat down on a blanket-covered case 'Everything you need to go on leave Tommy, just help yourself you know your size'.

I soon had my little pile picked out and I turned to her saying 'that's my lot sister,' when I was surprised to see her leaning back with her eyes closed.

'What's the matter sister?' I asked 'are you feeling poorly?'

She smiled and stood up 'Oh I'm all right, are you pleased to be leaving us Tommy?'

I hesitated and then I replied 'I'm pleased to be going home sister, but I can't honestly say I'm pleased to be leaving Kitebrook.

I'll always be grateful for what you've done for me, and I've been very very happy while I've been with you'.

She shrugged her shoulders 'It's a strange life isn't it, we just have time to become attached to you fellows and then away you go'.

'You know what I would like sister, ten days leave and then return to Kitebrook; that would do me fine'.

~ Tommy ~

She shook her head 'That's not the drill, boy; its ten days leave and then you rejoin your regiment, there's only one way back to places like Kitebrook for chaps like you'.

Faintly to my mind came the memory of tramping boots on cobbled roads, the smell of sweat, the weight of equipment, and the distant everlasting booming of the guns, the road back!

Every day now would bring that nearer once more.

I shrugged 'Oh well, we'll take it as it comes, I suppose I'm lucky to be here at all'.

'You've got a girl waiting for you haven't you?' she said swiftly changing the subject.

'Well I don't know sister, really,' I answered lamely 'a girlfriend if you like'.

'You liked nurse Ranston didn't you?'

I stared at her; she seemed to know a hell of a lot.

'Yes sister, I liked nurse Ranston a lot, but I've lost touch with her'.

She nodded 'Yes I know, it's a pity about that girl'.

I picked up my bundle; I didn't want to be reminded of Ruby.

Sister O'Brien laid a hand on my arm and her eyes had a strange glitter as she looked at me 'I wonder if you remember after your operation Tommy, how we worked to save your hand and your arm?'

'By jove yes, you were great, sister'.

'And do you remember what you threatened me with?'

I stared at her 'I threatened you sister? I don't know, - oh, good lord sister, that wasn't a threat, it was a promise!'

I dropped my bundle, took her in my arms and kissed her full on the lips, for a moment she hugged me fiercely and then she pushed me away. To me it was a kiss of gratitude but I knew I had kissed, under a sister's uniform, a love hungry woman old enough to be my mother. 'Go back to your ward, boy!' she ordered and I picked up my bundle and made my way back to the place where I belonged, feeling rather like a kid who has been trespassing. She visited the ward that evening but once again she was the sister on duty and neither word nor look denoted anything.

The following day I spent most of my time doing the rounds of the hospital and saying 'so-long,' to the patients and nurses I knew, and in the evening I was at Moreton-in-Marsh to say farewell to Flo's mother. A maid at the hospital had polished my buttons and cap badge and that night I stripped off my 'hospital blues,' for the last time. I was up bright and early the next morning and as I had breakfast sister O'Brien came along with my railway warrant and papers.

'Here's your papers and travelling warrant Tommy,' she said handing them over 'and here's some sandwiches for the journey, also a packet of cigarettes; the car is waiting to take you to the station, I think I'll just say goodbye now'. I stood up and held out my hand 'Goodbye sister and from the bottom of my heart, thanks for everything'.

Swiftly she looked round, the dining room was empty, she leaned forward and kissed my lightly on the cheek 'Goodbye Tommy, and God speed, I wish you luck', and she was gone.

I slung my haversack and made my way to the entrance where a car awaited me and a little group of nurses and patients to see me off. At the railway station, despite the early hour, I found Flo waiting and we spent our last few minutes together before the train arrived. 'You will come back, won't you Tommy?' Flo pleaded as I stood by the open carriage door.

'I would honestly like to Flo,' I replied 'this place will always be a happy memory, but there's a war on you know, I can't make useless promises when anything might happen'.

'You will write to me, please,' she said and tears began to fall.

'Yes Flo, I'll promise to write,' I replied leaning from the window.

The guards whistle blew and I kissed Flo goodbye as the train moved she cried 'After the war Tommy please come back I'll be waiting for you!'. A wave of the hand, the flutter of a tear stained handkerchief and the rumbling wheels carried me away from Moreton-in-Marsh. I was alone in the carriage and I felt thankful for it, I didn't know whether to feel pleased or sorry as I settled down for a long journey to the North of England.

It was longer than I expected and it wasn't until the following morning that I arrived at Newcastle, a two hours wait there gave me a chance to get a phone message home to let my mother know I was on my way. As the train steamed into my own station I saw, waiting on the platform, my father, my mother and Amy. I shook hands with my father, kissed my mother, then turned to Amy and acting on impulse I kissed her too, our first kiss. Home, after a year on active service and three months in hospital, the reaction was almost over powering until I got myself adjusted to it. My father was in his cavalry uniform and his Sergeant Majors crown was bright on his sleeve.

He looked at my bare sleeve 'I thought you were a Corporal Tommy, where are your chevrons?'

I pulled the stripes out of my pocket with a smile 'They're here, no time for those things in hospital'.

'Well that won't do, your mother will sew them on as soon as we get home'.

'So long as they are on for when I report back, that's all I care about, I'm free for ten days so I don't need them'.

'You must wear your badge of rank,' he retorted.

'Must nothing, I'm wearing civvies!' I answered.

'Good lord you can't do that!' he cried 'people will think you are a slacker'.

'They can think what they like, this tells a different story,' I replied holding up my still bandaged hand 'I've worn that uniform day and night for a year and now I want a change'.

I knew he didn't approve, he was the type who wouldn't, he would wear his uniform day and night, spurs and all, and glory in it, but I had a sneaking fancy that England was his happy hunting ground. A million weary feet could be treading the road to glory in France and Belgium, but not his, no sir, not his!

After tea I changed into my civvies and was surprised to find my clothes were tight on me 'Army life must be good for me'. I wandered round to find Amy at her sister's house and we spent the evening together, I again found happiness in her quaint, tranquil manner. During my leave my hand became swollen and I had it examined by a doctor at home, he advised a sling for a while so for the rest of my stay at home I wore a sling and it got no worse. Before my time to report back to duty I told Amy that I wanted her for more than a friend and in fairness to her I told her about Ruby.

'Poor girl,' she said 'Were you very fond of her, Tommy?'

'I would have been, Amy, if she had been at Kitebrook much longer,' I replied 'she was very like you in her ways'.

'Oh well, you can't have her so you'll just be satisfied with me?' Amy said with a laugh.

'No, that's not fair Amy,' I answered 'I liked you before I went overseas, I liked Ruby, and now that I'm home I like you more than ever'. She kissed me with a smile; 'All right Tommy if that's how you feel about it'.

The day came, all too soon, when once again I stood in khaki waiting for the train that would take me to Newcastle, and Amy stood by my side. 'How long do you think it will be, Tommy till you get another leave?' she asked.

'God knows Amy,' I replied shrugging my shoulders 'there's no telling what will happen or where I'll land up now'.

She smiled 'I'll be waiting when you come back Tommy'.

'That's just what you said before I went to France Amy'.

'Well, you came back, and I was waiting wasn't I?'

The train steamed in and I climbed aboard 'Well, cheerio Amy, I'll write as soon as I get settled'.

'Cheerio Tommy and good luck to you'.

A kiss and I was on my way, leaving behind a girl with a brave smiling face and never the sign of a tear, that was the spirit!

7.   RAW RECRUITS

I tramped through the gates of Newcastle barracks and handed in my papers to the Sergeant of the guard, he glanced through them and looked at me 'Just out of hospital Corporal, what's been the trouble?'

I held up my bandaged hand 'German lead poisoning,' I replied briefly. He laughed 'you chaps keep coming back for more,' he said 'all right, you know the ropes so just make yourself at home, I'll send your papers to the orderly room'.

I wandered away and stood watching a bunch of sweating recruits bashing it out on the Barrack Square.

'Back to the same old grind,' I thought with distaste.

'And what the hell do you think you're on?' barked a voice behind me.

I turned to see the over-size figure of a Regimental Sergeant Major glaring at me and I jumped to attention in the approved manner.

'Been in hospital with wounds sir,' I replied 'reporting back for duty'.

'What the hell duty can you do with that?' he barked pointing to my hand 'I don't want you, the bloody place is overrun with cripples, no bloody use to me!'

'I can go back home sir?' I said hopefully.

'You can, but you bloody well won't,' he rasped 'get yourself a mug of tea at the cook house and report to me at the orderly room in half an hour!'

I got my mug of tea and I was at the orderly room within the specified time to be greeted with 'Oh its you Corporal, right here's your papers, you'll get a train at 2 o'clock and report to a training reserve battalion at Hornsea, clear?'

'Where's Hornsea, sir?'

He looked at me 'Somewhere in Yorkshire me lad, but that doesn't matter, you get that 2 o'clock train!'

Well that was that, in the barracks at my depot and out again just like that; well it didn't matter, I didn't like barracks much. I had time for a snack at the station and then I was on the train bound for York. Here I had to change to a train that crawled its way to Hornsea and got me there by dusk. There was a cold wind blowing and a smell of the sea in the air as I made inquiries and found that the training reserve battalion was about four miles along the coast from the town. I tramped along the country road, wondering what I was heading for, and I got rather a shock when I saw the dull gleam of army bell tents in the gloom across the fields. Soon I came to the usual entrance to any army camp, the usual sentry on duty and the guard tent. The sentry informed me I had come to the right place and nodded to the tent 'Sergeant of the guard in there,' he said. The Sergeant looked at my papers by the light of a lantern and then he grunted 'Bit late to be reporting in isn't it Corporal, why didn't you leave it till the morning?'

'You'd better ask the 'Regimental,' that, at Newcastle,' I replied.

'Well its damned awkward getting you fixed up for the night'.

'In that case Sergeant I'll just kip here for the night, send one of these blokes for some blankets,' I said.

'Not much room in here for another man,' he moaned.

'I'll make room for myself, shuffle around you chaps, I'm staying, and you can like it or lump it'.

A chap was sent off and returned with a couple of blankets for me and I found a space to spread them and settled myself down in the guard tent, to the chap lying next to me I said 'Its a bit late in the year for camping isn't it?'

'If they keep us here much longer we'll all be in hospital,' he replied 'Gor when the winds off the sea its freezing, you back from France?'

'Yes,' I answered 'What sort of a mob is this?'

'Just been formed six weeks, nobody here been overseas, we're recruits'.

'Hell, I wonder what they sent me here for!' I exclaimed.

'I'm wondering that myself Corporal, what's it like in France?'

'You'll find out chum, you're in the right firm'.

I tried to settle myself to sleep, but after three months of soft living I found the ground pretty hard and the army blankets pretty rough. A dixie of tea at midnight for the guard was welcome, and I had my share, but by dawn I was cold and aching and pleased enough to get up and call it a night.

I found the camp was right on the edge of the cliffs overlooking the sea and it wasn't long before the smell of cooking attracted me to the cookhouse. 'Any chance of some breakfast chum?' I asked a chap in dirty white overalls with a couple of stripes on his arm.

'In the dining tent in two hours time,' he replied shortly.

'Listen chum, I'm not begging; I travelled all day yesterday without any rations and got here too late last night to get any, if you don't do something about it, I will'.

'Where you from?'

'I'm from a great big country called France where men are sharing their last crust of bread, do I get that breakfast?'

He looked at me and he looked at my bandaged hand 'I'll see what I can knock up for you, but its against regulations'.

'Its against regulations for a man to go without rations,' I replied.

I got my breakfast, a mug of tea, fried sausage and bread and afterwards reported to the marquee that was labelled battalion H.Q. The elderly Regimental Sergeant Major went through my papers and then gazed at me mournfully, stroking his moustache 'Don't know what the hell I'm going to do with you here, according to your papers you're awaiting a medical, what the hell did they post you here for?'

'I can't answer that one sir,' I replied 'but for goodness sake do something with me, I'm fed up wandering around like a lost sheep'.

'All right, all right,' he said testily 'take this chit to the quartermasters store and get your kit, then report to Company Sergeant Major Warren of B Company, I'll have to think up a job for you'.

I went to the stores and drew a full issue of kit, equipment, rifle, and two blankets that I piled in a heap in the corner and said 'I'll send a chap along to collect that lot'.

The quartermaster stared 'You can't do that, you have to take it with you!'

I held up my hand and grinned 'I can't manage that lot with one hand can I?' That damaged hand was useful after all. I found Sergeant Major Warren and he in turn passed me over to a Sergeant Levett who found me a home in B company lines. The chaps in the tent were busy with polish when I said to Sergeant Levett 'I want one of these chaps to collect my stuff from the stores, which one shall I send?'

The Sergeant gaped 'they're due on parade in five minutes,' he barked.

'All right, well excuse one of them from parade,' I replied.

'Can't you collect your own bloody gear?' growled the Sergeant.

'No, I can't,' I answered 'I can't hump that load'.

'I'll get it Sergeant,' volunteered a bright looking youngster.

'All right Smith, join the parade in half an hour'.

Smith brought my stuff to the tent and I told him to take his time and get it sorted out for me. He looked up as he was buckling the straps of my equipment 'The Sergeant said half an hour, Corporal!'

'Just you carry on my lad you're doing nicely,' I replied.

'What about the parade?'

'The parades doing fine without you,' I said.

'Suits me all right, I'm fed up with square bashing, you're back from France I hear Corporal'. I nodded my head. 'I wish they would hurry up and send us out, I want to do some real soldiering'.

'That's what I was saying a long time ago,' I replied 'Don't be impatient chum, it'll come soon enough'.

I spent the day lounging about the camp, nobody seemed to want me, the only soldier among six hundred in the camp who had been on active service, and I felt like an outcast. By nightfall I was in a savage mood 'All right,' I thought 'if that's the way they want it, they'll get it'.

Just before 'lights out,' the Sergeant poked his head in the tent 'Parade full marching order eight o'clock in the morning, everyone!'

'That include me Sergeant?' I asked.

'I said everyone!' he shouted.

'Right, but I'm not wearing any bloody equipment!' I retorted.

'Full marching order!' he yelled and stamped away.

The recruits in the tent were staring at me in silence.

'You'll go on parade won't you Corporal?' said Smith at last.

'Yes I'll go on their bloody parade,' I growled 'but that stuff will go in a bundle, just as it is'.

'What's the idea, Corporal?'

'I can't buckle up equipment with one hand can I?' I retorted.

'No, I suppose not,' replied Smith 'but I'll do it for you if you like, and then you can wear it'.

'You touch that equipment Smith and I'll skin you,' I replied hotly 'they've been bloody awkward with me and now I'm going to be bloody awkward with them!'

'Its C.O.'s inspection,' someone said 'the C.O. will have a fit'.

'The C.O. can have twins for all I care,' I answered.

During the bustle of getting ready for the parade the next morning I felt the boys watching me, expecting me to weaken at the last moment, but when the bugle sounded I tramped on to the parade ground with my rifle slung on my shoulder and my straps, belt and pouches stuffed in my pack. I 'fell in,' in my place with my rifle in my left hand and my equipment at my feet. Sergeant Levett took one look and nearly fell over backwards 'For God's sake, get that equipment on!' he cried hoarsely and I shook my head.

'Your rifle man, get it in your right hand!' he yelled and I waved my damaged mitt at him.

'You'll have to - -,' ' Parade - 'shun!' It was too late to do anything; the Regimental Sergeant Major was on parade. He stood at the far side of the parade ground, stiff as a pole, and his eyes travelled up and down the ranks. I suppose I must have stuck out like a sore thumb and suddenly the blast struck me 'Who the bloody hell is that man who's brought his bundle of washing on parade, what bloody army do you belong to with your rifle on the left side, why the hell don't you stand on your head and stuff your rifle up your arse, where's the N.C.O. in charge of the company - come here!'

Sergeant Levett doubled across the parade ground and stood at attention before the jury. What transpired I don't know but the Sergeant doubled back to me and shouted 'Pick up that pack and get off the parade quick, report to the orderly room right away!'

I slung my rifle, picked up the equipment, stepped to the rear and marched off the parade ground with the eyes of a raw battalion fixed on me in wonder. I dumped my gear in my tent and made my way to the orderly room where I hung around until the 'Regimental,' came off the parade.

'Come inside me lad,' he barked grimly 'I want a little word with you'. He threw himself into his chair and glowered at me across his desk 'Now what the blazes do you mean, coming on parade like that?'

'Orders were every man on parade with full marching order,' I replied 'and I did the best I could, I obeyed orders'.

'You should have gone sick if you couldn't wear your equipment!'

'I'm not sick sir, I just can't buckle up equipment or carry a rifle in my right hand'.

'We'll damned soon prove that,' he growled 'you'll report to the M.O. right away, and bring his report back to me here'.

'Very good sir'.

I made my way to the sick bay and reported to the doctor, an elderly grey haired officer with the three stars of a Captain on his shoulder. He looked too old to be in the army but his eyes twinkled as he said, 'I've heard all about it Corporal, lets have a look at that hand of yours, what are you trying to do, start a revolution or something?'

I shrugged 'Its not like that sir, the fatheads here don't seem to understand that I'm just out of hospital and I'm not up to scratch yet with that hand'.

He nodded his head as he examined my hand 'I understand son,' I yelped at his probing fingers 'did that hurt?'

'Yes sir, that hands tender'.

'I'll order a leather glove for you, that will protect it a bit until it toughens up, so the damn fools expect you to handle a rifle with that, I'll stop that game anyway!'

He sat down at his desk and wrote on a form which he handed to me 'Excused all parades, light duty only, pending a medical board; hand that in to the orderly room'.

'Thank you sir,' I replied accepting the form from him.

'Where did you get wounded Corporal?' he asked.

'Fricourt sector, the Somme,' I answered.

A shadow seemed to come over his face 'My only son is buried in that sector, he was killed on July 1st'.

I reported back to the orderly room and found the R.S.M. talking to a short stout built Captain and I clicked my heels as I came to attention in front of them.

The Captain looked me up and down with a glare.

'How long have you been in the army Corporal?' he barked.

'Two year's sir,' I replied.

'Don't you know to salute an officer?' he asked harshly.

'My right hand is injured sir, I saluted you by standing to attention'. I replied staring back at him and not liking what I saw.

'We've heard enough about that,' he snorted 'damn it, you've got another hand to salute with, haven't you?'

'Kings rules and regulations state a soldier will salute with his right hand only sir,' I quoted, and his face turned red.

'Have you got the M.O.'s report?' the R.S.M. butted in hastily, and I handed over the form.

'Excused all parades, light duty only,' the R.S.M. read from the form 'don't know what the hell we'll do with you here!'

'Better send him back where he came from,' snapped Captain Davis.

'I think I would sooner be in France than here sir,' I retorted.

Captain Davis stared at me long enough to make it uncomfortable, his legs apart and his belly stuck out and I stared back at the place on his tunic where there might have been a few coloured ribbons had he been a man. Suddenly his eyes gleamed and he turned to the R.S.M. 'Seeing that this N.C.O. is no use to us Sergeant Major, I would suggest that he should be reduced to the ranks, then he could be employed in the cook house or with the sanitary squad'.

'That's an idea sir,' said the Sergeant Major.

'Its an idea that won't work Sergeant Major,' I said taken aback at the viciousness of the attack.

'What do you mean, won't work?' snapped the R.S.M.

'I got these stripes in action on the field of battle,' I replied 'if you like to read up you Kings Rules and Regulations I think you'll find that only a general court martial can take them off me'.

Captain Davis snorted 'Is that right Sergeant Major?'

The R.S.M. nodded his head 'Afraid that's true sir'.

'Blast it!' stormed Captain Davis 'I'll have a word with the C.O. about this, this is no bloody home for cripples,' and he stamped away. The R.S.M. looked at me reproachfully.

'What the hell did you want to rile him like that for?' he growled.

'He riled himself,' I retorted 'He wants to get on a transport and do some soldiering on the other side, then he'd be worth a salute, maybe!'

'Look here Corporal, you seem to have got off on the wrong foot since you came here,' said the R.S.M. 'what's the matter with you?'

'I've been asking myself the same question about you lot,' I replied 'the trouble is Sergeant Major I'm a volunteer soldier with a year of active service under my belt and I've landed into a battalion of conscripts just learning to march, we won't mix!'

'Its no use you trying to back against the army Corporal,' said the R.S.M. 'better men than you have tried it and come a cropper, in the bible they called it 'kicking against the pricks!'

'I'm not kicking against anything Sergeant Major,' I replied 'I like soldiering, but I don't like being dumped in a mob like this and I don't like being messed about by a twerp like that Captain, who the hell does he think he is anyway?'

'He's your superior officer Corporal, and that's that!' retorted the R.S.M. 'What have you against this battalion anyway, they'll be going overseas same as you when they are ready'.

'I'll tell you what I have against them,' I replied 'most of them should have been in the army a couple of years ago that's what! I don't forget my winter in the line in Flanders, one man to about 30 yards of trench, and no rest due to shortage of men, while people like this sat on their arses in England and didn't care a damn about us until they were forced to join up by conscription'.

'Well you'd better make the best of a bad job,' sighed the R.S.M. 'I think I'll put you in charge of the rifle range while you are here, how will that suit you?'

'Just as you like Sergeant Major,' I replied and left him at that. And after that the parade ground saw no more of me, I spent my time in charge of the squads that came to the range to pass through their course of rifle shooting. I carried out my duties and made my reports direct to the R.S.M. and the Adjutant but I still had the feeling of a square peg in a round hole.

So far as it was possible in an encampment I gave Captain Davis a wide berth, I knew from the look in his eye, the few times we did meet, that he had my number chalked up and he came at me one day with all his guns cocked for trouble. I was approaching the main entrance of the camp on my way to the town when a voice barked 'Corporal!' I stopped and saw Captain Davis standing by the tent that housed the main guard and he cocked a finger at me. I marched over to him and stood to attention.

'Where are you going, Corporal?' he asked.

'Into the town sir,' I replied 'Duties finished for today'.

'So, just like that!' he rasped 'Damn it man you're improperly dressed!'.

I looked down at myself and felt the buttons of my tunic pockets and then the hooks of my collar but I could find nothing wrong, and I looked at him in bewilderment.

'Remove your head-gear!' he ordered and as I took off my hat he said to the sentry on duty 'Call the Sergeant of the guard'.

The Sergeant came at the double while I still stood with my hat in my hand trying to see what was wrong with it.

Sergeant, this N.C.O. is improperly dressed, make out a report on it and send it in to the orderly room'.

'Very good sir,' the Sergeant's eyes swept over me 'but I don't see'.

'You don't see!' roared Captain Davis 'That's the trouble with you NCOs, you don't see. Look at his cap badge and tell me, is that the cap badge of the battalion?'

I looked down at the silver cap badge of my regiment and then I realized what he was getting at. All training reserve battalions at that time wore a button as a cap badge while in training, and only got a regimental badge when they joined a unit.

'But this is my regimental badge sir,' I protested.

Captain Davis waved that aside 'You belong to this training battalion and you are no longer entitled to wear that badge. Remove it at once and get a proper cap badge at the stores. That's an order, and carry on with that report Sergeant!' he stamped away.

I looked down at the badge I had served under and fought under, and I looked up at the Sergeant with blazing eyes; 'I'll see him in hell first, the lousy bastard, this is my regimental badge!'

The Sergeant looked after the retreating figure of Captain Davis 'He's a swine, that one; I'm sorry Corporal but I'll have to make out the charge like he said, and my tip, take that cap badge out or he'll nail you for disobeying an order'.

I saw the sense in that and put my badge in my pocket as I made my way to the Q.M. stores and requested a button cap badge.

'What's the idea Corporal?' asked the Q.M. Sergeant, and I explained the position to him.

'Whew! He said scratching his ear 'Damned if I see how he can make that charge stick'.

'What's the C.O. like?' I asked him.

'One of the Indian Mutiny dugouts, but as straight as a die,' he replied.

'Good enough, you'll get this bloody button back tomorrow,' I promised.

That night the orderly Sergeant warned me for C.O.'s orderly room at 10 am the following morning and I was there on time for the R.S.M. to march me in. I pulled up in front of the C.O.'s desk and the Adjutant read out the charge sheet while this ancient relic of a soldier gazed at me through his glasses.

'Ahem! So you persist in wearing your regimental cap badge eh?'

'Yes sir I do'.

'Why?'

'I volunteered for service with this regiment when I joined the army sir, and I've served on active service with the regiment, I'm not a training reserve man'.

'Proud of your regiment eh?'

'I am sir, and I still belong to it'.

The Adjutant leaned over 'He's not transferred sir, he's attached'.

'Tut-tut! Who brought this charge to me?' asked the C.O.

'I did sir,' replied Captain Davies standing at the side of the C.O.'s desk 'I though you should know sir!'

The C.O. looked at him 'You thought I should know, did you, perhaps I know more than you think! Captain Davis remain here please, I want a word with you; Corporal, you are entitled to wear your regimental badge until such times as you are notified that you have been transferred to another unit, case dismissed!'

I left the orderly room with the R.S.M. and my first action was to replace my regimental cap badge in its proper place.

'Well that was soon settled and I'm pleased,' said the R.S.M. 'I'll bet Captain Davis is squirming before the old man is finished with him, but you watch your step Corporal, watch your step.

I didn't need to watch my step for very long, that weekend I had the pleasure of watching a draft of fifty men march off to the station on their way to France and at the head of the column marched Captain Davis. That was the last I saw of him.

The weather was cold now, with hard white frosts in the morning, and living under canvas on the edge of the sea didn't bring much joy. One night coming out of the Y.M.C.A. hut in Hornsea I bumped into a chap who was just entering 'Sorry!' I remarked and made to pass him when he grabbed my arm 'Hello, Tommy, how goes it?'

It was Fred Wake, the chap I had bandaged in a shell hole on the Somme and met again in Kitebrook hospital.

'Good Lord Fred where have you sprung from, we always seem to be meeting,' I exclaimed.

Over a mug of tea in the Y.M.C.A. he told me he had been back in France since leaving hospital and had again been wounded.

'Hell, Fred, that's quick work'.

He grinned 'I was put on a draft right away, but I only lasted a couple of weeks in France, I got this packet on the neck,' and he leaned forward to show me a nasty scar along the back of his neck.

'What are you doing in Hornsea, Fred?' I asked.

He shrugged 'I'm with an advance working party, my mob are at Alnwick and they're moving down here next week'.

We talked about the people we knew at Kitebrook and then Fred stood up 'I've got a date with a wench Tommy, care to come along with me?'

I grinned 'Don't be daft Fred, two's company you know'.

'Oh, there's two wenches at this house so you won't be in the way, you'll get a decent feed anyway, come on'.

Fred took charge of operations and led the way to the rear of a large house where a girl in a white overall answered his tap on the door. She greeted him with a smile and said 'Come in, Fred I've got a lovely meat pie for your supper, hello, who's your friend?'

Fred laughed 'This is the chap I keep meeting all over the place Millie, we met first in a shell hole on the Somme, then we met again in hospital in Gloucestershire, and now we've met once more in Hornsea, queer isn't it?'

'It must be fate,' said Millie looking me over 'anyway come in, a friend of Fred's is a friend of mine; I suppose you could do with a bit of supper'.

She led us into a nice clean kitchen and soon had us sitting at the table enjoying a big slice of meat pie and a cup of tea.

'What do you think of that for a meat pie Tommy?' asked Fred.

'Just about the best I ever tasted, Fred,' I replied with relish.

Fred grinned and winked at Millie 'Now he's paying you compliments Millie, tell him its your own make'.

Millie smiled at me 'I'm cook here,' she explained 'And the folk here like home cooked food.

'Well, if that's a sample I don't blame them,' I replied 'the flavour of that pie was delicious'.

As we sat and smoked the door opened and a girl in a black dress came in carrying a tray of dishes, as she put down the tray she looked at Millie and said 'what's this, an invasion?'

Millie laughed and answered 'Oh you know Fred all right, and this Corporal is a friend of his,' she turned to me and said 'This is Maud, she's parlour maid here'. And that's how I came to meet Maud in Hornsea.

We met a few times and I found her good company, it wasn't long before I discovered that she was an orphan girl, in fact so far as I could make out she seemed to be alone in the world. This might have had something to do with her attitude towards me, because I soon realized she was stressing the fact that wedding bells made sweet music and the sooner we heard them playing the better she would be pleased. However, my ideas didn't line up with hers at all, as a companion she was all right but the memory of Ruby and Amy put her right out of the running for anything more. The night I told Maud I was leaving Hornsea for Pocklington she rather overplayed her hand by throwing a rather realistic faint and subsiding in my arms. I don't know what she expected of me but I did the only thing I could think of, in the ring you pulled a chaps ears to bring him round, so I pulled Maud's ears and she made a swift recovery, but I don't think she approved at all.

The following day I made the journey inland to Pocklington where I reported to the orderly room and handed over my papers to the R.S.M. He was an elderly chap with the ribbons of South Africa on his tunic; he read my papers and then looked at me.

'Well Corporal back from France wounded and awaiting a medical eh?' he remarked 'What are you going to do here?'

'That's up to you sir,' I replied.

'Don't suppose you want any square bashing do you?'

I grinned 'Not if I can help it sir'.

He grunted 'Don't blame you, tell you what, act as orderly room Corporal here with me for a time, I'm getting too bloody old to go chasing all over the place'.

'What am I supposed to do sir?' I inquired.

'I'll find plenty for you to do, you report here at my desk at 8 am every morning, now go and get settled in one of the huts, find Sergeant Barlow, he'll put you right'.

I wandered round the huts making inquiries and at last found Sergeant Barlow and explained my instructions.

'Right, there's room in my hut, here it is,' he threw open the door of one of the huts and we entered 'get your bedding from the stores and settle down in here'.

He looked me over 'So old Warren is using you in the orderly room is he, what's the idea?'

'I'm waiting a medical, Sergeant,' I replied.

Barlow laughed 'Well he'll keep you busy Corporal, he likes to stay glued to his chair and let others do the running around'.

'Any overseas men here, Sergeant?' I inquired and I was pleased when he nodded his head 'They keep coming and going,' he replied.

I got along well with R.S.M. Warren and I found he was pretty easy going with anyone who had been on active service; his own active service had been against the Boers in South Africa and now his greatest regret was that age kept him in England.

'How would you like to go back to France, Corporal?' he asked me one day as we sat in the orderly room.

I looked out of the window of the hut and saw the squads of men tramping in the snow, men being hammered into shape by bawling N.C.O.'s, and I shook my head.

'I don't think I would like it, sir,' I replied.

'Why not?'

I shrugged my shoulders, 'I don't know really, but it all seems so different now. I was keen enough to go out with the battalion, but that battalion was wiped out and reformed since then. If I went back now I'd be among strangers'.

'You'd still be 'brethren-in-arms', Corporal,' he said 'and it must give you a thrill to be face to face with the enemy'.

'I don't know that I'm all that keen on thrills of that nature,' I replied 'there's a lot more to it than just fighting'.

I didn't do any parades at Pocklington, all I had to do was stick around the orderly room, make myself useful, and be at the beck and call of the R.S.M. and the Adjutant. As I got to know the chaps in my hut I noticed with interest a short thick set fellow decorated with the trade mark of the boxer who has been through the mill, a well flattened nose and an ear that looked like a battered mushroom.

'What's your name, chum?' I asked him.

'Private Reilly, Corporal,' he replied in a husky voice.

'All right, Private Reilly,' I said with a grin 'and what name did you fight under in civvy street?'

His small eyes gleamed as he replied 'Kid Reilly of Liverpool, bantamweight, suppose you could tell by my cauliflower!'

'Its a beauty, where did you collect that one?' I asked.

He shrugged 'It started in the boxing booth and then Mickey Munroe made a job of it when we fought in Leeds, they lanced it but it never went back into shape'.

I went over to get my shaving gear out of my haversack and I felt his eyes on me, and then he stepped in front of me 'Alf a mo,' Corporal,' he said 'You don't happen to have done a bit yourself, do you?'

I grinned 'Not your kind of stuff, Reilly, amateur, pure and simple'.

'Simon pure eh,' Reilly smiled 'well I've known some pretty good ones, get anywhere with it Corporal?'

'Battalion and brigade, and went down in the divisional final'.

'Hard luck, Corporal, still someone has to lose; had a go with any pro's in your time?'

'Two or three, the best one was George Dando, I was sparring partner for him once, before I joined up'.

Reilly's face lit up 'George Dando, holy mackerel, you're in the class, I wonder would you have a spar with me?'

I shook my head ruefully and raised my gloved right hand, I'm sorry Reilly, I'm afraid Jerry has put paid to my boxing'.

'Well now, that's a bloody shame,' said Reilly 'I was hoping you'd help me out for the sports. How about a bit of fast left handwork and no rough stuff'.

'Nothing doing Reilly,' I replied. 'I haven't boxed for months'.

It was left at that, I had no intention of attempting anything in the way of boxing, but two days later, after tea, my interest was aroused when I entered the hut and found the boys clearing the tables to make a space down the centre. Reilly was sitting on his bed and a set of boxing gloves were beside him.

'What's going on here?' I asked.

Reilly grinned cheerfully 'One or two of the boys are going to give me a bit of sparring, what about you Corporal?'

'No, not me Reilly, but I'll watch and find fault if you like'.

'That will suit me,' said Reilly 'lets get started, you fellows'.

Reilly was pretty fast and a strong body puncher but the fact that the chaps seemed scared of him made him look better than he was. He sparred with two chaps and further volunteers were lacking so he turned to me and said 'Any faults to find, Corporal?'

I nodded my head 'Yes, Reilly, you're dropping your guard where you come in to the body, a good left hooker would knock your block off'.

'But I'm coming in to throw punches, not to guard 'em,' he protested.

'You're punches wouldn't get there, I'm telling you'.

'Aw, never mind telling me, show me!' he challenged.

'Go on Corporal, show him!' echoed the grinning bunch of soldiers.

There was no way out for me so I stripped off my tunic and shirt, and gloves were pulled on, and I faced Kid Reilly to try and prove my statement. I had the advantage of height and reach, and I must have been about half a stone heavier, but I had been living pretty soft since my return to England and I knew what Reilly's body digs would do to me.

I just couldn't afford to take many of them. I moved around and jabbed out a few snappy lefts that jerked his head back, but I knew I was pretty slow, and he soon got wise, slipped under a left and came bustling in. A right under the ribs let me know he could hit and he grinned at me as I collared him and pushed him away. We fiddled around and I threw a miss, a deliberate miss with my right and as Reilly tore in he ran full into my favourite left hook. It cracked home on his chin and he dropped to his knees, shaking his head to clear the fog.

'See what I mean Reilly?' I said, and he looked up at me with a grin breaking out on his face.

'Yes, I see what you mean Corporal, hell, I thought you were kidding me; I never even saw it coming'.

There was a buzz of excitement from the onlookers as Reilly climbed to his feet and as I pulled off the gloves someone said 'Aw come on, give us some more'.

I shook my head 'Its no use boys, I'm out of training and I've only got one hand, that was only a bit of advice for Reilly'. However, that little episode told me that I was making a mistake in letting myself run to seed and I joined in with Reilly in his training, walking, running, punching bag, exercises, and sparring with my one good hand. He was a good sort and he never once took advantage of the fact that I was boxing under a handicap, actually he held out his chin and got me to try out my right on it. Then he would say dolefully 'You'd better tuck it away somewhere, its not much good to you'.

'I'm hoping it might improve in time,' I said.

'It might, but its going to take a long time,' he answered.

I was with the R.S.M. one day, busy in the orderly room when the duty orderly Sergeant walked in with the news that a lady wished to see me at the main entrance to the camp.

The R.S.M. cocked an eye at me and asked 'Expecting anyone?'

I shook my head 'No sir, I haven't a notion who it can be'.

'Well, you'd better go and find out what its all about,' he grunted 'And I hope to hell you haven't been up to any tricks'.

I made my way to the main gate and, greatly to my surprise, I found Maud from Hornsea awaiting me, under the eyes of a grinning sentry.

'Maud, what in the world are you doing here?' I asked.

She smiled shyly 'I've got a few days holiday, so I thought I would spend them at Pocklington, I hope you don't mind Tommy'.

'Ye Gods! What a hole to spend a few days holiday!'

'I don't mind Maud, why should I? But what's the big idea?'

'Oh, I thought it would be nice if we had a few more days together,' she simmered 'I've got fixed up with digs in Pocklington'.

'Well, I hope you enjoy it Maud,' I replied 'but I'm on orderly room duty and I don't get much time off so I'm afraid you won't see a great deal of me'.

'Oh dear, surely you'll get time off if you have a visitor,' she cried.

'Nothing doing Maud, there's no relationship,' I replied.

'Well what are we going to do?' asked Maud 'We can't just stand talking here, can we?'

'You hang around a bit, or wander down the road,' I said 'I'll slip back and see if I can get a pass out from the R.S.M.; its about tea time now so there shouldn't be any trouble'.

'Make it a late pass Tommy, the later the better!' said Maud, and the sentry grinned and nearly dropped his rifle.

I wasn't feeling too happy about it as I wandered back to the orderly room where I found the R.S.M. enthroned in his chair with his pipe going full blast.

'Well, what's the answer, Corporal?' he asked.

'Its girl I got to know in Hornsea sir,' I replied lamely 'and she's come here to see me'.

'I knew it, you bloody fool,' he snorted 'You've been playing about and now she's going to have a baby, out with it!

I stared at him 'No, nothing like that sir, she's got a holiday and she's spending it here in Pocklington that's honest'.

He grunted 'All right, but just you listen to me you young fool, I know women better than you do; you didn't put her in the family way in Hornsea so she's followed you here and she's hoping and praying you'll do it before she returns to Hornsea'.

I looked hurt 'Honestly sir, I have no intention --!

'You and your bloody intentions! He snorted 'I know what I'm talking about, I've seen it happen with good kids so often. A few hectic minutes behind a hedge and you're saddled with a wife and kid you don't want, for life! Look here son, are you in love with the lass?'

I shook my head 'No sir, I'm not'.

'Didn't think you were judging by the look of you. But mark my words, she's after your blood; what are you going to do about it?'

'What can I do about it?' I said glumly.

'Nothing son, nothing, just fall into the bloody trap I suppose,' he slapped his desk with a heavy hand 'By hell you don't, there's eight men leaving here tomorrow for Catterick and I'm detailing you to take charge of that party, understand?'

'Yes sir,' I replied, rather staggered at his swift decision 'and do I return here?'

'No, you don't, you'll stay at Catterick camp. I'll get your papers made out this evening,' he growled 'now where is this woman?'

'Waiting for me outside camp sir,' I replied 'Can I have a late pass sir?'

'No, you bloody well can't have a late pass, what the hell are you trying to do, put your head in the lions mouth?' he roared. He scribbled on a pass form and handed it to me 'That let's you free until 9 p.m. and if you haven't reported to the guardroom by then I'll skin you alive. Now away you go, and keep your buttons done up! I've got sons of my own in the army, that's why I want to keep you out of trouble see?'

'Yes sir, thank you,' and I wandered off with mixed feelings to join Maud, but those mixed feelings jolted into place as I turned a corner of the road and found Maud and a Sergeant laughing together at some joke the Sergeant had cracked. Maybe the old boy was right after all. The Sergeant gave me a smile and went on his way, while Maud joined me with 'I hope you've got a late pass Tommy!'

'No Maud, I've got to report back at 9 p.m.'.

'Oh that's not fair, what's the use of that! Sergeant's can get all night passes when their lady friends visit them'.

'Who told you that yarn, Maud?' I asked.

'Oh, that Sergeant I was talking to when you came along she replied with a toss of her head.

Pretty fast work, I though as we walked along.

'How about if I get an all night pass Maud?' I asked.

Her hand gripped my arm and she looked at me coyly 'Oh Tommy that would be lovely, will you?'

'I might,' I replied 'But it won't be in Pocklington, I'm leaving here in the morning for Catterick'.

Maud stopped dead in he tracks and stared at me. 'You're what?'

'The R.S.M. has just told me, I'm off to Catterick Bridge'.

'Where's that?'

'Somewhere in North Yorkshire I believe, I've heard of it but I've never been there,' I replied.

Then the storm broke, and I realized it was a storm of frustration as the tears rolled I lit a cigarette to cover my embarrassment. 'No use making a fuss Maud, its orders and I can't make better of it'.

'And what about me?' Maud flared 'I'm booked for four days in Pocklington and now its all no use, what am I going to do in this hole when you leave?'

I shrugged my shoulders 'You'll find something to do Maud, after all you came on your own, you know.'

We walked the three miles in the snow to Pocklington and had tea in a small cafe but I'm afraid neither of us felt very comfortable and I was pleased when I was able to tell her that it was time for me to get back to camp. More tears and pleadings that I would write long and often and then I was on my way back with a feeling of having got rid of a load off my shoulders. I handed in my pass and the Sergeant of the guard checked it against the clock; 'Fifteen minutes early Corporal,' he said with a smile 'Report to Sergeant Major Warren, he's in the Sergeant's Mess'. I reported at the Sergeants Mess hut and the R.S.M. came to me as I waited in the ante room. His eyes shot to the clock on the wall and he grinned 'Five minutes early eh', well that's all to the good; I want to tell you that everything is fixed up, you'll parade at seven o'clock in the morning with your kit, a horse transport will take you to the station for the eight o'clock train, all clear?'

'Yes sir'

'Good, you can change at York for Catterick, and what about the little lady?'

I felt, and I suppose I looked, a bit uncomfortable 'I'm beginning to think you might be right sir'.

'Might be right', he snorted 'I know damned well I'm right. Listen son, the country is lousy with females on the look out to get kids like you entangled, and I hate to see it. Watch your step in future and don't be a mug, goodbye and good luck'.

The party of eight men and myself boarded the train for York the following morning, seven rather helpless looking bewildered recruits and one elderly chap with ribbons on his chest. It was an unsociable squad that sat gazing out of the window of the train at the driving snow; the old soldier eyed me and said 'You know this place Catterick, Corporal?'

I shook my head 'No, do you?'

'I've heard of it,' he replied 'They reckon its a hell of a hole, break yer bloody heart in a matter of weeks,' his eyes roved over the listening recruits 'you'd be better off in the glass house'.

'Cheerful sort o,' cove, you are,' someone muttered.

'I'm telling yer,' said the old soldier 'I've heard tell there's a suicide among the 'rookies,' once a week, its murder!'

'And what about the old sweats?' a youngster asked.

'Oh, we're better off,' said the old soldier pointing to his ribbons 'they don't bash us around like they do you young 'uns, see'.

'What's your name?' I asked him.

'MacArdle, Private MacArdle,' he replied.

'All right Mac, you been to France?' I asked.

He stuck out his chest 'I went to France in 1914 Corporal'.

'Good lad, how long were you there?' I asked.

'Three weeks, got hit in the leg, I'll show you if you like'.

'It doesn't matter Mac,' I replied 'but I was over there for twelve months and I'm bloody sure Catterick is better than that'.

The recruits looked a bit relieved at that, and changing the subject Mac pulled a pay chit out of his pocket.

'Look at that Corporal,' he growled 'that's my bloody pay, one lousy solitary shilling for a weeks soldiering'.

The pay chit had to be signed by the soldier and handed in to any post office to be cashed, in transit soldiers often got pay chits instead of cash, stoppages had reduced Mac's pay.

I grinned at him 'You won't get drunk on that Mac!'

'Get drunk!' he growled 'it wouldn't buy the kid an ice cream'.

At York we disembarked and moved over to the platform for the train to Catterick Bridge where we found we had two hours to wait. I kept an eye on my herd but Mac was the only one who seemed to have any inclination to wander, up and down the platform he prowled, and then suddenly he just wasn't there any more.

'Where the hell has he gone?' I asked in anger and one of the recruits pointed to a door along the platform 'In there, Corporal'.

I knew only too well what it would mean for me if I arrived at Catterick one man short of the number I started off with and I hastened along the platform in a worried state. However, as I reached the door indicated, it opened and a grinning Mac limped out 'You bloody old pest,' I growled 'what the hell did you go off like that for?'

He raised his eyebrows 'You didn't think I'd done a bunk, did you?

'That's just what I did think'.

'Not so likely Corporal, I'm waiting for my ticket so you needn't worry. I'm not taking any chances, see!

'What the hell were you doing in there?' I asked him.

He winked at me and held out his pay chit 'What do you think of that bit of work, Corporal?'

I looked at it and saw where it had been filled in previously £. 1s. 0d. it was now filled in 1£ 1s. 0d. - and a very neat job he had made of it.

'I had to get the loan of a pen to do it proper,' he said with pride.

'That's forgery Mac,' I exclaimed 'they'll find out about it at the paymaster's office and then you'll be in the mush'.

'He waved his hand 'Aw to hell, it'll be weeks before it gets that far and I'll have my ticket by then 'sufficient unto the day, that's my motto me lad'.

'Oh well, its your funeral Mac,' I replied 'I know nothing about it'.

He grinned 'That's the boy, now what about me going out and getting it cashed while we're waiting here, and I'll bring a nice little bottle of the best back with me'.

'Yes, and once you're out of the station that's you away and I'm left with one man missing when I report to Catterick, Mac you old twist, do you think I've just joined up?'

Mac drew himself up 'Corporal, I swear on my honour, on the honour of the regiment, I'll be back to catch that train'.

His face was serious as he spoke and his eyes looked straight into mine. I shook my head 'You couldn't do it Mac, didn't you notice the red caps at the main entrance to the station?'

He sniffed 'Red caps, what the hell are they, just bloody toy soldiers, I'll be back Corporal, that's an old soldiers promise'.

'Half an hour Mac,' I said and I tramped along the platform so that I wouldn't see him depart.

It was half an hour of agony for me and I cursed myself for being such a damned fool, but Mac limped back with a bottle of whiskey and half a bottle of rum, and still money to jingle in his pocket.

'How in hell did you do it Mac?' I asked as I took a swig at the rum. He winked at me 'There's still people in this country who'll help an old soldier, and the bloke in that pub was one of them, you got to tell the tale, see?'

We travelled on to Catterick Bridge in the cold slow motion train, and the journey was the better for the spoils of war that old Mac had managed to supply us with. At Catterick Bridge I made inquiries about the camp and the answer was 'Five miles along that road, you can't miss it!'

We looked at our heavy kitbags, five miles, and I said 'What about it Mac?'

He shook his head 'You please yourself Corporal, but count me out. I've got a running wound and I couldn't do five miles to save my life, even without a blasted kitbag'.

As we debated the situation a transport driver came over to us, 'You chaps going to the camp?' he inquired.

'Yes,' I replied 'but it seems a hell of a long walk'.

'You're right, it is, especially with kit to hump,' he replied 'tell you what I'll do, you help me unload this wagon and I'll give you a lift back'. His horse transport stood loaded with boxes and I said 'What about it, chaps?'

The boys were willing so I set them to work while Mac and the driver finished off the last of the whiskey. As the horse plodded along the road to the camp I looked around the countryside and didn't feel much joy at the miles and miles of open snow covered ground.

'Where the hell do you go here for a night out?' I asked the driver.

'Richmond's over there,' he said waving his whip over the wide open spaces but as far as the eye could see there was nothing 'you might get there once a week, if you're lucky'.

'What's the camp like?' I asked him.

'Its hell, Corporal, just plain hell,' he replied 'must be about eight thousand men here and more coming in every day, and there's not accommodation for half that number; they're building huts all over the place but not fast enough, its a tough joint this camp'.

'There you are, I told you,' said Mac 'Before you've been here a bloody week you'll wish your mother had never met your dad'.

'Oh well, I suppose we'll get use to it,' I said.

'Not on your bloody life you won't,' said the transport driver 'nobody gets use to Catterick, you either stay here and go off your nut or you volunteer to go back to France, you mark my words Corporal, they'll break your bloody heart'.

The transport wagon pulled up at an entrance to the camp and when we dismounted a sentry directed me to an orderly room and I marched my party to the door of the hut. Inside, I handed over my papers to an officer and after glancing through them he called over a Sergeant with instructions to get my party bedded down. The Sergeant came outside with me and looked the party over 'Bright looking mob,' he grumbled 'what the hell did you bring them here for, Corporal?'

'Orders Sergeant,' I replied and he waved his hands 'All right I know, all the unwanted and unwashed in the bleeding army are being dumped at Catterick, pick up that kit and follow me'.

We picked up our kitbags and followed, trudging in the slush and snow through a maze of hutments. The Sergeant opened the door of a hut and bawled 'Sergeant Willis!' Out of the cubicle at the end of the hut a figure appeared in singlet and trousers, a huge bulky figure with more hair on his chest than on his head 'What the hells up now?' he roared.

'Here's some more rookies for you,' said our Sergeant with a grin.

'Don't want them, take them away and drown them, cut their bloody throats if you like, but don't leave them here,' shouted Sergeant Willis. He glared at us with baleful eyes and then he pointed to Mac 'I'll take that bloke, step out blast you!' and Mac hastily took one pace forward. The Sergeant's eyes roamed over me 'What are you wearing that glove for, busted hand?'

'Yes Sergeant, wounds,' I replied.

'Right, I can use you, step out!' he growled 'And you, Sergeant, can take the rest of these cows droppings out of my sight, this hut is now packed so I'm taking no more, shove off'.

The rest of the party moved off and Mac and I entered the hut with our kitbags while Sergeant Willis stood watching us and then he said with a grin 'I don't mind you chaps with a bit of service, you can fish for yourselves, I'm fed up acting wet nurse to rookies. You'll get your blankets and squeeze a sleeping place somewhere'.

We gazed down the hut, each side of which was ranged with sleeping boards on which rested folded blankets, the space between each bed being about one foot.

'Going to be a bit of a tight squeeze Sergeant,' I remarked.

'Well make room for yourselves, or sleep on the bloody doorstep if you like, its all the same to me,' he replied and he turned to Mac 'you go and get blankets, stores at the end of this line; and you come in here Corporal,' he opened the door of his cubicle and we entered.

He's cosy enough, I thought, as I looked around the little cubicle with its regulation army bed, table, shelves and cupboard.

'Nice little cuddy hole, Sergeant,' I remarked as he waved me to a chair and sat himself on the bed which squeaked under his weight.

'Not bad,' he grunted 'I'm making the best of a bad job, I'm stuck here now for the duration, this is a hell of a place and I reckon I'm entitled to what I've got see'.

My eyes fastened on the tunic that was hanging on a nail in the wall and I saw the ribbons of the D.C.M. and the M.M. along with another ribbon I didn't recognize.

'What's the third one Sergeant?' I asked.

'Eh?' his eyes followed mine 'Oh that, its a French gong I got early on, helped some Froggees out of trouble, have a fag?'

I took one and we lighted up.

'Now Corporal I'll tell you what I wanted you for,' he said, 'we do a hell of a lot of working parties in this dump and some of the work is a hell of a long way from here. The parties have to hoof it all the way and its getting me down, I can't do it like I use to, look at this'. He stood up and dropped his trousers, exposing a pair of huge hairy legs and I saw a long angry looking deep scar that ran right down one thigh.

'How the hell can a chap march with that?' he asked pulling his pants and sitting on the bed again.

'Its a nasty one Sergeant, surely the M.O.—'

He waved that aside 'M.O. be damned, they're not M.O.'s here, they're just bloody butchers in uniform, anything wrong with your legs?'

I shook my head 'No, my legs are all right'.

'Fine, well the drill is, when I've got a working party you'll take charge of it and give me a written report when you return see?'

'Suits me, Sergeant,' I replied 'but what about the officers?'

He snorted 'Balls to them! They don't know where they are in this place, so long as you're occupied, that's all that matters'.

So I took on the job of N.C.O. in charge of working parties and I found that most of the work was with pick and shovel on a rifle range that was being built beyond Catterick Village; that meant a march of six miles to the job and six miles back. Some of the chaps were fit recruits and it was all right for them, but some of them had been wounded and found it pretty hard going. I felt sorry for them and so far as I was able I detailed the work according to the physical capabilities of the men. This led to grumbling from the recruits, but it went no further than that. Things went pretty smoothly up to the day when I found myself in charge of a party of German prisoners detailed for work on the range and for this job I was given an armed escort.

I marched the escort to the barbed wire compound where the prisoners lived and reported to the officer in charge.

'All right Corporal, you'll have thirty of them and warn your escort to keep an eye open, they're going on this working party because of a little trouble they've given'.

'Very good, sir'.

'Oh, and transport has been arranged to take you on the job'.

I stared at him, an overgrown schoolboy in uniform making a valiant attempt to grow a moustache.

'We don't need transport sir, let them march'.

'It has already been arranged Corporal'.

'Well cancel it, sir'.

'Look here Corporal, I can't do that. You do as ordered'.

'Very good sir, but its all wrong. Our chaps, fit and wounded, march to that job in all weathers and now lousy Germans have transport laid on for them, its not right sir'.

'Just you carry out your orders Corporal!'

Transport took us to the rifle range and there I lined up the prisoners and barked at them 'Who speaks English?'

A big hulking Prussian type slouched forward with his hands deep in the pockets of his overcoat. 'I spik it,' he said with a grin.

I eyed him up and down and then I walked slowly round him. I was in a vicious temper at the injustice to our own troops, and I booted him as hard as I could on his fat behind. He yelped and jumped a foot in the air.

'Now get your hands out of your pockets, you bastard, when you're speaking to a British N.C.O.,' I yelled at him.

He withdrew his hands and looked at me reproachfully. 'British don't do that no,' he said 'I make report'.

'Well I've just done it see; and you make a report you bloody square head and I'll peg you for attempting to incite trouble'. I let that sink in while one of the escort murmured 'give him another for me, Corporal'.

'Now listen to me Jerry, just you inform your lousy pals that the first one who starts anything here will get a bullet through the guts and it will be a pleasure. Now get your coats off and graft, work like hell'.

To show them I meant business I ordered the grinning escort to load and the Germans eyed us with concern as the rifle bolts rattled. Work went on non-stop and trouble free that day, and it was a weary bunch of Germans I delivered back to the cage. I reported to Sergeant Willis that evening and told him what he could do with his working parties 'I'm taking no more ruddy square-heads riding on transports while our own troops have to walk Sergeant, and you can tell the C.O. Catterick Camp if you like'.

'If you drop this job Corporal they'll put you on something a damned site worse,' replied Sergeant Willis 'Dunno what you're belly-aching about, you've just had the satisfaction of kicking a Jerry up the arse!'

Two days later I was ordered to report to the medical hut and a doddering old fool in tartan trousers examined my hand and said 'I'm making you B2 Corporal awaiting a boards examination'.

Category B2 meant that I was fit for any work in England or overseas but not fit for the fighting line. Plenty of B2 men were being drafted to France; in fact judging by some of the drafts I saw limping away from Catterick Camp I am inclined to think that England was beginning to scrape the bottom of the manpower bucket. In France our troops had been hurled into attack after attack, heedless of the appalling losses of first rate fighting men and now the tide of battle had turned and once again the German jack boot was advancing over the blood soaked fields of the valley of the Somme.

However there was no joy at Catterick and if the worst came I felt I wouldn't be sorry to get away from it. In those days it was a land of queues, and hundreds of soldiers spent useless hours standing in a queue. You stood in a queue for a haircut, you stood in a queue for your pay, you stood in a queue at the Y.M.C.A. or the wet canteen, you stood in a queue for your meals, you stood in a queue for the latrines, in fact most of your time was spent standing in a queue. At long last orders came for me to move, I was detailed to take five men and report to an Army Service Corps Officer, Lieutenant Halliday, at Foss Island in York City. With joy in our hearts we boarded the train at Catterick Village and left Catterick with the hope that we would never return. In York station I contacted a red cap Sergeant and asked for directions 'Let's see your papers!' he ordered and I handed them over. After reading them he handed them back, 'Yes I know where you want to be,' and he directed me in the general direction of the section of York known as Foss Island, 'When you get there you'll find a place where the A.S.C. have built a lot of haystacks, report there for Lieutenant Halliday'. The five men I had with me were all wounded active service men so we took our time in reaching Foss Island, in fact we called in a pub and had a drop of nourishment to help us on our way, but eventually we got there and located a big area of land occupied by a lot of haystacks. The land was fenced in and following the fence we came to an entrance where a bored looking sentry stood on duty. 'I'm looking for Lieutenant Halliday,' I said to the sentry 'any idea where he is?'

He shook his head with a grin 'There's a hundred hotels in York and he might be in any one of 'em, we only see him on pay day'.

'Well who's in charge here?' I asked.

'Sergeant Duffy, Corporal, that's the man you want'.

'Right, where is Sergeant Duffy?'

The sentry looked vaguely around at the towering stacks of hay. 'Dunno Corporal, he'll be around somewhere'.

I turned to my little party 'All right, dump your kit and make yourselves comfortable, we're not trailing around this joint looking for anyone'. We sat on our kit and smoked and talked, after about half an hour the Sergeant strolled up and said 'Hello, who are you blokes?' I handed him the papers 'Reporting from Catterick Sergeant'. He was a small-wizened looking chap with a ginger moustache, he sported the cap badge of the Army Service Corps but he looked more like a racecourse tout than a Sergeant in the army. 'Oh, I see,' he said stuffing the papers in his pocket 'Well, you've come here to guard these stacks see, its cushy enough billet but you'll do most of your duty at night, its a patrol guard and you go round the stacks at night'. I looked at him to see if he was pulling my leg and then I looked at the haystacks 'What the hell do they want guards for?'

He grunted 'Suppose you've lived all your life in a town eh? Ain't you ever heard of haystacks taking fire that's what we've got to guard against. If this bloody lot got going in a wind it would just about burn York City down'.

'Well what the hell do they want to build them here for?' I asked 'There's plenty of room in the country for them'.

'Handy for transport,' replied the Sergeant 'Anyway don't ask silly questions, its nothing to do with us where they build the things; you'll be in private billets on this job; come on and I'll get you fixed up in this street'.

We picked up our kitbags and walked down the street with the Sergeant where he got each of us fixed up, the house I was posted to was occupied by an old lady and her married daughter and my room was a little attic at the top of the house. They supplied me with food and lodgings for which they were paid by the army and after my spell of tents and huts and army grub I felt quite satisfied with my little lot. The old lady was a decent sort but the married daughter was a bit of a snob, at my first meal with them she informed me that her husband had a commission, and the way she looked down her nose at my couple of stripes I knew just what she meant. However, we saw very little of each other, meal times was about the only time we met and then we were too busy eating to do much talking. After a wash and a meal I made my way back to the stack yard and met one of the chaps I had brought from Catterick, a fellow called Bill Sutton. A bullet wound in the leg made him walk with a stick and he limped over grinning.

'What's your billet like Corporal?'

'Not bad, I think I'll be comfortable enough'.

'I've got a corker, a soldiers dream,' he said 'Two daughters in the house and neither of 'em married, the eldest twenty three with a couple of kids, and the other one seventeen and one kid. They don't half know all the bedtime stories'.

'Hell! You'll have to watch your step, Sutton or you'll be in trouble'.

He laughed 'Not me Corporal, I've got a wife and kid waiting for me in 'Brum', I'll keep my nose clean'.

It wasn't his nose I was bothering about, all the same it was hardly fair putting a chap in with that much temptation. I contacted Sergeant Duffy and he explained to me the drill of plunging your arm into the haystacks to feel for any heat. 'We just fall the blokes in and check them at guard change times, no fancy parades or anything like that. I'll get your chaps on the duty roster and then you can make a start'.

'When will that be Sergeant?'

'Oh, I'll let you know tomorrow, have tonight off anyway'.

We slipped into the easy routine of looking after haystacks and most of it was night duty when we took turns of sleeping and patrolling. I suppose we were doing a job of work but I always had the feeling that the damned things would have been just as well without us. Off duty our time was our own and we found York City was a good place in which to spend your leisure, the trouble was we didn't have much else to spend. However in time we collected a little bunch of girls living in the locality of the stack yard and they had money to spend. They were working on munitions, and once a week on payday they rolled up to give us an evening out. It usually developed into a pub-crawl and it was their money that went down the drain, it was their idea of entertaining wounded soldiers. I found the going pretty hard at times; those dames could carry a cargo better than I could and I was usually sorry for myself the following day. I was no drinking man, but I just drifted with the tide.

I found myself doing a bit more than my share at the stack yard and Sergeant Duffy fading more and more into the background but this was due to the fact that the men stationed there were infantry men who had done active service and so was I. It was summed up in a remark I heard one day 'The Corporals all right, but I'm taking no orders from a bloody 'Alley Slopers,' bloke who don't know which end of a rifle a bullet comes out'. It was a happy billet at York and we made the best of it, as Bill Sutton once said 'We ain't alf lucky to be here Corporal, but for the grace of God we'd still be wallowing in the muck at Catterick'. The chaps started to apply for leave, and it was granted without any fuss; it was then that I suddenly realized that it was twelve months since I had my hospital leave. I filled in an application form and as I was writing it Sergeant Duffy said 'Putting in for some leave, Corporal?'

'Yes, it's a year since I was home,' I replied.

'A year, that's a hell of a long time, you're entitled to seven days and a free travelling warrant, where do you want to go?'

On the spur of the moment I replied 'Langham, in Norfolk'.

That was Amy's home, but I had no idea where it was.

Upon making inquiries I found that the railway station was a place called Holt, good enough for me, so I collected my pass and headed for York station the following morning.

'Change at Peterboro,' and away I went on a carefree journey into the unknown happy in the knowledge that I would find Amy at the end of my journey. It was late afternoon when I arrived at Holt and the ticket collector directed me on the road to Langham 'About seven miles, you can't miss it'.

Seven miles to walk, oh well, I was use to 'picking them up and putting them down,' so here goes; and I walked the seven miles of country lanes in Norfolk and never met a soul until I tramped into the village of my dreams.

'Where's the post office chum?' I asked the first country yokel I met, behind a drove of cows.

He grinned, looked me over, gazed at the sky, looked up and down the road and then said 'Just along past the church'.

I kept on along the village street past the church and then came to the general stores and post office, this was it. I pushed open the door and entered the shop to the jangling of the doorbell, closed the door and looked around. A stout built lady with fair gleaming hair stood behind the counter and looked at me enquiringly.

I smiled and said 'I'm looking for Amy'.

Her eyes went to my cap badge and then she cried 'Why, its Tommy isn't it?'

'That's right, how did you know?'

'Your badge bar, your regiment isn't in these parts, I'm Amy's mother, come through son,' and she raised the flap of the counter, put her arms round me and kissed me with a motherly welcome. And so I met the dearest, kindest soul in the whole wide world. 'Amy's out at present but she won't be long,' she informed me 'how on earth did you get here?'

'Train to Holt and then I walked,' I replied as I thankfully sat down in the living room.

'Oh, you poor boy, why didn't you write and say you were coming, we could have arranged someone to meet you,' she fussed around and laid out a plate of home cooked buns and a glass of cider. 'Amy will get a surprise when she sees you, Tommy,' she said 'how long are you staying?'

'Well I've got seven days leave,' I replied 'but I'm wondering now if it's convenient—'

Convenient - of course it is, we've got plenty of room here now that my boys are away. Stay as long as you can'.

She had four boys in the services, three in the army and one in the Royal Navy.

Just then Amy walked in and when she saw me she just stood and looked, then calm and unruffled as ever, she smiled and said 'Tommy! I thought I was dreaming'.

'No, its me all right,' I laughed and I kissed her and knew I had picked the right place for seven days leave.

Amy's father was just as dear a character as her mother, I found them to be a mildly religious family living in a little circle of love and friendship that made me realize what a lot of good things can be got out of life, if only you can live it the right way. I had a wonderful seven days, and they did everything to make my stay with them a happy one.

I left Langham in style, sitting in a trap behind a trolling horse, and Amy came to Holt station to see me off. Back to York and the same old grind, feeling a bit fed up at having to leave my happiness behind in a little Norfolk village. 'You're reporting to Strensall next week Corporal,' Sergeant Duffy informed me that night.

'Strensall! What the hell is this for?' I asked him 'I was at Strensall for a bit before I went overseas'.

'I dunno what its for,' he shrugged his shoulders 'Its always like this in the bloody army, you just get things nicely working and then you've got to start all over again with someone else'.

'Oh well, Strensall's not so bad,' I muttered 'damned sight better than Catterick anyway. We'll never win the war looking after haystacks anyway, will we?'

In due course I reported to Strensall camp and once more I was under canvas, but it was summer time so I didn't mind that. An interview with the Adjutant gave me an inkling of why I had been set to Strensall; he was a tall black haired public school type, reserved ad dignified, with the ribbon of the D.S.O. on his chest to prove he was a 'pukka officer'.

'Ah, Corporal, you did a course of bayonet fighting here before you went overseas, I believe,' he said quietly.

'That's correct sir,' I replied.

'Care for a job as instructor while you're here?'

'I can instruct sir, but I'm afraid I'll be handicapped a bit'

'How do you mean?'

'I won't be able to demonstrate sir, owing to my hand'.

'Oh, that's a pity,' he sat for a moment in thought then he said 'I'll tell you what Corporal, take it on and do your best for the time being, we're damned short of instructors for the moment, I'll switch you to another job later on'

'Very good sir, I'll do what I can,' I replied.

I quickly settled down at Strensall and I put all I had into the job handed over to me, to the sweating sorrow of the squads of men who passed through my hands. However, these were trained men, ready to depart overseas at any time, and I knew what was facing them when they moved up into the fighting line. Every little bit of extra knowledge of the use of the rifle and bayonet added up to a little bit extra chance of survival on the battlefield. They lumbered over rough ground, they crawled under or climbed over barbed wire, they pushed their way through woods with dense undergrowth, they jumped trenches and crawled along ditches and always they stabbed and hacked at dummy figures. I made them point and parry and use the rifle butt, I made them fight with dummy bayonets wearing leather protection and masks, I made them use their feet and swerve their bodies, impressing on them that this was no parade ground stuff and I taught them that at close quarter work a boot between the legs was just as effective as a bayonet thrust. I was confident that when I passed each squad over they were just a little better than when they started, and the Adjutant nodded his approval and said 'You're giving them a lot of stuff that isn't laid down in the drill book, Corporal, but I can see your point of view'. By the time they had finished their rifles were no longer cumbersome weapons, their rifles were part of them, and my creed was that you only became a good fighting man by coming master of your rifle.

It was in the wet canteen at Strensall one Friday night, pay night for the troops, that I got mixed up in a spot of bother. It was near to closing time and the place was crowded with soldiers, each of whom had indulged freely in the frothing ale. A commotion started at the bar and angry voices were raised, suddenly the crowd heaved back and there was the sodden thump of fists, a voice yelled 'Come on you English bastards, I'll show you what foightin,' is, up the Irish!' The scuffling went on beside the bar but I couldn't see anything but waving arms and a chap beside me cried 'Its that crazy Irishman Paddy Flynn'.

I had no idea who Paddy Flynn was but I could hear him howling his Irish war chant and judging by the sound of blows a first rate battle seemed to be brewing up.

'Spill an Irishman's beer would yer,' yelled Paddy 'I'll teach yer a bloody lesson, Hurrah for the Green, Ireland forever!'

There was the crash of bottles and glasses as a table went over and someone shouted 'Look out, here's the M.P.'s'. I saw a couple of military police at the door, a short stocky Sergeant and an unhappy looking Lance Corporal. 'What the hell's going on here?' roared the Sergeant 'Make way there, make way, come on Johnson!'

The crowd parted, making way for the police to the bar and leaning against the bar I saw a wild black haired chap in a torn shirt with a couple of soldiers laid at his feet.

He reared up as he caught sight of the two policemen and roared 'Polis,' is it? All right, call out the bloody marines if you like'. He swung his arm and a bottle flew through the air, the Sergeant ducked but the Lance Corporal got it on the side of the head and he folded up and lost all interest in the proceedings.

'That's enough Flynn, pack it up,' roared the Sergeant but the Irishman grinned and grabbed a glass off the bar. Deliberately he broke it on the counter and faced the police Sergeant with the deadly jagged piece in his hand. 'So its you, me broth of a boy,' he snarled 'Sure and I've been waiting,' for this chance. You've jugged me a few times Sergeant, but glory be, this is where I pay you back'.

The Sergeant stood motionless and there was fear in his eyes as the wild drunken Irishman advanced. As Flynn came nearer I elbowed the chaps on each side of me away; Flynn had to pass close to me to get at the Sergeant. 'Give me room,' I whispered and I set myself firmly on the balls of my feet. Flynn never saw me, his glassy stare was fixed on the Sergeant and I brought the punch from away behind putting all I had into it. It landed below the ear, and it was a good one, it sent Flynn weaving and his knees buckled, he dropped the broken glass but he didn't go down. He stood swaying, trying to focus his eyes and I stepped in and hooked him again, a hard left to the side of the mouth that brought blood, I think they were the two hardest punches I ever threw but still he didn't go down. However he was helpless, and the boys piled into him and carried him off to the guardroom with the M.P. Sergeant in full control. The other victims were taken to the M.O. but no harm had been done and they soon recovered, the Irish rebel looked sorry for himself the next day when he departed under escort for Aldershot. Fifty-six days detention was the price he had to pay, and I expect his Irish blood would be somewhat cooler by the time he came out. I never saw Paddy Flynn again.

The Regimental Police Sergeant was very effusive in his thanks. 'That crazy Irishman could have blinded me with that glass,' he said with a shudder.

'Yes, and worse Sergeant,' I agreed.

'Look here, Corporal,' he said 'I'm wanting you in my lot, I've put in an application for you'.

I stared at him 'Me, an M.P. oh, to hell with that Sergeant'.

'Now listen son,' he replied 'Its a damn good easy billet for you, what the hell do you want to go flogging your soul out for on this bayonet fighting racket, take things easy, man'.

I pointed to the cross swords on my sleeve 'Fighting is my job of work Sergeant, that's what I joined the army for'.

'You've done your share of fighting son, let someone else have a go,' he stood up 'anyway we'll see what H.Q. has to say about it'.

For three days I heard nothing further and then came instructions to report to the orderly room and once more I faced the Adjutant.

He smiled at me and said 'Congratulations, Corporal for assisting the Regimental Police the other evening. A nasty business. How would you like to carry out police duties at Strensall?'

'Its not my cup of tea, sir,' I replied.

'Well, no. I suppose not,' he leaned back in his chair 'Look here Corporal, I should advise you to take it on its a lot easier than the job you're on at present you know'.

I shook my head 'I'm all right as I am, I don't fancy it'.

'All right, I see what you mean, but in confidence, has Catterick Bridge any attractions for you?'

'Catterick Bridge, I hated the place sir'.

He nodded 'Most of us do. Well, the position is simply this, they're howling for instructors for Catterick and I'm afraid you'll be booked for there if you stay as you are. Anyway it's up to you'.

'I'll be a copper sir,' I replied 'Anything's better than Catterick'

'Good, report to Sergeant Richardson for duty,' and he dismissed me.

I didn't want to be a regimental policeman but I was thankful that the Adjutant had pointed out a loophole to avoid Catterick. I got my gear together and reported to Sergeant Richardson at the police tent, he greeted me with a smile 'Good boy, I thought you would come, put this arm band on and then you'll be one of us'. I pulled on the black armband with its red letters M.P., and thus I became a member of the most disliked mob in the British Army. Beside the police tent was a small barbed wire compound containing three bell tents, the residence of the chaps who broke the military law.

I found it a good billet, we patrolled the village and the country lanes, keeping a eye on the drunks and the chaps who couldn't tear themselves away from the entwining arms of love to get back to camp before 'Lights out', the drunks and the strays had to be chased back to camp and a few had to be carried back. We kept a strict eye on the gambling schools where the chaps who ran the 'Crown and Anchor,' boards and 'Housey,' flourished at the expense of the boys who liked a flutter, chaps leaving the camp improperly dressed, even one button undone, had to 'about turn,' and miss his evening out. We were responsible for the prisoners and had charge of the sorry squad on 'jankers,' while they sweated out their punishment in full marching order on the square. And although I dished out warnings and threats in plenty I never brought anyone up on a charge, I suppose I was a damned poor copper. It was while on duty at the crossroads outside Strensall village that I met Barbara; she was driving a bunch of cows to some farm over the hill and for some reason best known to themselves cows seem to have a habit of spreading out North, East, South and West when the opportunity arises. That opportunity arose at my crossroads and I watched with interest as the buxom wench dashed here and there thumping the cows with her stick.

Hot and bothered she cried to me 'Don't stand there grinning, come and give me a hand'.

'I don't know anything about those things,' I replied.

'Time you did, then,' she retorted with a toss of her dark curly hair 'now's your chance to learn'.

I was fed up hanging about at the crossroads so I gave her a hand to get the cows bunched together again 'Where are you taking them?' I asked her. She pointed along a road and by the sign post I saw it led to some place called Sheriff Hutton.

'A farm just over the hill,' she said 'thanks for your help'.

'I'm not doing any good here, I'll walk a bit of the way with you'. I offered and she smiled as we ambled along behind the cows. It was an hour before I got back to my post but there was no one about so I finished my turn of duty and returned to camp. I rather expected the Sergeant to bawl me out but apparently I hadn't been missed, being a freelance copper had its points after all. Barbara turned up in Strensall the next day and met me, this time without the cows and we spent a nice time together but I had to be back in camp at 6 p.m. to take over duty. We met a few times after that and I found Barbara was a sturdy healthy minded country lass, a farmer's daughter, whose soul interest seemed to be in horses and cows, chickens and geese, sheep and ducks and all the other things that go to make a farm. I was just becoming part of Strensall Camp when orders came once more and in the orderly room I received instructions to report to a Sergeant Major Drake in Leeds and I was handed an envelope with his name and address printed on it. I handed over my M.P. badge of office and departed from Strensall wondering what was in store for me in Leeds. I found the address to be a block of offices, and after climbing four flights of stairs I found a door with a label on it, Sergeant Major Drake, Army Service Corps. Hell! 'Alley Slopers,' mob, again!

I knocked and a voice bawled 'Come in!'

I entered and found a Sergeant Major sprawled at a desk in his shirtsleeves with a pile of papers in front of him.

'What do you want?'

I handed over the envelope 'Reporting from Strensall, sir'.

He grunted and read the contents of the letter 'Ho! I knew you were coming, but you're too bloody early, I don't need you yet. Dunno what I'm going to do with you at present, damned if I do'.

'Send me on leave sir!' I suggested hopefully.

'Can't do that, might be wanting you any time,' he looked at me for a moment, then he laughed 'You've been to France?'

'Yes sir'

'Good, then I'll tell you what to do,' he scribbled a note, put it in an envelope and wrote an address 'Give that to the landlord of that pub, he'll fix you up all right and if you don't hear from me report here on Friday for your pay. And take a tip from me boy, have a good time while you are in Leeds. Away you go'.

I reported to the landlord of the Commercial Arms and he read the letter I handed him 'Right you are son, we'll fix you up', and he beckoned to a girl in a black dress 'Alice, take this chap up to Room 14 and then get a meal ready for him, show him the dining room'. Alice looked me over and then with a gesture of her golden fluffy head beckoned me to follow. I followed, feeling in a bit of a daze.

Alice threw open a door along a passage 'Dining room,' she said 'When you get settled in, come down, and I'll have something ready, ham sandwiches all right for you?'

'That will do me fine,' I replied.

'And what about drink?' she asked 'Tea, or a pint of beer?'

'A pint of tea thanks,' I replied.

Another girl in the dining room looked up and said 'Hello Alice, what have you got there?'

'A soldier, billeted on us,' she turned away 'Come on Corporal, I'll show you your room'.

The girl in the dining room laughed 'Watch her Corporal when she gets you upstairs, she's a one, is Alice'.

'Jealousy!' replied Alice 'Don't you wish you had the job, Ann, dear?' 'Come on soldier, I'll show you your room'.

We climbed the stairs and it felt strange to me to be treading on carpets, along a passage of many doors Alice put a key in number 14, unlocked it and throwing open the door said 'There you are'. A nice single bed, a dressing table, a wardrobe, an easy chair, and a carpet on the floor, what comfort for a soldier.

'This is great!' I exclaimed, and in the doorway Alice shrugged.

'Bathroom along the passage, come down when you're ready'.

Alice left me and I took off my tunic and found the bathroom, what a joy after the tin basins in camp, I was wallowing in luxury. Back in my room I tried the bed, it was soft and yielding and the sheets were white, what a change to the hard boards and grey blankets I was use to. I made my way down to the dining room and Ann ushered me to a table set with a plate of ham sandwiches and cakes, a nice pot of tea, clean table linen and service. I tucked in and enjoyed my meal, I was sitting smoking when the landlord came in and approached my table.

'My names Weston,' he said 'How do you find things boy?'

'Just perfect Mr Weston,' I replied 'thanks for making me so comfortable!'

'No more than you chaps deserve,' he said 'Where did you get wounded?'

'On the Somme, when that show first started'.

He nodded 'Two of my lads were there, one of them won't come back, the other one is still in hospital, he's got a leg off and its not healing properly.

'I'm sorry to hear that, sir.

'Ah well, its the price I suppose,' he replied and he laid a key on the table 'that's a key for the door in case you're out late after we lock up for the night'.

'What time do you lock up Mr Weston?'

'Around midnight, usually'.

I laughed 'I won't be needing your key, I'm no night-hawk'.

He smiled 'Never mind, hang on to it in case, the bright lights of the city you know, and if there is anything you want just let me know. Have a good time Corporal when you've got the chance'.

He left me at that and Ann took the opportunity of telling me where there were good shows, but I wasn't biting at present. I pottered around a few of the nearby streets looking in the shop windows and then I returned to my own little room and all the comforts I had missed since leaving hospital. A nice bath and I rolled into that civilian bed with a thankful heart; I was just dozing off into peaceful sleep when a tap on the door brought me awake once more. 'Come in,' I called switching on the bed lamp. The door opened and Alice entered bearing a tray, on which there was a bottle of stout, a glass, and a plate of biscuits and cheese.

'I've brought you your nightcap Corporal,' she said as she set down the tray on the table.

'Oh good,' I said sitting up 'is this the usual thing Alice?'

She shook her head 'No it isn't, but Mr Weston says you have to get it every night while you are here'.

'Oh, so I can expect you every night at bed time, can I?'

'Me, or one of the other girls,' she replied 'Usually me, is it going to be hard for you to bear?'

I laughed 'No, not at all Alice, it makes life easier, I expect I'll sleep the better for it'.

'You mean for having the stout, or for seeing me?' she asked archly.

'Both Alice my sweet,' I played back at her 'after this little drink I'm sure I'll have sweet dreams of you'.

'And that I would consider a waste of time,' she replied with a smile 'are you quite comfy, anything more you want?'

'Everything's just perfect Alice,' I replied as she moved to the door and opened it. She paused there and looked at me 'Sure there's nothing more you want?'

'Not a thing Alice, not a thing, I'm very grateful to you'.

'Goodnight, Corporal,' and she was gone, perhaps I just imagined that she slammed the door a bit too hard. I didn't dream of Alice or Ann or any other female, I slept like a log and didn't awake until there was a knock on the door and a strange girl entered with a cup of tea.

'What time is it?' I asked her as she drew the curtains aside letting in the daylight.

'Eight o'clock and breakfast is in half an hour,' she replied 'You blokes can't half sleep'.

'Making up for what we've missed,' I replied.

She looked at me 'Some folk don't know what they've missed, until it's too late'. And she left me to think over that rather cryptic remark while I washed and dressed. I enjoyed a rich man's breakfast of sausage and bacon and egg, not bad for wartime Leeds, and then I set off to explore the City at my leisure. I had all the time in the world, my freedom at last. I was surprised at the few soldiers I saw in Leeds other than around the locality of the railway station, and I was agreeably surprised at the number of civilians who spoke to me in kindly greeting. I found that the trams were free to wounded soldiers, the shows were half price, and at a cafe I entered for a snack they waved aside the money I offered in payment. Leeds was good to me. As I sat on a bench in the city square one day an elderly lady handed me a box of fifty cigarettes, and one day when Alice was taking me on a trip to Roundhay Park we had just got on a tram when an officer turned in his seat and looked at us. He said something to the lady he was sitting with, rose and came over to me.

'Excuse me, Corporal, I see you've been wounded?'

'Yes sir, but I'm all right again,' I replied.

He smiled and pressed something into my left hand 'That will pay your fares wherever you're going'.

I looked down at the two half crowns in my hand 'But I don't pay fare sir,' I protested, and he smiled.

~ *Tommy* ~

'Never mind, treat the little lady to something,' he replied 'and good luck to you'.

I sat in a cafe with Ann and we enjoyed a good lunch, when I beckoned the waitress over and asked for my check she smiled and shook her head 'Your bill has been paid sir,' she replied.

A gentleman paid it at the cash desk on his way out'.

'What gentleman?' I asked looking around.

'I don't know sir, he's gone now'.

8.   HONOURABLE DISCHARGE

For two weeks I lived in idle luxury and then Sergeant Major Drake sent for me to report at his office.

'You're to report back at Strensall tomorrow, there's a medical board due and you're on it. Here's your papers Corporal, so get the train in the morning. How have you enjoyed your stay in Leeds?'

'Its been wonderful sir,' I replied 'But I still don't know why I was sent here'.

'Neither does anyone else,' he snorted 'but don't let that worry you 'ours not to reason why,' you know. Away you go and kiss all the little ladies goodbye'.

When I told Alice and Ann that I was leaving they both looked a bit down in the mouth and then Alice said 'Well, what about a farewell party tonight Tommy, lets all get blotto!'

'Five of us can come Tommy,' said Ann eagerly.

'Five girls, and me on my own!' I said aghast 'Have a heart Ann!'

Alice looked at me thoughtfully and said 'You know Tommy, you're a queer sort of soldier, I think you should be back at school'.

That remark rather shook me up, I prided myself I was a man, after all I had fought and held my own against other men with the gloves and with rifle, bayonet and bomb.

'I don't quite see what you mean by that, Alice,' I said.

She leaned across the table with a wordly look on her face 'All right Tommy, for your own good I'll tell you if you're so blind you can't see it for yourself. You've lived here for fourteen days and you've never realized that two can sleep nicely in a single bed. There's five girls working here and any one of them would have been only too happy to spend the night with you, its not the army you should be in its a bloody monastery. Now go back to Strensall and get some real soldiers to teach you the facts of life!'

I sat open mouthed as the two girls stood up and Ann said 'Oh Alice you shouldn't!'

'What about Mr Weston?' I exclaimed 'I couldn't turn his place into a house like that'.

'Mr Weston's not my keeper,' snapped Alice 'Anyway I've had my say, so goodnight and goodbye soldier!'

I went to bed rather sadly that night turning over in my mind the queer ways in which human nature can react, especially with the female of the species. If you do the wrong thing by a girl, its wrong, and if you do the right thing, its still wrong, so you're pretty helpless and hopeless whichever way you act.

'Oh, to hell with it,' I grunted and I turned over and slept the sleep of the just.

I departed the next morning with a handshake from Mr Weston but the girls of the establishment were conspicuous by their absence, I assumed I had been well discussed in their quarters.

It poured with rain during my journey and at Strensall it was coming down in torrents as I trudged from the station to the camp. The camp inside was a quagmire and I felt very depressed as I drew blankets and got settled down in a tent by then both myself and the blankets were in a sorry state. It rained and rained, that night I slept badly on the hard ground after my spell of comfort but it didn't worry me, I had known worse in the trenches. The following morning it still rained and I rose feeling pretty rotten, I was developing a heavy cold and I knew it. More wandering around in the rain and by tea time I felt all in, my breathing was sharp, I was coughing like a broken down horse, and my chest felt as though it was in an iron clamp. After tea I reported to the medical tent where a Sergeant went over me, took my temperature and said with popping eyes 'Good God!' Come this way Corporal, and see the M.O.'

We moved into an adjoining tent where the doctor sounded my chest and back and then announced 'Bronchitis. Get him to bed Sergeant, blankets and hot bottles'. I was put to bed in the ambulance tent, and for a week I was anchored there with nothing to do but cough and sit and listen to the rain hammer on the canvas overhead. After a week I was allowed to get up and potter around doing odd jobs to help the orderlies, and after another two days the M.O. examined me, stated I was clear, and instructed me to report for a medical board the following day.

A number of us paraded the following morning and we marched to a marquee where the doctor's were carrying out their inspection. One man at a time entered the marquee, and each man had to remove his boots before going in to see the doctors.

'What's the big idea, Sergeant?' I asked the N.C.O. in charge of the party, as I unfastened my bootlaces.

He grinned and said 'There's three doctors in there and, believe me, they're pretty tough on you blokes. All the same, they're not risking a kick in the teeth with ammunition boots'.

I had watched the boys coming out of that tent with expressions of disgust and agony on their faces; and then my name was called. I shuffled over the grass in my socks and entered the marquee to face three officer's sitting at three desks, and looking like three vultures awaiting their prey.

'Come over here!' snapped one of them and I moved over to stand at his desk 'What do you complain of?'

'I'm not complaining sir,' I replied.

He looked at some papers and then glowered at me 'You're marked category B2 do you want to go back to France?'

'That's up to you sir'.

'What do you mean by that?'

'I'll go where I'm ordered to go sir'.

'You won't volunteer?'

'No sir, I will not!'

'What's the matter with your hand?'

'Shrapnel wound sir'.

'Get that glove of, I want to see it'.

I stripped off the glove and held out my hand.

'That's healed up all right, open your fingers'.

I opened them half way, as far as they would go.

'Open them right out'

'I can't sir that's as far as I can get them; they'll close all right'.

'I don't want them closed damn it, I said open them!' he yelled 'move to the next desk'.

The second doctor peered at me through thick glasses and said 'Get your tunic and shirt off'.

He examined me and said 'Pretty good condition, any other wounds'.

'Just this bit in the forehead sir, no trouble there'.

'Can you use a rifle?'

'Haven't tried since when?'

'Since I used one killing German's sir'.

He picked up a rifle from behind his desk and handed it over to me 'Well, you can damn well try now, operate that bolt'.

'I operated the bolt and he snapped 'Now aim and fire!'

I brought the rifle up to my shoulder, squinted along the barrel, and pulled the trigger with my second finger.

'Well now, that's just splendid Corporal, just splendid, eh?'

'Yes sir, but there's one little thing you've missed,' I replied lowering the rifle butt.

'I'm always willing to learn,' he cackled 'what have I missed?'

'I couldn't grasp the small of the butt as I pulled the trigger, if that rifle had been loaded it would have jumped out of my hands'.

'You mean you couldn't hit a target?'

'Couldn't hit a haystack sir,' I replied cheerfully 'Try it yourself sometime, you'll see what I mean'.

'Move on, next desk,' he growled with a glare.

The third doctor was a young black haired type with a look on his face I didn't like.

'Where were you when you were wounded?' he rapped at me, looking at my hand and working it gently with his fingers.

'Place called Fricourt, on the Somme sir,' I replied.

'I see, and how long before it was attended to?'

'It got no proper attention until I got to Rouen'.

'Days after eh? I wonder why that was, I suppose you were hiding in some dugout, eh?'

'No sir,' the reply whipped out of me unthinking ' the reason was there isn't enough doctor's in France to handle casualties'.

His fingers kneaded at my hand and suddenly his grip tightened and he tried to force my fingers back. I yelped at the pain and he shouted 'Get those bloody fingers opened!'

I felt sweat on my face as he used pressure on my hand, it was torture while it lasted and I glared at him and balled my left into a fist. I couldn't stand it much longer, and then suddenly he let me go and pushed me aside.

'I suppose you think you'll get your ticket!' he sneered at me.

'All I think is, I'd like to get back among soldiers,' I gasped at him holding my throbbing hand.

'Get out of here,' he yelled, and I got.

That was my medical board at Strensall and I venture to state that sick animals get better treatment than wounded soldiers. For three more days I hung around in Strensall Camp doing nothing and then I received instructions to report back to Sergeant Major Drake in Leeds. Back I went and found the Sergeant Major sitting at the same desk in the same office. He greeted me with a smile 'Hello Corporal, back again. How did the medical board go?'

'Bloody awful,' I replied 'there's better doctors knocking around this country. I've been laid up with bronchitis since I left here'.

'Oh, so you won't feel like doing much eh?'

'Well, I'm not feeling 100%,' I replied 'what's the drill this time sir'.

He laughed 'The same as before, Corporal, you'll manage that, eh?'

An idea suddenly occurred to me and I said 'Where am I to be billeted sir?'

'Oh, let me see, you were at the Commercial last time I believe. No, you're going into a private house this time, here's the address in Woodhouse, you'll be all right there and report here on Friday for your pay'. I breathed a sigh of relief, I had no fancy for facing the females at the Commercial again; I found my new billet to my liking, an old lady with a married daughter and a younger daughter about 17 years old. The married daughters,' husband was an officer in the East Yorkshire Regiment; she told me that within five minutes of meeting her, with plenty of emphasis on the 'officer'. The younger daughter was a sweet youngster but a bit embarrassing with her hero worship for a wounded soldier. I had a nice little room and I had my food along with the family. Audrey, the younger girl, had just left school and started working on munitions and seeing that I was doing nothing she thought it was my duty to escort her to work and meet her when she had finished her daily toil. Audrey chatted away merrily as we tramped the streets, always keeping to the beaten track, and I found it rather refreshing to be in the company of a female without guile, that would come later I expect. My recent experiences had made me a bit wary.

Leeds was interesting in its way but I had a lot of time on my hands and no means of killing it. I found the days becoming long and a bit wearisome. One day as I sat on a bench in Roundhay Park a girl tripped over and asked me for a match. I handed her a box of matches and eyed her, she had everything, she was neat and dainty in her dress, slim and tall, with a rather narrow well shaped face and dark hair that glistened with the treatment it had.

'Mind if I sit down,' she said with a smile and I indicated the bench as hers if she wanted it.

'You seem lonely sitting here on your own,' she said, puffing at her cigarette 'Are you on leave?'

'No not exactly,' I replied 'I'm billeted in Leeds but don't ask me why because I don't know'.

She laughed and touched the gold braid stripe on my sleeve 'I see you've been wounded!'

'Yes, that was some time ago'.

'All the nicest boys are getting knocked about in this horrid war,' she said with a pout 'Will you be staying in Leeds long?'

'I'm sure I don't know,' I replied 'I just seem to be dumped'.

She moved a little closer to me 'Well, isn't that nice for you, my name is Mary, perhaps we could see each other a bit?'

I, looking, at the trim figure beside me thought that it could be interesting, very interesting, but at the same time she looked like a wench with expensive tastes.

'That would be nice, Mary,' I replied with a smile, but I'm afraid I don't live very high, Corporals don't get big pay you know'.

She shrugged her shoulders 'Oh I know that, actually I make a practice of going out with officers but there seems to be a scarcity at present so I have to do the next best thing'.

I gaped at her with my mouth open 'You don't mean to say you do this sort of thing regular, picking up chaps I mean!'

She burst out laughing 'Oh you silly boy, a girl must live you know'.

As I gazed at her in amazement, I could hardly believe the words she had uttered, a large ball rolled to a stop at our feet.

'Excuse me,' I said jumping to my feet and picking up the ball. I recognized it as a medicine ball, bigger than a football and used by athletes in training, and I threw it fast to the chap in slacks and white jersey who was running towards us.

'Thanks,' he shouted as he caught it and then 'look out,' and he hurled it back again. I had to run to catch it and this took me some distance away from Mary; by the time I recovered the ball the owner was beside me. 'You in training chum?' I asked looking at him with interest, he was a good looking youngster with jet black hair swept back from his forehead and the hard drawn look of the trained boxer about his face.

'Yes,' he replied with a grin 'I'm Nipper Neilson and I've got a fight in two weeks time.'

My eyes lit up as I replied 'Glad to meet you Nipper, I've done a bit myself'.

A heavier built chap also in sweater came trudging up to us and wiping his forehead he growled 'You travel too bloody fast for me Nipper, I'm getting past it'.

'My trainer Batt Kennedy, once Battling Kennedy and now a has been,' laughed Nipper Neilson 'Listen Batt this chap says he can use the gloves'.

Batt looked at me under furrowed brows and then his glance went to the bench where Mary still sat in solitary splendour.

'So you can do a bit eh?' he exclaimed 'Looks as if you're doing a bit already, you with that wench?'

I shook my head 'No I was sitting on that bench when she came and joined me'.

Batt snorted and said 'She would! Look son, see that bloke over there on the grass!' and pointed to a recumbent figure I hadn't noticed, some distance away 'That's the chap who's running her. Take my tip and lay off, she's a bad egg'.

'What about me joining you fellows?' I said eagerly, I could do with a spot of training'.

'Sure, come on,' cried Nipper and I waved my hand to Mary as we dashed away with the medicine ball.

We finished up a loft over a stable which Batt had rigged up as a gymnasium with punching balls, heavy bags, wall exercisers, skipping ropes and a well built boxing ring.

'What do you think of it?' said Batt Kennedy looking around with pride in his eye. 'Nice little place Batt,' I replied 'got many chaps coming here?'

He shrugged 'Not many, most of the useful boys are in the army, but I want to keep it going until after the war'.

'Nippers not in the army,' I pointed out.

'No, but he's due to go in a couple of months time blast it, now tell me what you've done with the mitts'.

Nipper had stripped off and he was shadow boxing in the ring as I told Batt my little story. 'Not bad for an amateur,' he commented 'pity you got that busted hand though, what about having a go with the Nipper?'

'I'm afraid I'm not much use to him,' I replied, 'I haven't boxed for ages, I've lost touch'.

'Well I'm not expecting a hell of a lot from you, me lad,' growled Batt 'but Nipper is short of sparring practice and anything's better than nothing. What about a couple of rounds to start with?'

'Oh all right, just a couple,' I replied taking off my tunic and shirt and removing my ammunition boots.

Nipper left his corner fast and jarred my head back with a couple of flashing lefts, he was fast and he could hit, I quickly realized that he was a bundle of high strung nervous energy and I was slow compared with him. I tried a left but his right counter to the chin rattled my teeth and I knew I couldn't out box him. I rushed but he side stepped smartly and again clipped me on the chin, then he tried another right that I weaved under and dug home a good one under the heart. We slammed away at close quarters and I was breathing heavy when Brett called time. One minute rest! Ten minutes would have suited me better. Time. Again Nipper came out fast and this time I met him, I couldn't out box him so I would have to fight him. We tossed punches back and forth merrily. I did manage to get home one that made him gulp, a left hook to the solar plexus and I ended the round with a trickle of blood from my nose.

'Try another one?' asked Batt.

'Hell no!' I gasped 'I'm out of wind!'

Nipper shook hands with me 'Thanks pal, I enjoyed that. Will you come round again?'

'I'll be here tomorrow Nipper,' I promised as I pulled on my tunic 'I've got a bit of ground to make up'.

I spent ten happy days at Batt Kennedy's gym and doing road work with Nipper Neilson. I found Nipper a likeable chap outside the ropes but once he stepped into the ring, even in the gym, his eyes turned hard and cold and every punch he threw meant business. He was one of those high strung nervy types who couldn't 'pull,' a punch if he tried, and he had me sore and aching until I realized I was a mug to try and meet him at his own game. I let him come at me and put all I knew into side stepping and shifting the head and body, and making him attack without much success. This tended to make him more and more aggressive and use up more energy, and as he came in my counter punching was most effective.

I never put the Nipper down, but he took plenty, and on one occasion I really shook him with a quick double left hook, both of which landed smack on the point. As he slid into a clinch he said 'That's a tidy left you've got Tommy!', and in the corner old Batt nodded his approval. Nipper hurt me at times and twice he had me on the floor wondering what had hit me, but it was all in the game. 'What's your candid opinion of the Nipper?' asked Batt one day as he rubbed me down 'Think he'll make it?'

I answered frankly 'He's too good for me Batt, I can manage 3 or 4 rounds with him but I reckon after six rounds he'd sweep me out of the ring in pieces. The only trouble with him is he's too nervy and impetuous, the class men will soon get wise and nail him'.

Batt nodded. 'That's what I'm frightened of, he's got to finish the job pretty quick or he burns himself up. I'm hoping he'll realize it himself soon.

He keeps promising to ease up but every time he goes in he's off like a bloody express train'. Nipper fought his battle with Lew Cohen, a Jewish boy from London at Liverpool stadium and stopped his man in the seventh round; but by then I had departed from Leeds once more.

I received orders to report at Catterick Camp and Audrey came to the station to see me off. I was feeling pretty gloomy about going back to Catterick and I was taken very much by surprise when Audrey threw her arms round my neck, kissed me, and burst into tears. Up to then I had looked upon Audrey as an overgrown schoolgirl, but it seems I was mistaken 'I'm going to miss you an awful lot, Tommy,' she sobbed into her handkerchief 'Promise you will write to me! Promise!'

'I'll promise you that Audrey,' I replied feeling a bit embarrassed at the youngsters woe, and then I was on my way. I kept that promise.

At Catterick Camp, just as forbidding as ever, I reported to the orderly room and after reading my papers the Adjutant looked at me with a puzzled frown.

'I don't know anything about you, Corporal,' he said 'I have no information about you coming here. You'd better hang around outside while I put a few inquires through'.

After a while a Sergeant came out of the orderly room and handed me an envelope with a grin 'You've come to the wrong bloody dump, its Strensall you should be at'.

'But my warrant was made out for Catterick,' I replied.

'I know, I know, it's a balls up at H.Q.'

'No wonder the bloody wars lasting a long time,' I groaned.

The Sergeant laughed 'First ten years are the worst, Corporal'.

'How the hell am I getting from here to Strensall?' I asked him.

'There's a transport going to Catterick village in time for the train to York, but you might be stuck in York station for the night. Why not stay here and go on in the morning!'

'Sergeant,' I replied 'As much as I like the look of you the sooner I can get away from Catterick the better I'll like it. Where's my travelling warrant?'

'I'll make it out right away,' he said and went back into the orderly room. Within a few minutes the warrant was in my hand and the Sergeant said 'The transport will pick you up in a few minutes, so-long'.

Soon the heavy transport was lumbering down the road and I sat in the back and had all kinds of thoughts about army organization. I caught the train all right and got as far as York where I was stuck until 8 o'clock the following morning, but I slept in the waiting room rolled up in my greatcoat with a contented mind. Catterick camp gave me a pain in the neck. At Strensall camp I handed my papers over to the Regimental Sergeant Major at the orderly room, and, checking a list on his desk he said 'You should have been here yesterday, where have you been?'

'Chasing all over Yorkshire looking for someone to own me,' I replied 'Sent to Catterick by mistake, spent the night in York station, and now I'm here. I hope I'm right this time'.

He laughed 'Yes, you're at the right place this time, but it won't be for long, Corporal'.

'I'm getting like a Cooks tourist,' I groaned 'Where am I booked for now sir?'

'Home my lad, home sweet home,' he said with a smile 'The medical board have marked you C3 and you've got your ruddy ticket. You'll be away by the weekend'.

I stared at him 'You mean I'm discharged?' I gasped.

'That's what I mean my lad,' he replied 'No more parades, no more guards, no more fatigues, no more soldiering'.

For two more days I stayed at Strensall while they transformed me from a soldier to a civilian, I kept my shirt, socks and boots and they issued me with a grey suit that would have allowed an increase of at least two stones in my weight. Then I got my discharge papers and a railway warrant for home with instructions to clear out of camp the following morning. I watched a battalion march past, men swinging along at the slope behind a military band and standing there in civilian suit I somehow felt an outcast, and I no longer belonged!

I listened to the drums and bugles sounding the retreat and I watched the flag slowly lowered to the ground; the plaintive notes of the last post echoed across the camp and somehow I had a feeling of sadness that I had come to the end of a long, hard road. In the morning the stirring call of reveille roused me and another discharge in the bed next to me grunted and said 'That bloody row won't waken me tomorrow morning, I'll just cuddle up beside my old Dutch an,' say to hell with the army'.

'We're going to miss it,' I mused, and he stared at me.

'Don't tell me you're sorry to be out of it!' he cried.

'I don't know, honestly I don't know,' I replied.

After breakfast we made our way to Strensall station, about a dozen of us, looking more like a bunch of tramps in our ill fitting civvies than ex-soldiers, and at York we split up to go our separate ways. My first port of call was a gent's outfitter to buy myself a collar and tie; I felt a bit better wearing a collar. I thought of going to Foss Island to visit the boys on guard duty at the haystacks and then I tossed the idea to one side saying to myself 'To hell with it, I'll be bursting into tears next'. I moved back into the crowds at York station and watched the troops bustling around but no one took any notice of me and I felt, as I suppose I looked a lonely hard up civilian. I climbed aboard the train bound for Newcastle and found an empty compartment, but just before the train moved off an elderly well dressed chap entered, followed by an elderly lady. I looked at them and then turned to gaze out of the window at the passing sentry; I could tell by their desultory conversation that they were strangers to each other, but neither of them spoke to me. I sat and thought how strange things were, I had felt very happy and contented with my lot when I joined the army, but now that I was leaving it things didn't feel right with me at all. Strange to say I wasn't looking forward to returning home to civilian life and I just couldn't understand my own attitude, during my service everyone had talked of the day they would get their ticket, dreamed of it, lived for it.

'Are you on your way to join the army, young man?' the elderly lady remarked, looking at me.

'No,' I replied 'I'm not'.

She sniffed 'Well, I must say you look young enough and fit enough, I've got two sons serving in the forces'.

'Perhaps the young man is on munitions,' said the elderly gent in a gruff voice.

'No, I'm not on munitions,' I replied shortly 'I'm not anything'.

'Are you out of a job young man?' asked the elderly man and when I nodded my head they both concentrated their gaze on me as though I was something nasty the dog had left on the doorstep.

'Not in the services and not at work of national importance!' cried the old lady 'Young man, you surprise me'.

'The Government should do something about it,' growled the man.

I sighed wearily and stretched my legs 'The Government have done something about it, if its any of your business I've just completed three years in the infantry and I'm chucked out due to wounds. Does that make you happy?'

Their attitude changed at once 'Why didn't you say so, my boy?' said the man, giving me a toothy smile.

I shrugged 'You folks should ask your Government to get ex-service men to carry a placard round their necks'.

And the rest of the journey to Newcastle was spent in stony silence. On Newcastle station I had a cup of tea and a bun as I watched a fully equipped battalion of the Royal Scots march on to a platform, headed by drums and pipers, to start their journey overseas. 'And I wonder how many of them will come back!' I mused as the train steamed out, bearing them away to the storm of shellfire and misery that awaited them over there; 'after all I'm lucky to be here'. I caught the slow train for home and as I saw the old familiar places my interest quickened, but at the back of my mind I felt sorry that Amy would not be there, she was still in Norfolk. As I tramped the two miles to my home I realized that although the place was familiar the faces were not, I had been away nearly three years and I had lost touch. All my old pals would be gone, either serving in the forces or gone forever, so it looked as though I would find things a bit difficult at first. Going back to civvy street wasn't going to be easy.

~ *Tommy* ~

I only met one person I knew on that walk through my own hometown, a chap called Jimmy Boyd who walked with a bad limp. He had gone down the pit to work at fourteen years of age, suffered an accident at fifteen and now he was a cripple for life.

I hardly knew you Tommy,' he greeted me with a grin and a handshake, 'You'll be pleased to get home again, I expect?'

I looked up and down the dingy street 'I don't know Jimmy, it doesn't seem much to come back to'.

He laughed 'Wait till you get settled down, you'll soon be in the swim again, even though most of the boys are away'.

That was the trouble, most of the boys were away, even my brother Jack[4] would not be at home, he had left a couple of weeks ago to join the Northumberland Fusiliers. I came to my street and I came to my house, I opened the door and walked into the living room, and then I got a shock that pulled me up dead. A young lady stood by the fire, a complete stranger to me, and she looked at me with a half smile on her lips. 'Good lord, I'm sorry,' I exclaimed 'I must have come to the wrong house'.

She laughed 'I suppose you're Tommy, in which case you're at the right, house all right. Your mother said you were coming home but she expected you later in the day. She's out at present'.

I looked around, yes; it was the same old furniture. 'Yes, I see its the same old place,' I replied 'But you're an addition since I was last at home, just where do you come in?'

'Perhaps I'd better introduce myself,' she said 'My name is McCrae, Mary McCrae and I come from the Shetlands'.

'Oh, that's all right Mary,' I answered her 'I suppose you are a friend of mother's?'

'Well, not exactly,' she replied 'I'm a teacher and I got a post at the same school where your mother teaches. I had to find digs and your mother said I could come and live here with her'.

'You're living here?' I exclaimed.

'Yes, for a time anyway, do you mind?'

'Good lord no, it'll be queer having a girl in the house but I suppose I'll get use to it,' I replied with a grin.

'I think we'll get along all right Tommy, I'll get you some tea ready,' she said.

'That's fine Mary, but I'm going to get changed first, I feel like a discharged prisoner in these clothes'.

'You'll find your things in the big room at the back,' she said as I made for the stairs 'The small room is mine'.

She had even pinched my bedroom.

---

[4] Jack Crawford (Northumberland Fusiliers) also survived the war

~ Tommy ~

As I washed and changed I listened to the chink of the cups and saucers downstairs and gave a thought to Mary McCrae, it was a name with a lilt in it, like her voice, and I began to think that my home might be interesting after all. Mary wasn't a pretty girl, she was too raw boned for that, but she had jet-black hair and brown eyes that did something to you. 'Pity she's a schoolteacher,' I mused 'but my mother could have done worse, much worse'.

I made my way down to the living room to find the table laid for tea and a pair of brown eyes looked me over.

'The eggs will be ready in a minute,' said Mary 'You look a bit better in your own clothes Tommy'.

I smiled 'My things are a bit tight on me but they'll do for now'.

As we munched our boiled eggs Mary said 'I suppose you'll be pleased to be out of the army Tommy, how long did you serve?'

'Oh there's worse places Mary, I've had about three years of it and I've had some good times, and some bad ones'.

'When were you home last?'

'A year ago when I came out of hospital'.

'You should have had more leave than that surely, in this country?'

I grinned at her 'Prying into my secret life already, Mary?' I replied 'As a matter of fact I did have seven days in between but I spent it at a girl's home, a girl I knew very well'.

'Oh, a big romance!' she cried with sparkling eyes 'Tell me all about it Tommy'.

'Its secret, don't you mention it to my mother'.

'Cross my heart, not a word to a soul'.

And I told her the story of my seven happy days in Norfolk.

'Did you get engaged to the girl Tommy?' and when I shook my head she said 'And why ever not?'

'Good lord Mary, I didn't have the price of a packet of fags much less a ring, and now I'm back home I don't know what the future holds with regard to a job'.

'Oh, I don't think you need worry about that, there's plenty of jobs for chaps like you'.

I shrugged 'Maybe, but I'm making sure I've got a future before I tie someone else up with me'.

Mary laughed 'Silly of you Tommy, my boyfriend said we had to get engaged the day he joined the army,' and she showed me her ring.

'What's he in, Mary?'

'The Scottish Highlanders, he's over in France now'.

Just then my mother walked in and stared when she saw me 'I wasn't expecting you until the late train Tommy, why didn't you let me know when you would arrive?'

I greeted her with a kiss and replied 'I didn't know myself, and why didn't you let me know we had an addition to the family?'

'I hope you don't mind?'

'Good heavens no, it brightens the old place up a bit,' I answered 'Mary and I are getting along fine'.

For a few days I hung around at home, amusing myself by rigging up a punching ball and a heavy bag and going for long walks to get myself into shape and I contacted the brigade people and came up against their request for my services as an instructor for the boys. I accepted the post and on the first parade night I was struck by changes in the company. 'You're not a patch on the company we had before the war,' I told them 'but I promise you I'll knock you into shape'. The biggest chap in the company was a fellow called Val Turner and I discovered that he had made a place for himself with the gloves and he gave boxing lessons to any of the boys who were keen.

'Some night you and I will have a little spar, Val,' I told him and being bigger and heavier than me he readily agreed.

When the time came for us to cross gloves I found he was pretty classy as a boxer and after making me miss a few times he slammed in a really good hard right to the stomach.

'If that hurt you I'll ease up a bit,' he said, with a smile to the group of boys who were watching us. I stared at him, he really meant it!

'No come on Val, we haven't started yet,' I replied and I moved out of a gentle spar into top gear. Soon it developed into a right merry mill and Val did his best but it wasn't quite enough. A quick change of feet and a left to the solar plexus made him gasp, followed by a left to the chin that made his knees wobble, and then a short chopping right put him down in a heap.

Val was satisfied that he had had enough, and I was satisfied that my injured right hand wasn't so bad after all.

The worst experience of my homecoming was the day when I called to see Jacky Barrett's mother. Jacky, my pal of school days and brigade camps and in my section in the army, posted missing in the Battle of the Somme. I found myself tongue-tied and uncomfortable and I was pleased when the ordeal was over. I soon got fed up with hanging around and I called on Mr Welsh to find out what my position was with regard to starting work. I found that Mr Welsh had retired and I was advised to see a Mr Eccles. In due course I met him and was informed that the only vacancy at the moment was assistant in the blacksmiths shop 'Later on of course there may be an electrical vacancy,' he informed me vaguely 'You've been out of touch a long time you know'.

'Yes,' I replied rather bitterly 'I suppose all the decent jobs are filled now by people who are dodging the army. All right I'll take it, until I find something better'.

~ Tommy ~

I started the following week in the blacksmith's shop, lighting fires, blowing bellows, and repairing underground tubs, and I didn't like it at all. After about a month of this I happened to meet the electrical foreman who had been on the job before the war and he stared at me 'Hello Tommy, I didn't know you were back, what are you doing?'

'I'm in the smithy,' I told him 'and I hate the bloody place, I'm packing in first chance I get'.

'Aw to hell with that, you should have come back to me, I'll damned soon change that for you, its not fair'.

Two days after I was transferred to another colliery where I was put in charge of the sub-station. I was back on electrical work but the fact that I had returned from active service to be dumped in a blacksmith's shop still riled me.

My mother was fond of attending whist drives and she had Mary to accompany her, on me fell the doubtful pleasure of escorting them to and from the places where the whist drives were held. I always became bored stiff at the cups of tea and small talk that went on at these affairs but things could become a bit interesting on the rare occasions when I escorted Mary home on her own. One night we were caught in a real downpour of rain, neither of us had coats but fortunately Mary had an umbrella and we huddled close together as we trudged along the road for home. She looked rather sweet as the lightning lit up the sky and in one dizzy moment I held her and kissed her, much to my own disgust.

'Mary, I'm sorry,' I said 'That was a rotten thing for me to do'.

'What do you mean by that Tommy?' she asked.

'Good lord, you're engaged to a chap who's having a rough time in France, it's not fair to him'.

'I see what you mean Tommy,' she replied 'But honestly I'm lonely and fed up with this place, first chance I get I'm leaving'.

'Well to be quite candid I feel the same way myself,' I told her 'I wouldn't mind going back into the army again. However, Mary, we won't improve matters by making fools of ourselves will we?'

'How could you go back when you've been discharged?'

'They're asking for ex-service men for the Army Service Corps'.

'Don't do that Tommy, something better will turn up before long'.

She was an interesting girl and we remained good pals, my moment of forgetfulness seemed to be a thing of the past until early one cold winter morning I was roused from sleep by someone shaking me. I opened my eyes and saw Mary standing by my bed wearing only a nightdress and a dressing gown over her shoulders.

'What's up?' I grunted sleepily.

'Your alarm went off ages ago, its time you were up for work'.

I squinted at the clock and saw I had fifteen minutes to get dressed and reach the colliery a mile away.

'Oh to hell with it, I'm tired,' and I snuggled down again in the bed.

Mary leaned over, put her arms around me and kissed me 'That will waken you up,' she murmured and was gone. It woke me up all right in more ways than one, I began to realize that things were beginning to get a bit out of hand despite the fact that Amy on the one hand and the Seaforth chap on the other had up to now acted as a brake.

However it all smoothed itself out nicely, two days later when I came home from work Mary greeted me with a glowing face 'Wonderful news Tommy, Ian is coming on leave'.

And Ian arrived in all the glory of kilt and sporran, he stayed at our house for a few days and he and Mary appeared to have a pretty good time together. He was a decent young chap and I liked what I saw of him and the next thing I heard was that Mary had packed up her post and they were leaving for the Shetlands together to get married. I never heard of them again, but that's how it goes in time of war, I've got to admit I missed Mary McCrae.

Time went on and I grew more and more unsettled with conditions as I found them in civilian life. My mother continued her work at school and as a result I found my home life lonely and meals were mostly out of tins. At work I found obstacles in my way due to the fact that I was an ex-service man, an example of this came my way when I was moved into the power station. The chaps on the job had not been in the services; they were of military age but exempt owing to their work of national importance. They would tell me nothing about the running of the power plant because they knew that once I had a grasp of the work, I would be able to take over a shift and one of them would be released for the army. I found solace in the company of a fair haired doll like wench called Millie, but Millie went off to be a nurse and surprised me by returning home a week later on leave in all the glory of a red cross nurses uniform. I couldn't understand this at all until a young friend of hers called Jenny told me that Millie only wore the uniform from the ladies room on Newcastle station to her home.

'She's not a nurse really, Tommy,' Jenny explained 'She's a maid in the hospital and she changes into uniform to show off at home'.

'I don't believe that Jenny,' I said.

'All right, you suggest going to Newcastle with her and you'll see'.

I did suggest it, next time Millie came home, and the girl went into a panic and turned my offer down flat. There was no more Millie for me after that, but I found myself going out with Jenny now and again but there was really no joy in that either. She was a nice kid, but still at the technical school, seventeen years old, and full of hero worship so I soon chucked that too.

Then I met the recruiting Sergeant one day and told him I was thinking of going back into the Army Service Corps. He knew me well enough, he had known me as a kid, and he said 'What's the trouble, Tommy?'

'Oh, I'm fed up with civvy street,' I replied 'I'm not getting anywhere at work and I'm missing the boys'.

He nodded his head 'I know how you feel son, we'll have you back quick enough in the Army Service Corps, we're scraping the bottom of the barrel for men, but why not let some of these bloody slackers have a go? My advice is, give civvy street another three months and if you're still not happy come back and we'll have you in khaki again'.

'When I think of the comradeship and the good times I've had in the army I can't understand why chaps funk it,' I said.

He looked at me and grinned 'You seem to have a yen for soldiering boy, but don't forget the other side of the picture, the slogging marches when your pack weighs you down and your rifle feels like lead, the blast of shellfire and the snarl of bullets, the rain and the cold, the mud and the blood, take it easy in civvy street for a while'.

In my heart I knew he was right, but I also knew that I wasn't going to stay in the civvy street I had returned to, much longer.

I met a girl called Emily who told me she was going with my brother Jack, she was fair and pretty but there was something about her that didn't seem to ring quite true. However, that was Jack's affair and I didn't see much of her. Then, one day I came across an advertisement in the local paper, ex-service men wanted to undergo a course of practical and theoretical training to city and guilds standard, men of sound education and knowledge of electrical engineering apply to the North Eastern Electric Supply Company. My application went in that night and two days later I received word to report for an interview at Wallsend-on-Tyne.

Once more I'm back in 'Civvy Street,' that land of which I've dreamed
And now I've got some funny thoughts, its not quite what it seemed.
They issued me with civvies and they told me I could go
I said 'so-long,' to Tom and Jack, to Harry, Bert, and Joe.
No more falling in at dawn upon the barrack square
No more spit and polish for the Sergeant's baleful glare,
No more drilling, no more marching, no more guard at night
No more 'now we'll try again - and THIS time do it RIGHT!'
No more peeling dirty spuds, no more 'make your bed'
No more 'come on, pick 'em up,' - those feet like lumps of lead,
No more falling in for this - and falling in for that
I'm back in civvy street my lads, I've got my bowler hat!
But memories come creeping back - in the fireside glow
Memories of the happy boys that I use to know,
And faintly in my memory I hear the roll of drums
And once more I'm 'falling in,' beside my soldier chums.
And back here in civvy street I somehow feel alone
Like a dog that's got to hide up to keep its blinking bone.
And I'm thinking that civvy street has nothing to compare

with the pals I've left behind me on the barrack square.
I'm going to miss the P.T. blokes for whom we skipped and ran
I'm going to miss the smell of bacon in the cookhouse pan,
I'm going to miss the slap of rifles on parade
And N.C.O.'s who tell you 'that's how soldier men are made'.
I'm going to miss those happy times in the village pub at night
When the boys are singing 'fit to bust,' and everything looks bright,
I'm going to miss 'Reveille,' and I'm going to miss 'Retreat'
I'm going to miss the rhythm and the crunch of marching feet,
I'm going to miss the mail from home, that feeling when it comes,
But most of all, in civvy street, I'm going to miss my chums!

I reported for my interview at Wallsend-on-Tyne and found that, if accepted, I would be given a six months course with an intermediate examination at the end of three months and a final at the end of six months. During training I would be paid a salary that would cover my lodging expenses and on the completion of the course I would be posted to one of the company supply stations on full salary. It sounded all right to me and I accepted those conditions. I answered all the questions of the panel who were examining me and in another room I sat down to complete a written test of elementary electricity and mechanics, followed by a test of maths. I found the electricity and mechanics to my liking but the maths paper disturbed me a bit, you don't do maths when you're soldiering and I soon realized I was pretty rusty. When I handed the completed papers over to the supervisor I told him the maths had given me a bit of a pain but he smiled and said 'Don't worry son, we make allowances for you chaps who have been serving'.

Back home I went and three days later I received a letter to say that my application had been successful and would I report for duty as early as convenient at Carville Power Station, Wallsend-on-Tyne. I told my mother I was handing in my notice at the colliery and I was leaving home, she didn't mind herself she said 'but what about your dad; he might not like it'.

'Well, he'll just have to lump it,' I replied 'I've got my own life to live and this looks like a promising start'.

I had to see Mr Eccles at the colliery when I handed in my notice and he didn't seem very pleased about it.

'Why do you wish to go to these people?' he asked.

'Because I think my prospects will be better,' I replied.

'Oh, I don't know. If you stay here you will get on, in time'.

'In time, perhaps,' I said 'but I don't want to get on 'in time', I want to get on now'.

'Well, being in the army for three years has held you back you know'.

'No, Mr Eccles, I don't agree with you,' I replied 'Having been in the army is holding me back and will continue to hold me back as long as the war lasts. Your chaps are scared stiff that an ex-service man will qualify to step into their shoes. I don't like their attitude and we'll leave it at that'.

'You wasted three years in the army,' he said lamely.

'Well I don't intend wasting any more hanging around the pits,' I answered him, 'Perhaps my three years didn't do me any good but I like to think it did my country a bit of good'.

'I hope you realize that I won't be able to reinstate you?'

I grinned at him 'I'll be in a hell of a bad shape before I ask you for that, I'm leaving here for good'.

The following weekend saw me on my way to Wallsend where I got fixed up in digs and I reported for duty at Carville on the Monday. There were sixteen of us, all ex-service men, and it was the beginning of a hard grind, 9 am to 12.30 p.m. in the classroom, 1.30 p.m. to 5.30 p.m. in the various power stations, substations, and workshops of the company, and always about 3 hours homework at night. I found a gym run by an ex boxer called Sam Minto of Wallsend, and it was here that I found my only relaxation; sometimes an hour sometimes only half an hour of training but the exercise did me good and I found myself doing a couple of rounds with the gloves with boys who were getting their names on the bills at various boxing halls on the Tyneside.

At the end of the three months period we reported at Rutherford College to sit our intermediate, and I felt a bit of a fool when I entered the classroom sporting a gorgeous black eye, it had been handed out to me the previous evening in the gym by an up and coming boy called Willie Westoll. He knew a bit too much for me and the eye proved it. There was a marked silence in the room as I made my way to my desk, but I felt every eye on me, and when the examiner was handing out our papers he spoke to me quietly 'I sincerely hope your damaged eye will not affect you, 'er reading the questions correctly'.

'Not in the least, sir,' I replied, squinting at him 'its feeling better now'.

'Oh! 'er quite!'

The exam over we broke up for four days and went off to our various home towns on leave and on my arrival my mother looked at my eye of many hues and remarked 'I thought you were training for engineering?'

'So I am!'

'Well you should keep your face out of the way of the engines'

I grinned 'That engine wore a boxing glove, mother'.

'Your dad's coming home on leave tomorrow, he's got a commission'.

'Oh, that's good. Where is he now?'

'He's at Howden in Yorkshire, he's transferred to the air force'.

He arrived the following day and I must admit he looked pretty good in a new blue uniform of fine serge with a lovely crease down the trousers and kid gloves on his hands. As I looked him over I thought to myself 'He'd pass all right, if only he would keep his big mouth shut'.

How right I was! He had only got the commission that week but he was soon expounding on the art of flying, and looping, and rolling, and how to attack a Jerry on the blind side.

'Do you think you've been wise in packing up at the colliery?' he asked me.

'Very wise, its tough at present but I'm learning,' I replied.

'What happens if you don't pass these exams?'

'If I pass I'm in, if I don't I'm out, so I'm going to pass'.

'I still think it's a bit risky, you might not pass'.

'In that case I'll have a crack at something else, but no more pits for me'.

Back I went to Wallsend to learn that I was through the intermediate safely and I settled down to another three months of toil. I kept on with my boxing at the gym in Wallsend and I found I was regaining the form I had enjoyed when boxing in the army; at the same time I began to realize my limitations against boys who were tough and rugged fighters. They were professionals, used to battling ten, fifteen, and twenty rounds and I was finding it hard going to stand up for three rounds with them. By 'boxing clever,' I found I could manage it, but if I tried 'mixing it,' I usually landed in trouble. However, they were good sports and I enjoyed my time with them and I went with them at times to act as 'second,' in the corner at places like St. James's hall and Sunderland stadium. One day as I stood in Grey Street in Newcastle a tramcar pulled up at the other side of the road and the driver seemed to be playing a merry tune on his gong.

'That bloke seems to want you,' said a man standing beside me, and as I looked across the road the driver waved his arm at me.

I walked across the road, wondering what it was all about, and then suddenly I recognised him, Dicky Knight, the bloke who had joined up with me, travelled to Barnard Castle with me, and soldiered with me until he was carried away on a stretcher.

'Good lord, Dicky, its good to see you,' I cried.

'Come on Tommy, jump up beside me; I'm holding up the traffic,' he said and I climbed into the cab beside him. He started up and away we went laughing and talking and recalling the old days with the battalion.

'How's the wound Dicky?' I asked him.

'Oh not so bad, they took some bone away so I'll always have a limp, but it could have been a damned sight worse,' he replied with a grin.

'I'll bet there's not many of the old battalion left now, Dicky,' I said.

He looked at me 'Do you remember Mitchell, the company runner?'

I nodded my head, and he went on 'I met him the other day, home on leave, he's been wounded twice and back in France again, he reckons there's not a couple of dozen of the chaps left of the battalion that marched away from 'Barny'.

I travelled with Dicky until an inspector stopped the tram and informed us that it was strictly forbidden for anyone to be in the cabin with the driver, so I dismounted and said 'so-long,' to Dicky; I had to pay my fare on the return trip to Newcastle but it was worth it, it was good to meet an old comrade-in-arms. We never met again.

Some time later I went to North Shields for the day, and as I strolled along the sea front I suddenly remembered that this was the place where Fred Wake lived, the Tyneside Scot I had met in France, in Kitebrook, and in Hornsea. I made inquiries at the police station and they directed me to the post office where I was lucky enough to find a postman who knew his address. I made my way there and saw a chap with one arm pottering about in the little front garden.

'I leaned over the fence and said 'Hello Fred, how goes it?'

He straightened up and stared at me, then he dropped his trowel and cried 'Blimey, its Tommy. Gosh, I'm pleased to see you'.

We had a wonderful day together talking over the old days in hospital, and that was the fourth and the last time we met.

I buried myself deep in my work and I felt satisfied at the way things were going, my workshop practice and operational work on power station routine put me well ahead but I had a struggle with mechanical drawings and maths. Still, the other chaps were in the same boat, the trouble was that our war service had blotted out everything else for the time and it was hard to get our brains adjusted to the stuff we had left behind in the schoolrooms. Only when I was home for the weekend I met the local recruiting Sergeant and he greeted me with 'Well Tommy, have you thought any more about the Army Service Corps?'

I shook my head, 'Nothing doing Sergeant, if I go anywhere now, it will be the engine room of a ship. I've wasted enough time in my life'.

'Oh well, I don't blame you; anyway it looks as though the war won't go on much longer'.

That was true enough, the tide had turned in France and the German front seemed to be cracking beyond recovery. As time went on I found it pretty hard to make ends meet, my salary just covered my lodgings and my army pension of fifteen shillings per week went on text books, fares, and cigarettes, but at long last the course was completed and after sitting our finals we were sent home to await the results. After a week of waiting I received word that I had passed grade B and I was instructed to report to Durham City to take up duties at the generating station in that city. Upon arriving there I learned that only one chap in the class had passed grade A, three had passed grade B, seven had passed grade C, and five had failed to make the grade. Two grade B men and two grade C men were allotted to Durham where we had to put in a couple of weeks before taking charge of a shift. The other grade B chap informed me that he was fixed up in good digs in Durham and there was room for another, so I went along with him and soon got settled down. The landlady was good to us and she certainly knew how to cook, Harry and I got along well together and it was a good billet.

After a couple of weeks on probation an engineer arrived from Newcastle and put us through our paces with the plant we were to control, reported us satisfactory and henceforth we were on our own. At long last I was on a living wage with a few shillings to spare each week, I liked my work, and I was very fond of the fine old city where I lived. I wasn't very happy about my grade B so I continued with a course of study and as a result I was able to sit and pass grade A after a period of about twelve months. This swallowed up my 'spare shillings,' but I considered it worthwhile.

Meanwhile, two months after taking up residence in Durham City the war came to an end, and there was a bewildering feeling of emptiness everywhere. Before people recovered from the 'shock of peace,' the 'Spanish Flu,' struck the country and thousands died of it, but I was one of the lucky ones. While it raged throughout the land there seemed to be as much death in peace as in war. I received word from Any to say that she was coming North to stay with her sister and, although this was sixteen miles from Durham City I was delighted at the news. I decided that the best way to overcome the sixteen miles would be a motorbike and in due course I bought a second hand job, a two stroke with belt drive. It wasn't so hot but it got me there and back, even though I had to run alongside at times to help it up the hills. I had a few 'near misses,' on that bike but it served its purpose.

It was in Durham City that I met Tommy Lancaster, an ex middleweight who had fought for and lost the middleweight title at one time in his career as a glove slinger. He had retired from the ring and now ran a pub in Durham and a gym where all the local talent gathered to talk and train. Once more I was drawn into the game and soon I was busy with ball, and bag, and gloves; it did me a heap of good because there wasn't much in the way of hard work at Durham. I walked into a bagful of trouble at the gym one evening when I offered to do three rounds with Buller Brodie. Buller was training for a fight at West Hartlepool and his punch was heavy, he was strong and tough with a little the better of me in weight. However I had been going pretty good myself and I felt in grand condition, so I thought I could 'box clever,' for three rounds with Buller and keep clear of serious trouble. During the first round I venture to state I gave Buller a boxing lesson, I used all the speed I had and my left was never out of his face; but I had the feeling I was hitting a stone wall, it seemed to have no effect on him. He came out for the second round hunched up, bobbing and weaving and then it happened, he got me with one in the middle that nearly broke me in two and followed with a right to the chin that dumped me on the floor. After that I was 'receiver in general,' he draped me over the ropes, dumped me on the floor again, and hit me with everything but the stool, and by the end of that second round I was pleased to call it a day. I knew when I had had enough, and I knew nothing I could do would stop that whirlwind of leather. They say it was good while it lasted, I dare say it was good, but only from outside the ropes.

Eight weeks later I again stepped inside the ropes with Buller, this time he was booked for a fight in Glasgow and it was his request. I went in with a 'do or die,' feeling and I used all the room in that ring to make him miss. Again I out boxed him in the first round, and I stepped out for the second resolved to make myself hard to catch. I drew a trickle of blood from his nose and things were going nicely until he got me with a left hook that slammed me back into a corner. He came in fast and crowded me and when we came out of the mix up he had a gash over his eye. The bout was stopped and after inspection it was decided to call off his fight in Glasgow, and Buller swore I caught him with my elbow, and his manager was far from pleased with me 'That's cost us twenty bleedin,' quid,' he moaned. I couldn't say whether I caught him with my elbow or my foot, in a mix up like that anything can happen, but I knew that Buller was too tough for me to handle and I left it at that.

Now that Amy was back in my home town I travelled there every chance I had, I was at home more than I was in my digs at Durham and I found a lot of happiness and contentment in company of that girl from Norfolk. The war was over, I had a decent job, and the future seemed to be fairly good and as time went on we decided to become engaged and to get married in June. I made inquiries around Durham City and found the best I could do at the moment was one room and the use of a kitchen. We accepted this, we could live anywhere so long as we were together, and we didn't have a care in the world.

I suppose in my own small way I had faced up to quite a few things during my brief life. I had faced up to boys and men with the gloves, I had faced up to shellfire and men with rifles and bayonets, but facing up to the person on that bright day of June was, without doubt, the finest job I had ever done. I had joined hands with someone who walked beside me through life, facing good luck and misfortune without a word of complaint, and never let me down. For six wonderful months we lived in our one roomed garden of Eden in Durham City and then I was brought back to earth with a jerk when we realized that you couldn't very well have a baby when living in one room. We hunted around in Durham but couldn't make better of it and eventually had to accept an offer of two rooms in Hebburn-on-Tyne with Amy's elder sister. I sold my motorbike in order to buy our first piece of furniture, a bed, and we moved to Hebburn, where we were comfortable. The snag was travelling daily to work in Durham, this was a matter of thirty six miles and involved a lot of extra time and expense; for instance I had to be up at 4.30 am to catch a train at 5.30 am in order to be on duty at 8.00 am. However we made the best of things and when Amy's brother in law died her sister decided to return to her home in Norfolk. We bought the furniture and household goods and took over the house in

~ *Tommy* ~

Hebburn, and, although it took all the cash we had we were happy to have a home of our own.

Young Tommy was born in that house in Hebburn-on-Tyne and our happiness was complete excepting for the fact that I had to spend so much time and money on travelling, seventy two miles a day was a lot. About this time I had a medical board and my army pension was cut to seven shillings and sixpence a week so that made matters a bit more sticky. I applied for a transfer nearer home and was informed there were no vacancies on the Tyneside at present but my name would be kept on the list for future reference, and that was that.

I discovered a gym in Jarrow-on-Tyne where I was able to get in some useful glove slinging, but I was finding it hard going among the professionals on the Tyneside, and, although I toyed with the idea of turning professional myself in order to make a bit extra cash, common sense prevailed. I realized that these chaps could take me to pieces over the longer distances of ten and fifteen rounds. So for three years we slogged along making the best of the circumstances but only just paying our way. Meanwhile my father had been discharged from the air force and after a period of idleness he bought a manufacturing confectionery business in Sunderland and a seven-roomed house. Once again my mother was occupied in attending to the clerical side of the business while my father drifted around the area getting orders, my brother Jack came home to take up teaching at a school outside Sunderland and for a time things went well with them. Then my mother realized that she couldn't run the home and run the business, and she offered us three rooms, rent free, if Amy would attend to household duties. We talked it over and saw the advantages; it meant cutting down my travelling from seventy-two miles a day to forty miles and day and no rent to pay. In the end we decided to accept the offer and we moved from Hebburn to Sunderland, but in doing so we made a mistake, our life was happier on our own in Hebburn than ever it was in Sunderland. Once you are married it pays to cut your family ties and paddle your own canoe, even if you are hard up. However the die was cast and once more we made the best of it and the one who benefited most was the youngster, my mother thought the world of him and he went short of nothing. Soon I was able to buy another motorbike, a new one this time, and it was a trusty machine that served me well on the road from Sunderland to Durham.

I soon discovered a gym in Sunderland, run by 'Duggy,' Morton and used by quite a number of useful North country boxers. 'Duggy,' was a canny soul who charged you a nominal fee to join his gym and he raked in a percentage from the boxers for supervising their training, getting them fights, and acting as a second in the corner. When I applied for membership 'Duggy,' looked me over and said 'Keen on boxing are you?'

'That's right, I like to have a go,' I replied.

'All right, I'll try you out with one or two of the boys, if you're any good I'll get you fixed up'.

'Half a minute, I'm not a professional,' I answered 'I just like the game as an amateur'.

He sniffed 'Hell, there's not much fun in that or money either, have you done any boxing, son?'

I nodded 'Done a bit in the army'.

'Oh well, here you are, try a couple of rounds with this bloke Private Bob Robson,' and I shook hands with a grinning, flat nosed cauliflower eared chap who had been busy with skipping ropes. And that's how I met Private Bob Robson, an up and coming North country boxer who was one of the best natured chaps I ever met either in or out of the ring. I belted out a couple of rounds with private Robson and found the going pretty hard due to lack of training, but 'Duggy,' said 'Not bad, with a bit of training you'll be all right'. Robson grinned at me and said 'That's a pretty nifty left hand you've got mate'. Private Bob Robson and I became pals, I did roadwork with him and I sparred many rounds with him, gradually I became fitter and faster and soon I found Bob turning to me for advice on various points of training and moves in boxing.

9.   GOING BACK

From the *Harrogate Herald*:

After 62 years, a Harrogate veteran has re-visited the Somme battlefields of his youth.

Tommy Crawford was just 18 when he disobeyed his father's instructions to stay at home to look after his mother, lied about his age, and went to France with the 15th Durham Light Infantry.

That was in September 1915. He arrived in France just in time to take part in the battle of Loos.

Tom served in France for less than a year, but in that time he fought in Loos, wintered in Flanders, marched down to the Somme, where he took part on the first tragic day of that battle.

He was wounded on the Somme - his right hand was damaged when a bullet hit his rifle, and he was hit in the forehead. When he looked out of the shell hole in which he was hiding, he was hit in the mouth. He was sent back to hospital and returned to England.

He did not return to France again until June of this year, now aged not 18 but 81, thanks to two military historians, Major and Mrs. Tonie Holt, who organise tours of the battlefields, Tom left his home in Woodfield Road, Harrogate to spend three days reliving old memories and remembering old comrades

Carnage

Not that they had ever been forgotten. Nor had the scenes of carnage which had forcibly imprinted themselves on his mind 'You try to forget it, yet somehow it keeps cropping up in your memory', he said.

Returning to the battlefield of the Somme, he told me that he remembered that time, 62 years before, when '60,000 khaki bundles were lying about the field'. It was a ghastly affair from beginning to end.

He was again reminded of his comrades who gave their lives when the tour took the party to the Menin Gate at Ypres, to witness a ceremony which has been performed there each evening for 60 years.

Watching the Belgium trumpeters sound the Last Post to the memory of 56,000 British soldiers who died holding Ypres throughout the war, Tom felt it was sad, and even pitiful, that these same men should be remembered only once a year at the Cenotaph.

Freedom

'People today may not appreciate the freedom they have nowadays but it is only due to these men that they have that freedom', he said with some feeling.

And yet, although his memories were tinged with sadness, there were occasional touches which amused him. For instance, the trenches visible today at Passchendaele - unlike the trenches Tom remembered - had sandbags filled with concrete rather than sand.

And, as he remarked with a wry grin, 'you could stand on top of these trenches without any bullets flying around your ears'.

The France he visited this year was not quite the France he remembered, however. 'What were only tree stumps in those days, were now grown trees again. Property was all smashed down in our time, Ypres was just a bundle of fire and rubble. Ypres today has been completely rebuilt'.

Nor were the prices the same. In 1915 he bought a souvenir made out of shell cases from a wounded Belgian soldier for five francs. Now, similar souvenirs are selling for 400 francs!

Dawn suddens up and still I hear
The crimson chorus of the guns
Look! Like a ball of blood the sun
Hangs o'er the scene of wrath and
wrong.
Quick!
Stretcher-bearers on the run!
Oh Prince of Peace!
How Long, how Long?
From a poem by Tommy Crawford.

Perhaps, for Tom, and many other old soldiers, the most noticeable piece of restoration was the 'Golden Madonna'. During the war this statue of the Virgin and Child, on top of the church in Albert, was damaged by shell-fire, until it balanced, precariously, at right angles to the church steeple. The soldiers used to say that when she finally fell down, the war would end.

The statue has now been restored to its correct, upright position. It had also been painted gold - hence its new name - and now forms a landmark over the whole of the surrounding countryside.

He was struck by the flatness of this surrounding land. 'How anyone advanced over that ground, with machine gun fire against them, I do not know'.

Cemeteries

The other thing which caught his attention, was the immaculate condition of the war cemeteries. 'You would not see a blade of grass out of line', he told me, with admiration for the work of the War Graves Commission.

Tom was one of the lucky ones. Sixty thousand men fell on the first day of the Somme alone. Millions altogether were killed. As Tom said: 'When you look around those places, and you remember the type of fellows they were, young lads of 17, 18 and 19, it's a crying shame that it ever happened - it should never have been'.

But, above all, his thoughts were of the comradeship between the soldiers.

'It wasn't all bad times, you got out and once you were away from the trenches, the bad times were smoothed over by the comradeship of the people you were with. They were all volunteers'.

It was the comradeship that Tom missed when he left the army in 1917. Things were not the same in 'civvy street'. He had difficulty getting a job, although he had served his time as an electrician in the collier near his native Durham before the war. Eventually he got a job in the colliery power stations in various parts of the country until he retired 16 years ago and moved to Harrogate with his wife and two sons.

Tom Crawford comes from a military background - his grandfather fought in the Boer War, his father was a Hussar, he himself served in two world wars (he had a temporary commission in the last war), his two sons by his first marriage served in the R.A.F., and his second son by his present marriage served with the army in Northern Ireland.

But, as he told me very firmly, but I suspect, with a twinkle in his eye, if there should, heaven forbid, be a Third World War, he would be quite content to remain an interested bystander.

His wife looked as if she couldn't quite believe him. She was probably right to be sceptical.

Just as at 18 he couldn't stay at home, so, even at 81, it would be difficult to imagine Tom standing on the sidelines if his country were in danger.

A letter to Brian

Having visited the Somme battlefield Tommy Crawford wrote the following letter to his son, Brian on 24th June 1978:

Dear Brian,

I arrived home on Tuesday evening and it's taken until now for me to get up steam to write. I suppose at my age when you are 'bushed,' it takes time to recover. When I set off for my tour Peter, Barbara and Maria[5] met me at Kings Cross and escorted me to their place at Eastcote where I stayed the night. I had to be at Victoria at 9 a.m. the next morning so that meant up at 7 a.m. for the tube during the busy time.

Again Peter escorted me and we found the coach where Major Holt and his wife warmly greeted us. The coach was filled up by ex-service men and wives, but only 6 World War One veterans, and it turned out I was the only 1915 amongst them - Senior Man!

We arrived at Dover and went aboard for a good crossing and a good lunch was laid on en route for Calais. After lunch Major Holt asked me to go with him up to the 'Holy of Holies,' the Captain had invited me onto the bridge. I found it very interesting.

I bought 200 fags and a bottle of rum before landing and tucked them away in my case but there was no trouble with customs at Calais.

We pushed on to Poperinghe to visit Toc H. and then we took the well-remembered road we tramped so long ago to arrive at Ypres in time for the Last Post ceremony at the Menin Gate. We laid a wreath of poppies and Belgium Buglers sounded the ' Last Post', two minutes later ' Reveille,' and during this all traffic stopped.

We all felt rather sad that the Menin Gate Ceremony could be carried out by Belgium every evening in respect to British soldiers who died in thousands at Ypres while our own Cenotaph in Whitehall stands silent and forlorn for all but one day of the year.

Then we took the road once more and arrived at Bruges in Belgium at 10 p.m. for dinner at a large first class hotel and stayed overnight, good rooms, television, telephone, bathroom and toilet in every room. However after such a full day all we wanted was bed after dinner as it was about midnight and had to be ready for the road at 7 a.m. next morning.

---

[5] Peter is Tommy's Grandson and Maria Great-Granddaughter from his first marriage to Amy

We made the journey back to Ypres and on the way stopped a short while at the crossroads we knew as ' Hell Fire Corner', all quiet now, but during our war an evil place where shell fire never ceased. The Cloth Hall and buildings around the market place was a mass of ruins and fire in our time, now it is all rebuilt and not easy for us to recall.

We covered the Ypres salient including Sanctuary Wood and the trenches at Passchendale and Tyne Cot, needless to say, not the trenches as I knew them. I had a couple of bottles of stout and a casket of chips in Ypres market place. I saw some crossed cartridges (like I have at home) and was informed the price was 400 francs. I told the bloke mine had cost me 5 francs and the answer was '1915 was a long time ago'.

We visited the Canadian Memorial Park, the trenches and underground tunnels of Vimy Ridge. The Germans held Vimy Ridge from 1914 to 1917 and the French lost 130,000 men in attempts to capture it and failed. The Canadians took it in 1917 for the loss of 10,600 men.

The whole of the ridge is honeycombed with deep underground tunnels where hundreds of troops could shelter safe from shellfire and in every direction the ground was open and gave the enemy a wonderful field of fire. By the time I had tramped through the tunnels and climbed the stairways I was on my last legs, but Major Holt's wife helped me to recover and as we sat and talked she asked me if I could I remember any incidents of the war. I recited a little poem I wrote and unbeknown to me she had a tape recorder in a haversack, which she switched on.

It was played on the coach on our way to Longeau (Somme area) to my discomfort but greeted with applause by the coach party.

We stayed overnight and the following morning took the road to Bray, Fricourt, Contalmaison, Pozieres, Thiepval, Beaumont Hamel and Albert.

At Fricourt your glasses were very useful, from this village I could look back towards Albert and follow our line of advance on July 1ˢᵗ 1916. It was strange to remember the hell that broke out over this ground which was now so quiet and peaceful.

At Albert all the ruins have been rebuilt and the Golden Madonna is once more standing upright over looking the battlefields of the Some where 460,000 were lost.

The most outstanding part of the whole tour was the immaculate condition of the cemeteries, large and small, not a blade of grass out of place and memorials to every Regiment of the British Army.

We took the road to Calais and the crossing was a bit rough but a good lunch was laid on before we saw the white cliffs of Dover. I bought another 200 fags (total 400) and a bottle of John Haig for Colin plus the usual perfume for Mum. Then I found I had too much, and Dover Customs I was told was pretty tight, I didn't fancy doing anytime in clink so I got a lady in the party to do a spot of smuggling for me.

We got to Victoria at 9 p.m. and I was pleased to see Peter waiting with his car to take me to his home. By then I knew I had reached the limit, and it was due to the rest I had with Peter and Barbara that enabled me to make the journey to Harrogate on Tuesday.

Everyone in the party was very considerate and helped me on my way, Major Holt and his wife did all they could for me, Peter and Barbara were wonderful.

For me it was a wonderful trip back down memory lane but I was pleased to know I was home again when Mum arrived home at 11.30 p.m. from her trip to Scotland.

The coach driver said we had covered 900 miles during the tour.

Now I'm tired of writing so I must close, hoping you are keeping well, I was pleased to see a letter from you when I arrived home.

With Love from
Dad

10. FINAL THOUGHTS

Tommy Crawford wrote the following at 82 years of age.

Will someone tell me where and when we carried out this 'Lovely War' they used to sing about and now shown on the television.

Perhaps at 82 my memory is a bit dim, but I served in 1915, 1916, 1917, Ypres, 'Plug Street', Loos, the Somme and all I can remember is the rain, the mud, the cold, rats, and the feeling of sorrow for the dead, the mutilated, the blinded and gassed. Line after line of British civilian soldiers formed up as on parade moving across open ground swept by German machine gun and rifle fire.

It was a long time before the brass hats realized that British breasts could make no headway against a never ending storm of fire from behind the masses of German wire. The boys sang their marching songs in 1915, 1916 when moving from sector to sector, but after the Somme there wasn't much singing. The brass hats must have had a 'lovely war' 20 miles behind the fighting line but I wouldn't know about that, during my time I only saw one of them.

Churchill said 'we are losing about 5000 men a day and taking a few yards of French farmland, will someone tell me what is Haig's objective?'.

There is not and never has been 'A lovely war' for the boys who came from Manor House, Factory and Slum to form a half trained civilian soldier army.

And when it was over I saw ex-soldiers selling boxes of matches and shoelaces in the streets.

A country fit for heroes to live in!